AF352764

Bidjara   Garingbal   Karingbal

Carnarvon Gorge Section, Carnarvon Gorge
    National Park, Queensland, Australia
A spiritual homeland
Many generations of caretakers
Many Aboriginal families have upheld and
    maintained reverence for this place and its
    many stories

I openly and wholeheartedly acknowledge that
    there are many Aboriginal people who claim
    their birthrights to the place we now call
    Carnarvon Gorge
Many Aboriginal people and their families who
    I have not met, and do not know of

I acknowledge you
I express my respect to your families
I offer my care for your ancestors

Groups of Aboriginal families who I have
    met, and Countrymen who have been doing
    the work

I acknowledge you
I express my respect to your families
I offer my care for your ancestors

The creek is nourished by many sources

An introductory interview

Artist Dale Harding in conversation with curator Hannah Mathews about <u>Through a lens of visitation</u>, which was hosted by Monash University Museum of Art (MUMA) from 28 April to 26 June 2021. This discussion took place via email throughout January and February of the same year.

HM Let's begin at the beginning—the title, <u>Through a lens of visitation</u>. You've had this title in mind since the project's early days. The project encompasses three parts: a new series of works made by you and your mother Kate Harding (also an artist); the exhibition of these works alongside a selection of your existing works at MUMA; and this publication, which brings together new and old writing on Carnarvon Gorge and its resonances within Australian modernism. Could you extrapolate on your choice of title and its meaning?

DH From 2017 through to early 2019 a number of colleagues had been sharing their knowledge of Sidney Nolan and Margaret Preston's visits to the broader region that is locally referred to as The Carnarvons. A key early moment was when Conservator Paula Dredge contacted me about Sidney Nolan's visit to Carnarvon Gorge. After discussions with Paula, I began researching and talking with peers about emerging links and Curator Tim Walsh showed me the page in an Art Gallery of New South Wales publication on Margaret Preston with an image of a Carnarvon Gorge Rock Art site. I'd been gathering any references I could to get a sense of the unfolding stories of artists visiting the region, and I felt an immediate response to Nolan's <u>Landscape Carnarvon Range</u>, 1948.

Dealing with growing personal frustrations about tourism inside The Gorge, and after my mother's sister Karen Lawton was the last family member (at the time) to leave her employment as a Queensland Parks and Wildlife Service (QPWS) Indigenous Ranger at The Gorge Section, I was interrogating the idea of being a visitor myself.

In 2019, in an attempt to make sense of my experience of moving among varied conversations regarding Carnarvon Gorge, I made a direct appropriation of <u>Landscape Carnarvon Range</u>, 1948, onto the walls of my studio. These walls are where I make studies for wall paintings and where I put ideas for the time being. Underneath the Nolan copy I claimed my studio space by writing 'through a lens of visitation'.

My perception was that so many people claim Carnarvon Gorge, and the Ancestral Cultural Sites that live there, as their own. Whether they were on their first visit, their second camping trip, or came since the road was sealed and they could drive to The Gorge on bitumen all the way from any capital city, my perception was that they were always visitors. And that the local people returned as visitors also, by way of Government Management and jurisdiction.

HM The project's title implies a location that remains unspoken, unread, unidentified. People may think of the museum. But what is apparent at the heart of your work is Country, specifically your mother's Country of Carnarvon Gorge, in what is also widely known as Central Queensland. It has been important that Country be at the centre of this project too. Could you speak to your (active) relationship with the Gorge?

DH Further to all the oral teachings, histories and memories of Carnarvon Gorge that came to me through my grandparents and bigger families, an entry point here might be via the block-mounted poster of a photo of one of the internal sites of The Gorge that hung between the dining table and kitchen in Nanna and Grandad's house. This place was familiar to me before I was taken out there, and Nanna would speak to the poster as normal to those who visited, in the way of speaking to sacredness in diaspora.

At this moment, in 2021, I would like to offer that my relationship with The Gorge is active from a distance. I am very often within walking distance of the Gorge, and yet I have chosen to not visit it unless for a specific purpose—I have visited only a small number of times in the past couple of years. I have enjoyed being nearby, while a couple of my cousin-sisters contribute to a largely female group of Bidjara and Garingbal/Karingbal people involved in Cultural Heritage Management and relational discussions. It has been important for me to hear about the Gorge from women in my community, and to develop my relationships in other parts of The Carnarvons and around Central Queensland.

HM You purposefully sought the contributions of senior women with specialist knowledge to this publication. Could you speak to this choice in terms of protocol, gender and the potential that lies in revisiting the past?

DH In discussions early on we were aware of the presence of Eldership and I was interested in seeking the contributions of the 'Elders' in the field. The voices of senior Art Historians were my first choice when approaching this research, and it was easy to point towards the senior writers on the artists Margaret Preston and Sidney Nolan—Nancy Underhill, a Brisbane local and Nolan scholar; and Deborah Edwards, who had identified the images of Carnarvon Gorge in the book she co-wrote on Preston. It was important to me that the fragments of connections between Carnarvon Gorge and these two artists be investigated by writers who could build on their histories, and for me to test my gut-instinct that there were very familiar parts of their Modernist art practices that I could read as post–Carnarvon Gorge.

Ann Stephen's expertise in the field of Australian Conceptualism and Minimalism was sought as a foundation for exploring the ways these discoveries blend among contemporary art practices to influence my work in the pursuit of contemporary Central Queensland 'modernisms'. The three experts all know of each other's work, share overlapping study, and were my dream team for this research project that builds up the stories of how Central Queensland Aboriginal artforms might be involved in Modernist and Australian Contemporary Art.

I was amazed in 2020 to read Dr Jackie Huggins's essay from 1993 on her Mother's born country at Carnarvon Gorge, and to read of her very familiar questioning and critiques of non-Aboriginal visitation to The Gorge—partly because Aunty Jackie and her Uncle Fred Conway are still having those conversations in 2021, decades later. As a Bidjara scholar, writer and activist, Aunty Jackie's original essay and new preface are like the roots of the grass for our work with MUMA.

Professor Paul Taçon's 2019 report, written on the request of a group of involved Bidjara and Garingbal/Karingbal people, is also republished here. According to my understanding, Paul maintains the care of country and cultural heritage shared for Carnarvon Gorge through his writing and presenting on the fire damaged Rock Art Site, Baloon Cave, Carnarvon National Park and Carnarvon Gorge Section, and he has agreement to uphold this story in his work. It is not surprising to me, and is a source of inspiration, that expertise and experience is gathered in this publication from the work of women leaders in their fields.

My mother Kate chaired a meeting of Bidjara and Garingbal/Karingbal community members with QPWS hierarchy a couple of summers ago, just like her mother (and father) who would join those meetings for the benefit of The Gorge country. I celebrate the work of Bidjara women including Kristine Sloman, Aunty Jackie Huggins, Ljudan Michaelis-Thorpe, Michelle Hobbs and my cousin-sisters Melissa Lawton-Mills and Jamie-Lee Clark for their work towards the care and maintenance of our Ancestors' stories in and around The Gorge.

While a number of our male Elders have maintained unbroken relationships and insisted on connection to Carnarvon Gorge and surrounding country, it is important to note that much of my recent contact has been among leaderly female company.

HM You're interested in establishing and contributing to a discourse of Indigenous modernisms and have long been interested in the visits of Australian artists, Margaret Preston and Sidney Nolan to the Gorge in 1940 and 1947 respectively. Also Mike Parr in 1975. You find resonances of the rock art specific to the Gorge in the practices of these iconic artists who have been canonised within the early and middle periods of Western modernism. Where do you see these influences specifically and what does this mean in terms of broadening our understanding of art history?

DH Minimal form and reduced aesthetic values have long been present in Aboriginal expressions in what is now called the Central Queensland region, or more specifically, the places where the Mari Language groups originate. What we call minimal, conceptual and reductive art practices also belong to cultures where codification and distillation are normal, both prior to and post the Colonial Frontier settlers arriving from Brisbane and Sydney just before the middle of the nineteenth century.

Mike Parr's work, <u>Identification no. 1 (Rib markings in the Carnarvon Ranges, North-West Queensland</u>) from 1975 is now included in the canon of Aboriginal artforms that endure across the Central Queensland Sandstone Belt. His photographs are the remnants of actions embodied in situ.

And when I first saw Nolan's costume designs for <u>The rite of spring</u> performed in London in 1962, I saw that they were derived from rock art. Although he did not explicitly acknowledge this influence, it is fair to ask questions about it on a methodological basis: Nolan, an educated Australian artist, chose to manufacture templates in the shape of human hands and wrists, making negative stencilled images by the application of atomised liquid pigment sprayed over the templates with his own breath, to convey narrative subject matter of communal rites at a time when Modernist Primitivism was present in the air.

Art students are asked questions about influence and methodology all the time, and this often helps to recognise and even acknowledge the presence of subconscious imitation and referencing of other artists and their work. I have often been startled to recognise the influence of a colleague's work on my own, and I openly acknowledge and honour the ways that someone else's practice has grown my own. These artists know who they are.

There is a precise series of choices that an artist makes in order to create negative hand stencils blown by breath. With the exception of the little metal apparatus used by artists to project atomised liquid pigment by the propulsion of human breath (which eliminates the need to put substances in the mouth), breath-blown negative hand stencils have been in practice consistently in the art of the Central Queensland Sandstone Belt for longer than wheels have been round.

I now know that Sidney Nolan visited Carnarvon Gorge a quarter of a century before the promotional photos documenting him posing with all the components involved in making negative hand stencils for his <u>Rite of spring</u> costumes were taken by Axel Poignant.

On another branch of the research tree, I began to feel that my mother, Kate Harding, had been doing and living what I perceived Margaret Preston was trying to achieve. Many Aboriginal people do these kinds of things as consolidated cultural practices and I was interested to see if Preston's motivation wasn't all bad.

HM Your work often pays particular homage to matrilineal female figures in your family—engaging and bringing forth their stories. For this project you have worked with your mother Kate Harding. Could you speak to why this relationship was particularly important to this project and the kinds of conversations you had with Kate as it evolved?

DH Kate and I have been involved in conversations for a long time about her parents' cultural knowledges, and about home and country and artmaking. Kate's own quilt-making practice was already exploring and experimenting with new ways of decoupling from American and Northern European quilting conventions, while my work was looking more closely at Preston's intentions and her legacies.

Gordon Bennett's bodies of work after Preston were becoming illuminated for me and I was learning more about the shades of Preston's conviction as a Cultural Appropriationist. Mandy Quadrio, Jan Oliver and Dr Carol McGregor all have expertise in the fields where Kate was taking her own work and, through support garnered by MUMA for this project, Kate was able to share studio time with Mandy and Jan who have learned ways of generating self-determined art practices. So Kate and I mostly shared conversations around her motivation and intention to move into a stronger, self-chosen position through her use of materials, content and knowledge sharing.

I worked to keep Preston and Nolan in my studio as Kate developed her bodies of work for <u>Through a lens of visitation</u>. And when Kate conversed with Deborah Edwards, and Deborah shared her book on Preston, the research was becoming evident in the momentum and motivations behind Kate's work. We talked and asked questions around what her parents intended for Country and cultural knowledges, and it became clear that what Kate and I had been doing in our work together was very different from other people's interest in a National Art. This work begins in the home and for Kate and me it is a Bidjara, Ghungalu and Garingbal continuum.

HM You reflected recently that you felt you were at a point within your practice where you could look back and see the distinct focuses and chapters that have led you to now. Could you share more about this, and why it is important for the future?

DH Kate's parents lived through diaspora and each of them never gave up their beliefs in the sacredness of the Ancestral cultural sites that they described in mine sites, in buffel grass paddocks, behind handrails and in untold other locations.

I believe that it has been important, if not necessary at times, to share cultural stories and places with others, in the ways decided as best at the time, for the benefit of the bigger picture. Kate's parents were involved in establishing the Dreamtime Cultural Centre in Rockhampton, Central Queensland for the benefit of, as I put it, making visible the people and ongoing cultural stories of the greater region. So making contemporary art, and sharing this in galleries and museums, might be understood as part of an extremely long lineage of consolidated practices by Aboriginal people who feel that Central Queensland is home.

I have made choices as an artist that have offered big lessons and have led me to focus now on generative practices and constructive modes of resistance. Also, I would like to see the wider public develop some fluency, or visual literacy, in the cultures and expressions that are maintained across Central Queensland.

I used to work among what I described as 'the burden of truth that is shouldered by those who are silenced'. Perhaps I have learned that there are negotiations to be held when the opportunity to be witnessed and when urgencies of social and climate challenges are experienced simultaneously in the site of performance. Because these experiences are, I suggest, distinct from consolidated practices and places of being.

My biggest hope is that we will witness more and more cultural forms being generated, shared, lived and consolidated among the daily and seasonal lives of Aboriginal people throughout Central Queensland. I choose the word consolidated with priority. I propose that spectators are an auxiliary motivation for living cultural lives, and that contemporary art is an extension or continuation of the home lives and social lives of communities. This is a challenge I propose for myself and those around me.

Along with my colleagues and family, I have sought to participate in exhibitions in ways that enable us to do more outside of the gallery, before and after the shows and audiences—this is what I see as generative practices. I love my life as an artist and I love it when what we do as professionals contributes to building upon what was there before the exhibition.

Reflecting on my different bodies of work, over what is only a tiny period of time, I would say that I have been motivated by the immediate conversations around me, including Woorabinda oral histories and my own personal experiences. Of late the conversations around me have been about making art in the home.

Until there is powerful and meaningful Aboriginal management of the Carnarvon Gorge Section of Carnarvon National Park, temporary visitation and work with contemporary art galleries and museums are among the ways that cultural continuums might be embedded and consolidated.

What might happen if more of Central Queensland's Murri community see themselves within the histories of Australian Art rather than through the lenses of people who came, saw and left again?

In my quest towards establishing a national art, I would like regional expressions to be strengthened and nourished to the benefit of the art forms present in my daily experience.

Kooramindanjie:
Place and the postcolonial
by Jackie Huggins,
Rita Huggins
and Jane M. Jacobs (1995)
WITH 2020 Preface
by Jackie Huggins

It's hard to believe that this article was written over twenty-five years ago. Time elapses but certain situations still remain. For example, the biggest debacle for Aboriginal people remains in the Native Title arena. It was so new back in 1995, just a year after the Mabo judgement, and prospects of resolution seemed so positive and exciting—like a shiny toy. Everyone was trying to get involved to work things out and receive some due justice in land rights. Unfortunately for some, power and greed reared their ugly heads. The best outcomes of this crusade have been the creation of economic opportunities and the tracing of families and bloodlines.

I had heard people say that there would be the 'haves and have-nots' in the Native Title process. Although it would make us less disadvantaged, the result would be a divide between the privileged and the poor. I mentioned in the article that there were six groups with claims to Carnarvon Gorge but under ethnocentric legislation there can be only one victor. Uninterrupted occupation and traditional knowledge privilege Aboriginal claims. But tragically clans had been removed from their Country to missions and reserves across Queensland under the notorious *Aboriginals Protection and Restriction of the Sale of Opium Act 1897*.

My Bidjara people are still in the fight and have cultural heritage ownership over the Gorge. A number of descendants including Dr Dale Harding and I have been involved in preserving the rock art and protecting what is left of our magnificent Country through our Working Group spearheaded by our Elders Fred Conway and Bill Lawton. Uncle Fred has been a ranger here for over thirty years. Both he and Uncle Bill have expert knowledge of the area and they pass this learning down to their families.

The Department of Environment and Heritage are engaged with us, as are the rangers who work on the site and the surrounding area. There is a new cultural building and visitors centre where updated knowledge is on display. Previously the paths and signs,

made by the Queensland Parks and Wildlife Service, used little
Aboriginal language. Today it is a different story, with traditional
names being used in abundance for walkways and other sites. But
there is still a long way to go.

My family visit the Gorge as much as possible to keep our
spiritual connection strong. Just recently my son John Henry (the
young boy in the article, now a grown man) and I returned to feel the
earth and gain our energy and sustenance in the ancient homeland
where we were born. Sadly my beloved mother Rita Huggins passed
on in 1996, a year after this article was published.

Accessibility has improved. The road into the Gorge is now fully
sealed, unlike when we visited in 1995. There are now a small
number of accommodation places. These are mostly for dedicated
campers in tents, however more upmarket and luxury suites in lodges
are also available. Tourism has markedly increased as a result of these
measures. Covid-19 has made more people travel within Australia and
has enabled more Australians to explore this wonderland. The
perception that Carnarvon Gorge is a hidden treasure is now
disappearing.

The place is still as majestic as when we first experienced it.
The paths are a little downtrodden from the numbers of tourists who
visit every year, and, tragically, a recent fire burned out some
invaluable and cherished rock art, which can never be replaced.
Restoration of this cave continues with the traditional owners.

There are toilet and telecommunications upgrades occurring to
keep up with modern developments. Aboriginal rangers have been
employed, a long overdue action from the state government.
Training is desperately needed as well as on-the-job guidance from
more experienced workers.

When I visit Carnarvon Gorge I get the feeling I have when
I am in Uluru, except this is MY Country. The Country that has
nurtured me and my families for generations. That feeling is
indescribable; a deep sense of respect and love overcomes you,
similar to seeing your children arrive on this planet. You are shrouded
in the warmth of your ancestors surrounding your presence and
showing you around, protecting and caring for you.

This was how I felt on my most recent visit a month ago.
The Gorge was dry and dusty then, but after we left plentiful rains
occurred as if to replenish the soul and provide the renewal it so
deserves. I feel tempted to visit again in a few weeks. One of the
most noticeable differences is the abundant signage around the
visitors centre at the commencement of the main walking track
acknowledging the First Peoples and announcing that this is truly
Aboriginal Country. So, twenty-five years on some improvements have
happened, but like the bigger story of Aboriginal affairs, there is still
a long way to go.

Dr Jackie Huggins AM FAHA

'Kooramindanjie: Place and the postcolonial' was first published
in *History Workshop Journal*, no. 39, Spring 1995, pp. 165–81.

HISTORY WORKSHOP JOURNAL

ISSUE 39   **SPRING 1995**

EDITORIALS

ARTICLES AND ESSAYS

E. P. THOMPSON AND THE USES OF HISTORY

SPATIAL HISTORY: RETHINKING THE IDEA OF PLACE

HISTORY AT LARGE

UNDER VICE-REGAL PATRONAGE

Carnarvon Ranges

RIOTOUS SCENES OF GRANDEUR

Absorbing description of the Wonders of Carnarvon National Park with Glorious Coloured Pictures.

City Hall, Monday, November 7th, 1938
AT 8 P.M.

By D. A. O'Brien F.R.G.S.A., Leader of the C. R. Expeditions of 1937 and 1938

Historical, Educational, Entertaining

1. Archibald Meston—"A land of enchantment, of romance-the parent of golden dreams-a paradise of hills and streams, of rocks and caves, of birds and flowers, of lake and vale. A fit mausoleum of the old dead Myall race."

2. Ruth Timbury—"The roof of Queensland 4000 feet up, the 250 mile tangle of peaks and gullies between the Lynd and the Warrego Ranges."

3. Dr. H. I. Jensen D. Sc.—"If irrigation can be applied ... one of the greatest producing areas in Australia. Gold, Coal, Opal, Agate, Sulphur, Oil, Felspar."

4. Sir Thos. Mitchell named The Claude and Lake Salvator after the immortal painters.

5. Mr. V. Grenning, Director of Forests, Queensland.—"Slowly but surely the beauty and grandeur of the Carnarvon National Park is being realised. Gorges, the richness and grandeur of which adds yet another brilliant jewel to Queensland scenic attractions, finds no parallel in any other part of Queensland."

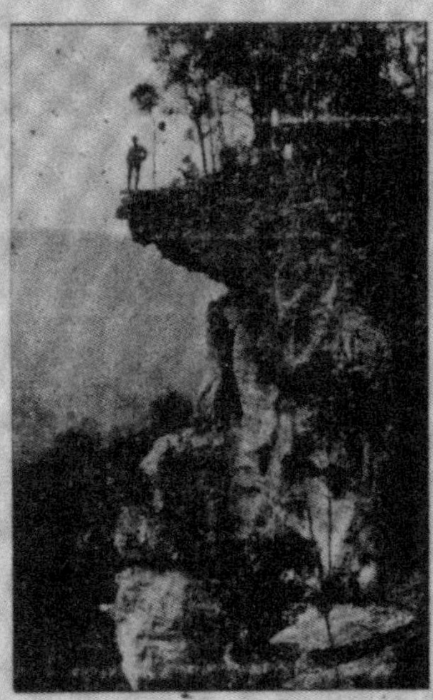

Underground river and hidden water falls, salt and fresh water crystal springs. Thrilling 3000 feet descent from Great Dividing Range.

One of Australia's unknown beauty spots. See it and know your country. Don't miss this display.

The Rt. Hon. the Lord Mayor will preside.

ADMISSION 2/- & 1/- **Box Plans at Palings**

Carnarvon Ranges: Riotous Scenes of Grandeur, 1938. The Royal Geographical Society actively promoted the scenic in the attempt to invent a tourist destination.

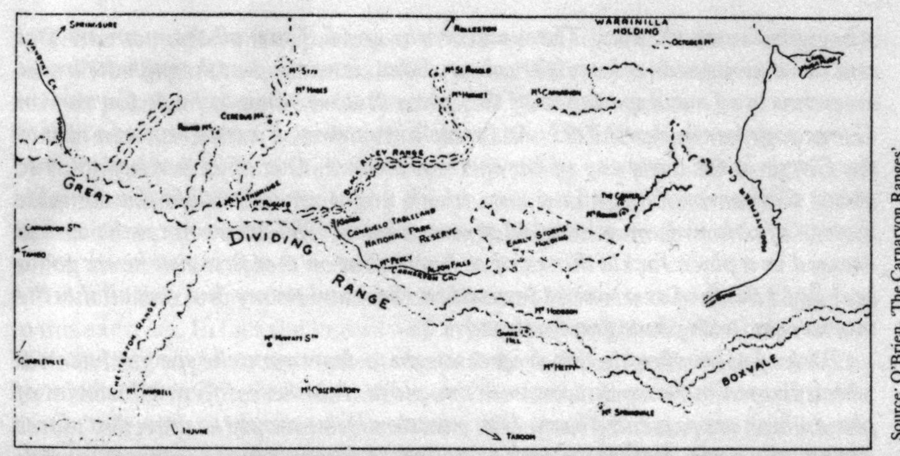

Sketch map of the Carnarvon Ranges. The map shows that the early Carnarvon Gorge 'expeditions' were entering country which was far from unknown or un-named.

Kooramindanjie: Place and the Postcolonial
by *Jackie Huggins, Rita Huggins and Jane M. Jacobs*

Touring Aboriginal Land

In Carnarvon Gorge National Park, Central Queensland, a rock art trail guides visitors to an Aboriginal place in the past. The interpretative sign suggests that if the visitors had arrived a little earlier – some 10,000 years, it says – then they may have 'followed a family group of Aboriginals across the dry plain to this oasis gorge'.[1] It is April 1993 and I (Jane Jacobs) am following 'a family group of Aboriginals' (Jackie Huggins, her mother 'Auntie Rita' and her son, young John Henry), across the plain, to the oasis gorge and down this very trail. I do not have to project into the past to move through this country in the manner recommended by the National Parks' sign.

This journey was the result of a collaborative writing project between myself and historian Jackie Huggins whose family is from the Carnarvon Gorge area. During 1992 Jackie and I were colleagues at the same academic institution. We discussed our work and in the course of those discussions realized that we had both made our first and, at that time, only visits to Carnarvon Gorge in 1985. Jackie had gone to the Gorge to see her mother's country. On that visit Jackie never made it into the Gorge itself because of torrential rains. My visit was a result of my involvement in a research project for the Australian Heritage Commission on the impact of tourism on

Aboriginal rock art sites. The weather was good. I saw all the main art sites and came away with at least 200 colour slides. It was in part through the ironic unevenness of our experience of this place that we came to be in Carnarvon Gorge together in April 1993. At Jackie's invitation, I joined her on a visit to the Gorge in the company of her son and mother. Our objective was to write about Carnarvon Gorge in a way which might render visible the complex history of colonialism as enacted at one point in 1985 when our paths almost crossed in a place Jackie thinks of as home (but on that first visit never got to see) and I think of as a tourist destination (and saw on my first visit all that the tourist sees, with photographs to prove it).

Each of us involved in this project sought to draw upon the specific histories which shaped our associations with this place. It is these differing histories of place which are presented here. Our intention is not simply to show that places have many pasts. Rather we seek to politicize the notion of a 'sense of place', to reveal the power relations which not only shape meanings of place but also the very way in which we might dwell (or not dwell) in place. We set conditions. Jackie did not want me to be the ethnographer, the expert on her culture. But then I did not want to be her ethnographer, I wanted to think and write about my place here.

My land
Kooramindanjie (Carnarvon Gorge) is 600 kilometres north west of Brisbane in the sandstone tablelands of the Great Dividing Range of Australia. It is an oasis in the desert plains and Aboriginal people would travel many hundreds of miles to visit this place for water, food, shelter and ceremonies. It is the country of Rita my mother and my maternal grandmothers, it is Bidjara country.

Our people lived in this area for over 19,000 years (archaeologically speaking) in the maze of gorges, ranges and tablelands. Other tribal groups living around the area were Kairi, Nuri, Karingbal, Longabulla, Jiman and Wadja. However since the government removals policy, descendants from these tribal groups are now scattered over wide areas of Queensland and northern New South Wales.

Non-Aboriginals must understand their cultural and ethical limitations in studying, researching and writing about Blacks. They must learn to step back in areas where they are not welcome, although they often think and presume they are, where they are intruders not accomplices. Otherwise, they can do great damage to Aboriginal people and our struggles, adding to the burden rather than alleviating it. Binney suggests that we cannot translate others' histories into our own – we can merely juxtapose them.[2] Translation is detrimental to the integrity of one or the other, or to both historical traditions. Rather than trying to understand the past on its own terms, some academics have sought to explain Aboriginal pasts in terms of a contemporary ethnographical present which they confront but do not fully comprehend.

There are different experiences of the world, different bases of experience. If we begin our understanding as we actually experience the world, it is at least possible to see how we are located. What is known of the 'other' is conditional upon that 'other's' relative location. Whites must not ignore this by taking advantage of their privileged speaking positions to construct an external version of 'us' which may pass for our 'reality'. There must be limits to the ways our worlds are re-written or placed in conceptual frameworks which are not our own.

I don't have to say to Jane that I didn't want her to be the big white expert in this exercise. In fact she knows well my feelings on that topic. But I can see she's itching to get to that spiral notepad. In fact my mother asks me 'Why isn't she taking notes?'. She told everyone about Jane when we returned home, referring to her as another writer, like myself, but she was bewildered at Jane's refusal to take notes.

Ambiguous senses of place

The interpretative sign on the walking trail at Carnarvan Gorge directs the visitor to 'pause . . . reflect and wonder at the ways of those who wandered this land before us'. The Huggins family group and I – their trailing tourist – thought more about the ambiguous status of those of us who wander the land now. We discussed the history of violence and dispossession that resulted in large numbers of Aboriginals in the area being massacred late last century and those who were left being relocated earlier this century. As we walked the trail, Jackie and I discussed the fact that this visit is one of only a few ever made to the area by Auntie Rita – even though it is her homeland. I talked of my first visit to the Gorge in 1985 as an 'expert' on the management of rock art sites suffering the pressure of tourism. I wondered uncomfortably if my recommendations had manifested themselves on the ground in the form of this time-tunnel interpretative trail. Many attempts to narrate a sense of place presume the necessity of embeddedness, permanence, presence. In contrast, our presence in Carnarvon Gorge is surely constituted by our intersecting senses of displacement.

> Within 50 years of the first visit by a white man to Carnarvon, few traces survived of the culture of the Aboriginals who had inhabited this land. Only a sketchy picture of their lives and long history in the area remains.[3]

Auntie Rita's born country[4]

I was only a small child when we were taken from my born country. I only remember a little of those times there but my memories are very precious to me. Most of my life has been spent away from my country . . . but I remember about the land I come from. It will always be home, the place I belong to.

My born country is the land of the Bidjara-Pitjara people, and is known now as Carnarvon Gorge. . . . There were huge cliffs and rocks, riddled with caves where many of my people's paintings were. Most caves and rock faces showed my people's stencilled hands, weapons and tools, and there were engravings here, too. Fertility symbols and the giant serpent tells us of the spiritual significance of the place. This place is old. My people and their art were here long before the whiteman came.

The caves were cool places in summer and warm places in winter, and offered shelter when the days were windy or when there was rain. They offered a safe place for the women bringing new life into the world. As had happened for my mother and her mother before her, going back generation after generation, I was born in the sanctuary of one of those caves. My mother would tell us how my grandmother would wash my mother's newborn babies in the nearby creek, place them in a cooliman and carry them back to suckle on my exhausted mother's breast. . . .

My mother, Rose, had a Bidjara-Pitjara mother known as Lucy Conway from the Maranoa River and a white father who was never married to her mother. I never knew who her father was. I don't know much about the contact my mother had with whites. She had a whiteman's name, but she also had a tribal name, Gylma, and she spoke language and knew the old ways. My father, Albert Holt, was the son of a Yurri woman known as Maggie Bundle and a white man, the owner of Wealwandangie Station. My father was named after that man. . . . Dadda was brought up on the station, away from his mother's people. When he grew up he wanted to be with Aboriginal people, and started visiting the camps. He saw my mother there and wanted to marry her. After that, he stayed in the camp with her, and then the children started coming.

One winter's night, troopers came riding through our camp. My father went to see what was happening, and my mother stayed with her children to try to stop us from being so frightened. One trooper I remember clearly. Perhaps he was sorry for what he was doing, because he gave me some fruit – a banana, something as unknown to me as the whiteman who offered it. My mother saw and cried out to me, 'Barjun! Barjun!'

Dadda and some of the older men were shouting angrily at the officials. We were being taken away from our lands. We didn't know why, nor imagined what place we would be taken to. I saw the distressed look on my parents' faces and knew something was terribly wrong. We never had time to gather up any belongings. Our camp was turned into a scattered mess – the fire embers still burning.

What was to appear next out of the bush took us all by surprise and we nearly turned white with fright. It was a huge cage with four round things on it which, when moved by the man in the cabin in front, made a deafening sound, shifting the ground and flattening the grass, stones and twigs beneath it. We had never seen a cattle truck before. A strong smell surrounded us when we entered the truck and we saw brown stains on the wooden floor. . . .

The truck went on, travelling for two terrible days, going further south. As if in a funeral procession, we were loud in our silence. We were all in mourning. I can't remember what we had to eat or drink, or where we stopped on the journey, and by the time we reached our destination we were numb with cold, tiredness and hunger. And this new country was so different from our country – flat, no hills, and valleys, arid and cleared of trees.

It was Barambah Reserve (renamed Cherbourg in 1932). . . . Here we were separated from each other into rough houses – buildings that seemed so strange to me then, with their walls so straight. Each family was fenced off from the other into their own two little rooms where you ate and slept. The houses were little cells all next to each other in little rows. A prison. . . . The place in fact had its own gaol. A prison in a prison. There were white and Aboriginal areas.

No one had the right to remove us from our traditional lands and to do what they did to us. We were once the proud custodians of our land and now our way of life became controlled by insensitive people who knew nothing about us but thought they knew everything. They even chose how and where we could live. We had to stay in one place now while the whiteman could roam free.

Dis-place-ment
During the late 1920s Rita and her family were rounded up by the troopers and sent on the back of a cattle truck to the then Barambah Aboriginal Reserve, later known as Cherbourg. Rita reminisces about the time of traditional Aboriginal existence in a manner which most people would find beautiful. Her stories are glimpses of a pristine past prior to the white invasion. She tells me:

My mother would make soap from the leaves of a tree and unfortunately for us there was no excuse not to take a bogey. Goanna fat was used for cuts and scratches on bare feet and limbs as well as soothing treatment for aches and pains, eucalyptus leaves for coughs and bark for rashes and open wounds. Witchetty grubs for babies' teething while charcoal was used for cleaning teeth. Bush tucker also thrived in this environment and we were never left with empty bellies. The men would go hunting for kangaroos, goannas, lizards, snakes, porcupines with their spears, boomerangs and nulla nullas while the women gathered berries, grubs, yams, edible roots, wild plums, honey and waterlilies with digging sticks. Children always accompanied the women as there was less likelihood that animals would run away when disturbed. The creeks supplied an abundant and rich source of fish – jew, yellow belly, perches and eels.[5]

While my mother recalls an idyllic Carnarvon Gorge her memories efface a history of an opposite kind; the bloody massacres which occurred not only here but right across the continent. They were acts of violence intended to demonstrate white superiority and power.

The perpetrators were seen as heroic pioneers who had entered into the place they saw as 'wild' but which we called home. Their quest was to tame the 'natives' and possess the land. Their greed cost my people dearly. There was only one thing they could do with us – get rid of us completely so they would not have anybody else to consider. Then our tranquil home could become their fortresses and their recreational areas. They did this through force and theft, by poisoning flour and waterholes, burying Blackfellas alive, tying them to trees for shooting practice, and much more. The scarcity of white women in colonial times meant that the colonizers sexually exploited Aboriginal women. The result was rape and 'half-caste' children who were usually disowned by their white 'fathers'. The conquerors killed Aboriginal dogs and game, they dispossessed us of our hunting grounds and destroyed our sacred sites.

In 1857 the Jiman people whose country bordered Carnarvon Gorge retaliated against the invaders.[6] They attacked and killed those who lived and worked on the Fraser homestead of Hornet Bank Station. This acted as the catalyst for what became known as the six months 'little war' which was waged against the Jiman and other Aboriginals in the Central Queensland area by white vigilantes. Many Aboriginal people – men, women and children – in the area were shot down as punishment for the killing of the Fraser family. The reprisals developed into an uncontrollable rage and resulted in the wholesale slaughter of innocent human lives. No effort was ever made to bring the white murderers to court. The killings and mutual hatred created during this period went on long after, and all over Australia.

The people of my mother's generation display a profound lack of bitterness about their lot, something which I find both frustrating and amazing. This trait has often polarized old and young Aboriginals. It has encouraged so many of my generation to become active about the continuing injustices occurring to Aboriginal people. We were once the proud custodians of our nation and then our way of life was irreversibly shattered by the controlling hand of colonialism. Aboriginal people could not choose how or where to live again. Under the powers of the Queensland Aborigines Protection and Restriction of Opium Act 1897, we were dictated to by government officials and told to stay in one place. If we wanted to go off the reserves set aside for us we had to get clearance from the reserve officials. This clearance was known as a permit and the system was standard practice in Queensland from late last century until the 1980s. It was only through the permit system that we were allowed 'freedom' from the reserves. Aboriginal people had to stay put now while the whiteman could roam free. We became like prisoners or occasional tourists in our own country.

Geography and imperialism

The discipline of Geography has a problematic relationship with the historical process of colonisation. Geographical knowledges of 'other' lands were crucial tools in the building of empires and provided practical guides for dispossessing 'others' of their space. The colonial history of nation-states such as Australia testifies to the symbolic and practical possession enacted through the map. Contemporary geographers and historians have begun to re-read the map in this historic context.[7] Paul Carter tells us that the naming of places and the making of maps, created a colonized place out of a pre-modern Aboriginal space. In Carter's terms this is the process whereby the 'haze' of space is turned into the 'clear outlines' of place.[8]

For the map and the act of mapping/naming to be positioned as the signifier of colonialism is a most seductive notion for a geographer. But in the critical appraisal of the map as a 'state of geographical knowledge' it is important that it does not remain 'alone on stage'. De Certeau argues that cartographic knowledge dis-places other knowledges and practices which are essential to the very production of maps. He makes a plea for the inclusion of the 'tour describers', an insertion of the 'itineraries' of occupation which give rise to and make use of the map.[9] This concern with 'tour describers' returns us to Carter's spatial history which foregrounds the ambiguous itineraries of colonisation – the journeyings of explorers, travel writers and others, and their encounters with Aboriginals. Such journeyings led at times to the making of maps, at other times depended upon the knowledges of maps and yet at other times darted away from the structures of knowledge and power held within the map. What is central here is the idea of 'travel' of movements into and out of places, what the anthropologist James Clifford describes as the processes of dwelling and travel.[10] In the Australian nation dwelling and travel have an ironic resonance. For many Aboriginal Australians the experience of being under colonialism has been one of dispossession and forced movement, that is, dwelling out of place. For non-Aboriginal Australians, occupation is in part constituted out of travel: the early travel to and through the interior, but also the transient engagements most contemporary coastal-hugging Australians have with the interior of the nation as tourists.

To think about dwelling and travel allows the relationship between identity and place to be understood as more than an unproblemized, unruptured notion of 'sense of place' (perhaps derived from the notion of being-in-place)[11] which is frequently said to be undermined by the alienating power of, say, commodification (including tourism).[12] A more productive notion of identity and place might attempt to reconcile these two possibilities, and to

*recognise a certain co-habitation between the global and the local, the com-
modified and the vernacular, the mediated and the 'real'.*[13] *Doreen Massey's
'progressive sense of place', for example, argues against a sense of place
which is artificially bounded and localized and for a sense of place constituted out of the relationship between the local and the non-local.*[14] *But this
'friendly' co-habitation may not be deconstructive enough to accommodate
the often ambiguous 'senses of place' which are generated in contemporary
settler Australia and which are forced into a political space by the arbi-
trations of Aboriginal eligibility to land rights.*

*The land rights provisions of this nation, including the most recent Native
Titles provisions, still privilege Aboriginal claims which are supported by
traditional place-specific knowledges and often uninterrupted occupation.
Yet many contemporary Aboriginal Australians have an uncanny sense of
place. Colonialism has rendered their country, their home, unfamiliar to
them.*[15] *In 1993 Jackie, Auntie Rita, John Henry and I were guided through
Carnarvon Gorge by paths and signs made by the Queensland National
Parks and Wildlife Service. We practiced a map, followed an itinerary,
which had been devised by the National Parks authority as a means of
presenting this place – as a scene – to the visitor. Carnarvon Gorge may well
have been Jackie and Auntie Rita's country, but the path of their return was
made for viewers other than themselves. A truly postcolonial land rights provision might accommodate such estrangements and presume its goal to be
the provision of the means for places to once again be rendered familiar.
This is an active and inventive land rights, not a compensatory land rights of
loss.*

Lost in place

I felt out of place at Carnarvon Gorge. Jane and I actually thought we were
lost in the area at one stage. I felt I should know this place but could not get
us out of the mess we had found ourselves in; we did not know where we
were as we drove along the dirt track in the darkness of night. I could sense
that Jane was too frightened to offer directions – directions I had expected,
her being a geographer and all.

*On the first of our many walks to various cultural sites a certain confusion
arose. It was a journey which began with the wrong name. We set out for a
site Auntie Rita had referred to as 'what I think they call "Hemisphere"'.
Having been to the Gorge before, and being a geographer and reading my
maps, I knew there was no site called 'Hemisphere' but that there was one
called 'The Amphitheatre'. Close enough. We set out the next day to the
place on the map called 'The Amphitheatre'. When we arrived at the site it
was not the place Auntie Rita had visited before and wanted us to see. This
place had no rock art. Auntie Rita was greatly distressed, thinking this was
the place but that it no longer had any art. With my geography and my translation we had come to the wrong place.*

Indigenous touring

The 'uncanny' might also describe contemporary non-Aboriginal experiences of this place. Non-Aboriginal tourists were clearly unsettled when they confronted 'indigenous tourists' walking along the Carnarvon Gorge trails – even more so when Aunty Rita struck up a conversation and announced 'I was born here, this is my country'. This is not to say that non-Aboriginal tourists do not expect or want to meet Aboriginal people when out in the bush. Most do, and throughout Australia National Park authorities and mainstream tourist ventures are busily 're-Aboriginalizing' place in the service of the tourist industry. Aboriginal communities are often actively engaged in this process, producing arts and crafts for the tourist, running their own 'indigenous Australia' tours, and in some areas owning and managing the areas open to the tourist.

But in Carnarvon Gorge the Huggins family seems 'out of place'. This is a place rendered in popular literatures, including current park brochures, as devoid of living Aboriginal people but rich in Aboriginal 'heritage'. Official brochures mention the 'passing' of local Aboriginals but not the local massacres. Aboriginality is presented in Carnarvon Gorge through the rock art which, safe and static, hugs the walls of the Gorge. The Huggins family's claims of belonging and ownership, along with their presence as 'tourists' in the Gorge, are rendered unbelievable by the myth of a place thoroughly cleared of Aboriginals.

Their passing is marked only by the fragile art on the sandstone cliffs. This is damaged if the fine dust at the base of the rock wall is disturbed. To enable you to view the art, boardwalks have been constructed at the three art sites. . . . Keep to these to protect a valuable and irreplaceable part of our heritage. . . . Please look without touching. The artists are gone and it would be a further tragedy to lose the heritage they left. By keeping on the boardwalk you will see the art to the best possible advantage.[16]

Carnarvon Gorge is a place occupied by tourists, shaped by tourism. There is a transitory but continual occupation of the Gorge by tourists. In 1993 some 400 visitors each weekend confirmed this is no longer Bidjara country, but a public space, a National Park. The National Parks sign we confronted on our first walk together through the Gorge directed the tourist to gaze upon an imaginary Aboriginal time, in what is now an ambiguously Aboriginal place. Imagine if the National Parks interpretation sign directed the visitor's gaze not to an Aboriginal pre-history but to a more recent colonial history. Here we might see the imaginative projections which have ensured that this place became a tourist space, serving the transient in search of an authentic experiences of inland Australia.

When I set out to write about Carnarvon Gorge from my own non-Aboriginal positioning, I never imagined that I'd find a colonial history so close to my professional identity as a geographer. For Carnarvon Gorge, tourist destination, was created through the vision of an amateur geographer, Danny O'Brien, who was a member (and later Director and General Secretary) of the Royal Geographical Society of Australasia (Queensland Branch) from the 1930s through to the mid 1960s.

The first expedition by the Royal Geographical Society of Australasia (Queensland Branch) to the Carnarvon Ranges left Brisbane on July 6, 1937 with 11 members to 'explore that vast area known as the Carnarvon Ranges'.[17] It was led by the enthusiastic but undoubtedly eccentric society member, Danny O'Brien. It was the first of at least fourteen expeditions to the sandstone tablelands between 1937 and 1958. O'Brien was a controversial figure in the Queensland Society. He is remembered today less as an heroic advocate of the Carnarvons, the maker of an inland service industry resource, than as a 'abrasive' and 'self-indulgent' personality who seriously damaged the reputation of the Society among scientists. Indeed, the government is reported to have complained that under his leadership the Society was no longer serving its function of providing geographical information for the administration of Queensland.[18]

O'Brien's expeditions were representative of a modern Australia, a modernising Australia. The group travelled not by horseback, but by train and car. Trails were not carved through unknown lands. The groups travelled with local guides from nearby pastoral leases and frequently arranged ritualistic ceremonies of governmentality, various civic welcomes and fare-wells, to mark their passage through the area. By this stage in the settlement and development of modern Australia, this place at best could be described by O'Brien as 'little known land'.[19]

In this history 'the geographer' is not simply the maker of maps; the area had already been surveyed and mapped by the time the Society came to Carnarvon Gorge, no frontier cartography was necessary. Less than ten years after the first expedition, the Carnarvons was captured on an aerial photograph run. All major natural features were already named, even renamed, as O'Brien's own account testifies:

> *We stood on Consuelo Tableland . . . and viewed the great valley of Lethbridges' Pocket with its deep walls. . . . We saw in the distance, Tyson's Nugget, Mount Lethbridge (also known as Keniff's Lookout), Vandyke Creek, veering away towards Springsure and Mount Sugarloaf.[20]*

All that was left to name for this mimic explorer were overlooked geographical features or newly-constructed engineering works. O'Brien immodestly named after himself a road he had lobbied local authorities to grade and a makeshift causeway made by the members of one of his expeditions.

O'Brien did not just lead expeditions to these areas; he wrote about, photographed and filmed them. These 'explorers' did not harbour the reluctance for photography Paul Carter noted in their predecessors.[21] O'Brien's writings appeared in special Society publications and his visual records of the Gorge were presented in lantern slide and film showings in Brisbane and regional centres throughout Queensland. O'Brien's writings on his visits to Carnarvon Gorge are not part of that genre of information which might help us reconstruct the 'real' geography of Carnarvon Gorge, but they are important in reconstructing an imaginative geography of desire. His writings are more aptly described as travelogues than scientific treatises. They are fledging promotional documents with descriptions of place more romantic than systematic. O'Brien's activities on behalf of the Royal Geographical Society during the 1930s and 1940s thus mark a moment when the geographical imagination shifts from the cartographic to the scenic, in the quest to invent a tourist destination.

O'Brien's 'pioneer expedition' was considered a triumph less because of the new knowledges it established than the verification that the gorge could be reached by car over level country, and that, if an all-weather road was built, the Gorge could be reached in a 'comfortable' two-day motor trip from Brisbane. In his writings O'Brien was self consciously constructing a place which was to have a particular role in the on-going development of Australia and the state of Queensland. His 1942 publication entitled 'Carnarvons' was written 'for the development of the state' and copies were duly posted to President F. D. Roosevelt, Henry Ford, David Lloyd George and Prime Minister Menzies.[22] He was, by his own description, 'the honorary advocate of Carnarvon range development' and his rewards were 'the knowledge that there now exists a tourist traffic to Carnarvon National Park'.[23]

In creating this tourist destination, O'Brien's depictions of Carnarvon Gorge sought to reinvent a frontier land, an unoccupied land open to 'discovery'. In relation to Aboriginal occupation, O'Brien did not have to rely on imaginative constructs like terra nullius *(land unoccupied), which was the founding myth of the colonization of Australia. In this part of Queensland the fiction of land unoccupied had (almost) become fact through the massacres in the area and the forced removal of Aboriginal families to reserve areas. When O'Brien described his 1937 visit to the Gorge he referred to the 'old Dead Myall race'.[24] But the area was not empty of Aboriginals: there were families that still worked and lived on nearby pastoral leases and there was still a small community camped on the edge of Springsure. On one of the early expeditions, O'Brien discovered that a local Aboriginal population did exist, but noted that it was confined to a camp on the edge of the nearby town of Springsure and that the group was mainly 'mixed blood'. Under the supervision of a police officer the expedition visited the camp. Although it is very probable there were quite a large number of Aboriginals at this camp, O'Brien was only interested in photographing a man he refered to as 'the Last of the Tribe group of Aboriginals'. King Chookey's photograph was to appear in the travelogues to be issued by the Society.*[25] *In the context of the travelogue this photograph functioned as an exotic curiosity. But King Chookey, 'last' of the tribal Aboriginals, would also provide an assurance to would-be travellers that Aboriginals of this kind were few and far between in this place. Prospective travellers were told in one promotional booklet that they might look forward to camping in an 'Aboriginal cave' but were assured that the Aboriginal inhabitants had disappeared 70 years ago.*[26] *O'Brien's erasure of a 'threatening' Aboriginal population was premised on the distinction he made between 'full blood' and 'mixed blood' Aborigines. The former he relegated to the 'relic', the latter he simply discounted. In almost all of his publications Aboriginality is presented in more 'comfortable' and aesthetically pleasing ways. It is the visually impressive rock art which lines the walls of Carnarvon Gorge which is to provide visitors with a calm and scenic experience of a pacified and naturalized Aboriginality.*

In O'Brien's quest to develop this place as a tourist destination for those seeking an experience of the interior it was also necessary to construct this place as untouched by non-Aboriginal settlers. O'Brien reaches Carnarvon Gorge through modern technology and engineering and relies on non-Aboriginal guides from the local pastoral leases. Yet he depicts the place as untouched by settlement – where 'the footprints of the white man are still missing from many of its most secluded places'.[27] *Discursively depopulated, O'Brien could label his first trip to the Gorge a 'pioneer expedition' and speak convincingly of the 'insurmountable difficulties' he faced in traversing 'new country'. His writings not only made a place but also render him the pioneer hero. But he was an explorer who, like many before him, followed in the paths of others.*

> *. . . we passed over a sloping razor back with only a few feet of even surface, and although but a few hundred yards in extent, it proved to be the most thrilling experience of our whole journey. There was a precipice on each side, hundreds of feet down without a stop. The expedition moved in single file. Our guide went on before us in a casual and unconcerned way, and we followed his lead.*[28]

His heroic possession of the 'undiscovered' Carnarvons were indeed a fiction. By the end of the nineteenth century the Carnarvon Range areas had been divided between the pastoral leases of Mt Moffatt, Carnarvon, Consuelo and Bandana. By 1932 the Gorge itself had been designated by the state authorities as National Park. His desire to re-invent the masculinist project of pioneering exploration was perhaps most seriously unsettled by the presence of a small travellers cottage at the mouth of the Gorge, which was built by the local Country Women's Association around the time of the Society's first expedition to the area.

O'Brien was beset with a nostalgia for an earlier age of exploration when geographical knowledges of description and mapping were on more solid ground. O'Brien and the Royal Geographical Society attempted to consolidate the precarious masculinity of their expeditions through reference to science and technology. The very description 'expedition', from the noun 'expedite', evokes an authorized, systematic venture with an intent of clearing difficulties, or hastening progress. O'Brien consciously brought modernity to the Gorge. His journeys were marked by orchestrated technological rituals which were later reported to the Society. He claimed to have made the first chartered air flight over the Gorge and the first wireless transmission from the Gorge. This performance of progress ultimately gave way to the pursuit of pleasure.

By 1956 a circular letter encouraging people to come on a Royal Geographical Society trip to the Gorge was still referring to the ventures as 'expeditions'. But the practice of 'expedition' was giving way other notions. The brochure which promoted the Society tours describes what travellers might expect:

'An outstanding feature of recent expeditions is that though we are not now attracting so many scientists, we are getting a great many intelligent younger people. Thus the real aims of our Society are being accomplished, and instead of geology, anthropology, etc., just being laborious subjects in the lecture room, they are now 'picnic' subjects – education by pleasure. Our students don't get nervous collapses caused by study, though some have collapses caused by Cupid. . . . This is Queensland's biggest picnic trip'.[29]

O'Brien's dream was being realized: the Society's visits to Carnarvon Gorge might well be seen as infant forms of niche tourism: an adventure tour, a cultural tour, an eco-tour, perhaps even Australia's first version of ClubMed.

Despite O'Brien's avid advocacy of Carnarvon Gorge and the early interest by the Queensland Tourism Bureau in the area this place, Carnarvon Gorge was received ambivalently. A post-war (1949) visit to the area by tourism officials and the press led to reports that the area was 'over-rated as a tourist attraction', had 'disappointing' scenery and poor accessibility. At best, it concluded, the area might serve as a cheap holiday destination for 'low income western residents'.[30]

Carnarvon Gorge has remained a relatively inaccessible place, a destination only for the keen long distance traveller or the local. Tourist numbers remain relatively modest when compared with the massive levels of tourism experienced by the more famous and spectacular National Parks of Kakadu or Uluru. The main road to the Gorge is still unsurfaced and there is no five-star hotel resort. The pace of recent tourist development of the area has been largely regulated by a local non-Aboriginal, a self appointed gatekeeper of Carnarvon, who works for the National Parks Service. O'Brien saw the opening up of the Gorge as dependent upon the intervention of engineering, the construction of roads, the building of resorts. The current manager of this site has used engineering and technology to different ends – to contain visitors to direct their paths through the Gorge. In the early 1980s military helicopters airlifted timber into the Gorge so that massive boardwalks, the first of their kind at art sites in Australia, might be built. The boardwalks were designed to keep tourists away from the art, they protect 'heritage'. But the boardwalks also opened the art to more precise and regulated scrutiny, directing where visitors go, drawing the visitor's attention to specific details, interpreting the art in terms of technique and meaning and presenting the signature of 'heritage' on the landscape of Carnarvon Gorge. These structures, built to protect the art, inscribe the on-going possession of this place by tourism.

The true meaning of the gorge to the Aboriginal people may never be explained. The Aborigines coexisted successfully with the environment in this area before the pyramids of Egypt were built, but they left no written record.[31]

Reclaiming Place

Returning to my mother's 'born country' complemented my own sense of identity and belonging, and my pride in this. It was important to me that we made this trip together as she had been insisting for quite some time, pining for her homelands. We shared a special furthering of our mother-daughter bond during this time, although we argued incessantly about nothing as usual or, as she calls it, 'fighting with our tongues'. I began to gain an insight into and understanding of her obvious attachment and relationship to her country and how our people cared for this place long before the Royal Geographical Society and park rangers ever clapped eyes on it. The way my mother moved around, kissed the earth and said her prayers will have a lasting effect on my soul and memory because she was paying homage and respect to her ancestors who had passed on long ago but whose presence we could both intensely feel.

This was our place, my sense of becoming. The land of my mother and my maternal grandmother is my land too. It will be passed down to my children and successive generations, spiritually, in the manner that has been carried out for thousands of years. As Rita's daughter, I not only share the celebration and the pain of her experience but also the land from which we were created.

Like most Aboriginal people it is my spiritual and religious belief that we come from this land hence the term 'the land my mother'. This land is our birthing place, our 'cradle'; it offers us connection with the creatures, the trees, the mountains, the rivers and all living things. This is the place of my dreaming. There are no stories of migration in our Dreamtime stories. Our creation stories link us intrinsically to the earth. This is why place and land is so important to us, it does not matter where and when we were born.

The High Court Mabo decision of 1992 and the subsequent Native Titles Act will attempt to rectify some of these injustices through the new land claim process. Claims are already being prepared on behalf of the Bidjara people for the Carnarvon Gorge area. Five other clan groups may also lay claim to it, as this place was used by a number of groups for ceremonial purposes. Tensions are mounting between the Aboriginal traditional owners and interest groups, pastoralists, National Parks and Wildlife Service and of course the white experts. Decisions made by the Aboriginal Land Claims Tribunal will need to consider the concerns of all interested parties and not just Aboriginal concerns. Any claims we Bidjara people make to this country under the provisions of the new Native Titles Act will have to counter the myths that there are no Aboriginal people for this place. The claims we as Aboriginal owners of this land can make are tainted by dispossession and its violence on our memories.

Rita and other elders will now be pressured to remember their childhood memories of their place to help prove our association with this country. Not so long ago the protectionist and assimilationist policies of the day pressured our elders to deny and forget. How ironic it is that now every detail must be recalled and told and that this remembering and this telling is now honourably encouraged and documented and forms the basis for land claims being won or lost. History finds a way of reinventing itself for Aboriginal people, for better or for worse.

In conclusion, I want to return to the early tourists. Their desire for tourist pleasure was always shadowed by the memory of violence. Mrs Hamlyn-Harris was one of the first women to go on a Royal Geographical Society Carnarvons expedition. She wrote a series of poems about this place as a tribute to the intrepid leader Danny O'Brien. In one of her poems, simply entitled 'Carnarvon Gorge', she contemplated the history that led to her coming to my place.

> Yes, what have we done?
> The past is dead by our own hand. The olden race is gone.
> They are but ghosts, those spirits of the wind and trees,
> That sigh such doleful threnodies!
> We of To-day by duty bound must wake
> And silence them with Joy's sweet laughter ringing,
> And children's voices singing!
> We must arise, and of this primal playground make
> A resting place for toiling families of the drought stricken west
> Needful of Nature's healing and of rest.
> Thus shall we at last
> Make humble expiation for the past.[32]

Turning Kooramindanjie Place into Queensland's 'biggest picnic ground' has not made 'humble expiation' for the past.

NOTES

1 Walking trail interpretation sign produced by Queensland National Parks and Wildlife Service, Baloon Cave, Carnarvon Gorge National Park (n.d.).

2 Judith Binney, 'Maori oral narratives, Pakeha written texts: two forms of telling history', *New Zealand Journal of History*, 21(1), 1987, pp. 30–32.

3 Queensland National Parks and Wildlife Service, *Carnarvon National Park: Park Guide*, QNPWS, 1991. By the QNPWS estimates, the area would have been clear of Aboriginals by the 1880s. Auntie Rita and her family were taken from her country in the 1920s.

4 The following section is reprinted in Rita Huggins and Jackie Huggins, *Auntie Rita*, Aboriginal Studies Press, for the Australian Institute of Aboriginal and Torres Strait Islander Studies, 1994, pp. 7–12.

5 Reprinted in Huggins and Huggins, *Auntie Rita*, pp. 7–8.

6 Gordon Reid, *A Nest of Hornets: The Massacre of the Fraser Family at Hornet Bank Station, Central Queensland 1857 and related events*. Oxford University Press, 1982; and Raymond Evans, Kay Saunders and Kathryn Cronin, *Race Relations in Colonial Queensland: A History of Exclusion, Exploitation and Extermination*, University of Queensland Press, St. Lucia, 1988.

7 See as examples J. Brian Harley, 'Maps, knowledge and power' in Denis Cosgrove and Steven Daniels (eds) *Iconography of Landscape*, Cambridge University Press, 1988, pp. 277–312: David N. Livingstone, *The Geographical Tradition*, Blackwell, 1992.

8 See for the more general point of mapping and naming Paul Carter, *The Road to Botany Bay*, Faber and Faber, 1987, pp. 320–352: Paul Carter, *Living In A New Country*, Faber and Faber, 1992, pp. 9–27 and p. 123–124.

9 Michel de Certeau, *The Practice of Everyday Life*, University of California Press, 1984, p. 121.

10 James Clifford, 'Traveling Cultures', in Lawrence Grossberg, Cary Nelson, Paula Treichler (eds), *Cultural Studies*, 1992, pp. 104–5.

11 Martin Heidegger, 'Building, Dwelling, Thinking', in Martin Heidegger, *Basic Writings*, Harper San Francisco, 1977, pp. 319–340.

12 Sharon Zukin, *Landscapes of Power: From Detroit to Disney World*, University of California Press, Berkeley, 1991.

13 David Harvey, 'From place to space and back again: Reflections on the condition of postmodernity', in Jon Bird, Barry Curtis, Tim Putnam, George Robertson and Lisa Tickner (eds), *Mapping the Futures: Local Cultures, Global Change*, Routledge, 1993, p. 11.

14 Doreen Massey, 'Power-geometry and a progressive sense of place' in Jon Bird, Barry Curtis, Tim Putnam, George Robertson and Lisa Tickner (eds), *Mapping the Futures: Local Cultures, Global Change*, Routledge, 1993, p. 64.

15 See Ken Gelder and Jane M. Jacobs, 'Uncanny Australia', *Ecumene*, forthcoming.

16 Queensland National Parks and Wildlife Service, *Carnarvon National Park: Park Guide*, QNPWS, 1991.

17 Danny O'Brien, *Carnarvons*. Published under the auspices of the Carnarvon Range Association, Brisbane. Records of the RGSA (Qld), 1942, p. 2.

18 P. D. Griggs, *A Dream in Trust: The Centenary of the Royal Geographical Society of Australiasia, Queensland, Incorporated*. Special issue: *Queensland Geographical Journal* 8, July 1985, pp. 82–84.

19 O'Brien, *Carnarvons*, p. 8.

20 Danny O'Brien, *The Carnarvon Ranges: Expedition of 31 all told, 18.9.'50 to 3.11.'50*. Unpublished manuscript. Records of the RGSA (Qld),1950, p. 2.

21 Paul Carter *Living in a New Country*, Faber and Faber, 1992, p. 31. Carter argues that there is an odd absence of photographical technologies in early exploration and geographical travels.

22 O'Brien, *Carnarvons*, p. 8.

23 O'Brien, *Carnarvons*, p. 36.

24 O'Brien, *Carnarvons*, p. 21.

25 O'Brien, *Carnarvon Pictorial*, p. 6.

26 Danny O'Brien, *The Carnarvon Ranges*, RGSA (Q), Records of the RGSA (Q), 1947, p. 12.

27 Danny O'Brien, quoted in Anon., Manuscript in Records of the RGSA (Q), n.d., p. 1.

28 O'Brien, *Carnarvons*, p. 5.

29 Circular letter from Peter Grant and Tom Denning, Joint Organisers of the 1956 RGSA (Qld) Carnarvon Expedition, to prospective participants, Records of the RGSA (Q), February 1956.

30 *Charleville Times*, 'The Carnarvon Ranges Fails as Tourist Attraction', 22 December, 1949.

31 Queensland National Parks and Wildlife Service, *Carnarvon National Park: Park Guide*, QNPWS, 1991.

32 M. Hamlyn-Harris, 'Carnarvon Journey and other Verses of the Series "Mid Highways and Byways of Queensland"'. Tribute to D. A. O'Brien from Friends RGSA. RGSA (Qld) Records, n.d.

Tracing connection: Margaret Preston and Kate Harding by Deborah Edwards

In an interview in 2017 Dale Harding spoke not only of his unbroken connection to Country and an ongoing responsibility to maintain systems of knowledge held through Bidjara, Ghungalu and Garingbal forebears, but also of the significance of women in the 'bigger stories' of his culture.[1] His mother, Kate Harding, who is in his words 'a very skilled maker in many different media', and who has worked materially with him over recent projects, has been engaged for over forty years with what is still referred to as the 'domestic' or (even) 'feminine' arts— sewing, crochet, Japanese beading, embroidery, appliqué and quilting.[2]

Kate and Dale Harding's connection to Kooramindanjie (the Carnarvon Ranges) is a heritage encompassing extraordinary expanses of Indigenous ochre stencils, rock engravings and freehand paintings. Taken to Carnarvon as a baby by her mother to be with a female Elder, Kate Harding has long been involved in the important matrilineal lines that deliver 'bigger stories' about her culture. During the past several years she has moved into new artistic territories, shifting her practice from the creation of functional domestic objects steeped in Western traditions of sewing to one that is centred on her identity, her family's history and her relationship to her Country.[3] Her recent works signal not only a decolonising and Indigenising of Western domestic arts, but a desire to create and locate her creations within both European and Indigenous traditions and forms.

It seems likely that early twentieth-century modernist Margaret Preston managed to visit Carnarvon Gorge in 1940.[4] For around three months from July to September, Preston travelled with her husband by plane and truck, viewing Indigenous rock-art sites in Arnhem Land, the

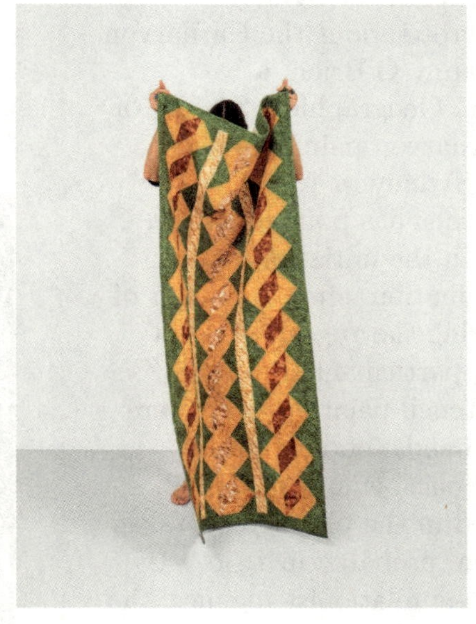

FIG 01
Kate Harding, *Cylinders* 2020, textile and appliqué, 187 × 100 cm, Courtesy of the artist. Photo: Carl Warner

1   Queensland Art Gallery and Gallery of Modern Art, 'Dale Harding introduces *Wall composition in Rickett's Blue*', 10 October 2017, YouTube, https://www.youtube.com/watch?v=b5YUwryn1KQ.

2   Dale Harding, 'Environment is part of who you are', 12 October 2019, YouTube, Tate, https://www.youtube.com/watch?v=-EA77G9UKIc.

3   Kate Harding, conversation with author, 16 September 2020.

4   While Preston did not publicly elaborate on a visit to Carnarvon, her husband William Preston's photograph of the stencil galleries of Carnarvon appears on the same page of a Preston photographic album (in the collection of the National Gallery of Australia) as those of Injalak Hill (Oenpelli), which Preston certainly did visit in 1940 and which she wrote about in a public article. To travel to Aboriginal reserves, missions and rock-art sites in the Northern Territory in 1940, after war had been declared, required special governmental permissions (which the Prestons were granted through business connections), yet there appear not to have been the same restrictions in place to travel to Queensland sites.

Kimberley, Bathurst and Melville Islands, Kakadu and probably Carnarvon Gorge. There she would have seen extensive stencil paintings in red, mauve, yellow, black and white ochres on white sandstone escarpments, and galleries of symbolic rock carvings—artworks which, as activist and scholar Marcia Langton has noted, can be recognised as a definition of territory and identity, and perhaps a form of census.[5]

Preston certainly attempted to see Carnarvon in 1943 and she did visit there in 1947[6] during a trip which encompassed rock-art sites in Central Queensland, the Kimberley, Groote Eylandt, Chasm Island, Rossel Island, Darwin and Alice Springs, and included travel over 'many miles of rough black soil roads impassable after rain' to view the spectacular galleries of Carnarvon Gorge.[7] It was on this trip that Preston collected ochres to grind into paint on her return to Sydney.

By 1940 Preston had been a student of Indigenous art for at least fifteen years and its impact had catalysed a profound reorientation of her art. It led to the creation of two major bodies of 'Indigenised' artwork: her designs for domestic crafts in the 1920s, and a set of major landscape paintings (and still lifes) in the 1940s.

The 1940 trip marked the beginning of Preston's decade-long methodical investigation of Indigenous rock-art sites across Australia. At one level this was a product of increasing interest among European Australians in rock painting and carving sites, which were documented in the 1930s by anthropologists such as Sydney based Frederick McCarthy, who wrote in 1939 of 'the astonishing wealth of drawings and paintings in rock shelters and caves throughout Australia'.[8] At the same time, the popular magazine *Walkabout* began to feature articles on the regions and rock art of Northern Australia (including the Carnarvons in 1941). Preston probably sourced information about visiting Carnarvon through her connection with members of the Anthropological Society of New South Wales, including prominent Sydney anthropologist A.P. Elkin who wrote about the Carnarvon paintings in *Oceania* in 1940. Danny O'Brien, a Queensland member of the Royal Geographical Society of Australasia, lectured on the Carnarvon paintings and carvings to Society members in Sydney in 1944.[9]

As geographer Jane M. Jacobs has pointed out, in the 1940s Carnarvon Gorge was in the initial phases of being developed as a tourist destination, after a number of non-Indigenous 'expeditions' during the 1930s.[10] After a 1937 trip led by Danny O'Brien, participant Reverend Hayes reported in the press on stencil paintings that were 'the finest he had ever seen'; of 'hands, boomerangs . . . nulla nullas, stone-axes . . . dilly bags, emu feet, human feet, tools'. Paintings are featured in the photograph taken by William Preston at Carnarvon, probably in 1940.[11] By this time, under colonialist and assimilationist regimes, the Indigenous owners of the Carnarvon Ranges had suffered decades of violence, systematic dispossession of their lands and relocation to missions or government-administered settlements such as Cherbourg and Woorabinda. Kate Harding's great grandmother, Ada Mummins, her grandmother and her mother, all spent significant parts of their lives in Woorabinda.[12]

Preston did not literally transpose the stencil imagery of Carnarvon artworks into her own prints and paintings, and less is known about her response to the Carnarvons than to several other rock-art sites she wrote publicly about. One assumes that descriptions of the impact of the Carnarvon artworks were featured in her 1948 manuscript, *Into the blue: a guide to Central and*

5   Marcia Langton, 'Prehistory', in *Marcia Langton: Welcome to Country*, Hardie Grant Travel, Richmond, Vic., 2018, p. 7.

6   In relation to her attempted visit in 1943, Preston reported that 'the powers say no', perhaps referring to wartime restrictions. Margaret Preston, letter to Clem Christensen, 25 August 1943, Preston archives, Art Gallery of New South Wales, Sydney.

7   See biographical notes in Deborah Edwards and Rose Peel with Denise Mimmocchi, *Margaret Preston*, Art Gallery of New South Wales, Sydney, 2005, p. 280. The trip included sites near the Rupert river in Central Queensland, as well as the Victoria, Katherine, Alligator and Roper river areas in the Northern Territory.

8   Frederick McCarthy, 'Aboriginal Art', *Art in Australia*, ser. 3, no. 77, 15 November 1939, pp. 53–62.

9   A.P. Elkin, 'Cave painting in the Carnarvon Ranges, South East Queensland', *Oceania*, vol. 11, no. 1, Sep 1940, pp. 114–15; Edwards, Peel and Mimmocchi, *Margaret Preston*, 2005, fn. 111, p. 295.

10   Jane M. Jacobs, in Jackie Huggins, Rita Huggins and Jane M. Jacobs, 'Kooramindanjie: Place and the postcolonial', *History Workshop Journal*, no. 39, Spring 1995, p. 175–76.

11   'Wonders of the Ranges. In Carnarvon Gorge', *The Northern Miner*, Charters Towers, 23 August 1937, p. 4; trip also cited in A.P. Elkin, 1940, p. 114.

12   Kate Harding, conversation with author, 16 September 2020.

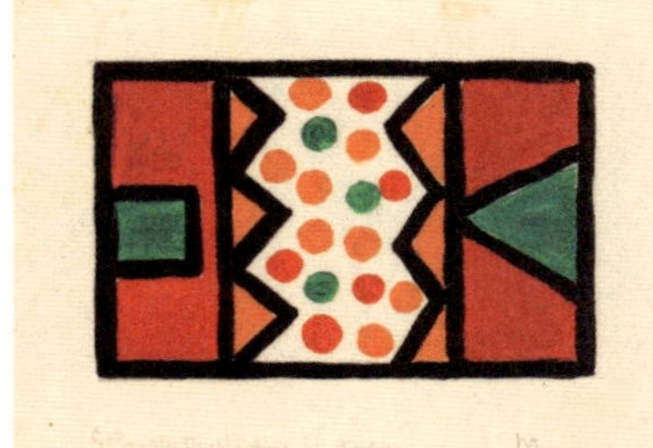

FIG 02
Margaret Preston, *Aboriginal design—Letter M: Design from a Golmary shield* c.1927, gouache on paper, 13.3 × 19.2 cm (sheet), 9 × 14.4 cm (image), State Art Collection, Art Gallery of Western Australia, Perth, Purchased through the Sir Claude Hotchin Art Foundation, Art Gallery of Western Australia Foundation, 1998. © Margaret Preston/ Copyright Agency, 2021

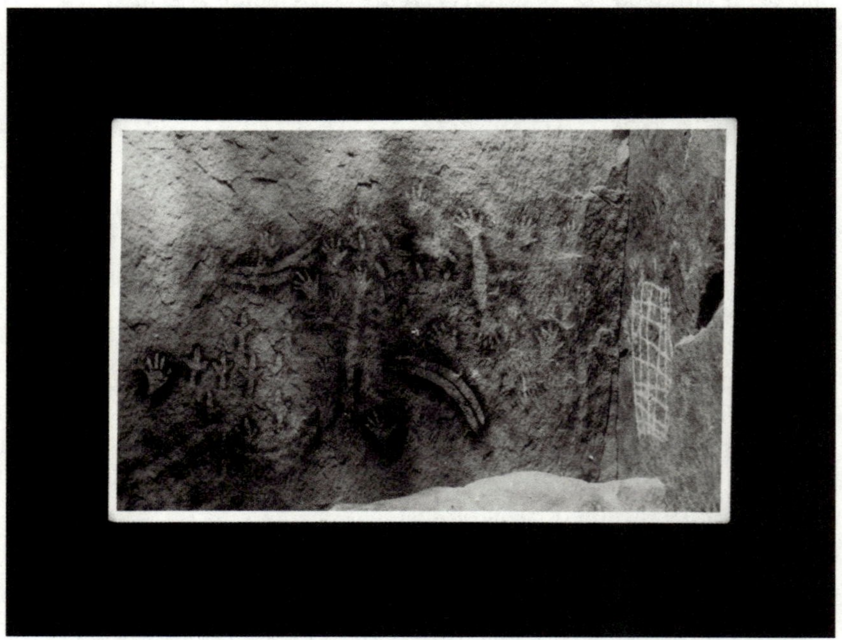

FIG 03
William Preston, *Rock art at Carnarvon Gorge* c.1940 or 1947, gelatin silver photograph, National Gallery of Australia, Canberra, Gift of Mrs L. Hawkins 1987, 1987.2196

Northern Australia (now lost), which was described at the time as 'an account of a six months' trip . . . through the far North and North-West of Australia . . . written by Mrs Preston and illustrated with . . . photographs by Mr Preston . . . [with] some of the photographs of rock and cave drawings in almost inaccessible places.'[13] In any case, there is little question that the combined impact of rock murals and rock-carving sites in Queensland and the Northern Territory, including Carnarvon (and Injalak Hill at Gunbalanya—previously Oenpelli) significantly affected Preston's art.

Preston's study of Indigenous art began at a time when there was widespread ignorance about its forms, and her research into rock-art sites across Australia was virtually unprecedented among Australian artists. Nonetheless, her trips were undertaken with explicitly appropriative aims, under the perception that Indigenous authenticity and expression could be taken and literally 'possessed' by her—an attitude which lays bare the relationship between modernism and colonialism.

On return from her 1940 trip Preston declared that 'the way is now open for Australia to develop a national art.'[14] Modernism, notwithstanding its aspirations to internationalism, did not absent itself from identity politics, and at the intersection of modernism and 'Aboriginalism' in Preston's art lay an emphatically nationalist agenda. This conformed to a wider global phenomenon of colonialist societies seeking, in the crisis of impending 'post-colonialist emptiness', to build national identity from Indigenous culture. Moreover, Preston's modernist/formalist search for the artistic truths of the Australian condition focused on the aesthetic surface. Advising craftspeople about 'Aboriginalised designs' in 1930, she wrote: 'Mythology and religious symbolism do not matter to the artist, only to the anthropologist'.[15] Her segregation of aesthetics from meaning and from any sense of the oppressive social realities for Indigenous people make her one of the first and most problematic appropriative artists in a history of cultural and social abuse. As Arrernte-Kalkadoon curator Hetti Perkins wrote: 'To Aboriginal eyes [Preston's work] reads as a scrambled orthography of vaguely familiar words or a discordant symphony where the notes don't ring quite true. Preston's passionate attempts, while well intentioned, were doomed to fail ultimately because they are meaningless to Aboriginal people—not unlike the contemporaneous government policy of assimilation.'[16] If Preston's artistic nationalism was exceptional in its focus on appropriations of Indigenous art and the marginalised discipline of the domestic arts, her ultimate contribution was not the work she created under these focuses, but her prescient foregrounding of Indigenous culture as one of the great (and living) art traditions of the world.

Margaret Preston and Kate Harding are artists from different times with radically different cultural perspectives. Yet there are connections which can be traced through their practices, in the context of a desire expressed by many artists for more constructive modes of existence which acknowledge synergies or intersections between previously separated histories. As Wiradjuri-Kamilaroi-European artist Jonathan Jones has written: 'There are two ideas of culture, Indigenous and non-Indigenous. There is an overlap even if people don't admit it . . . people constantly focus on things that are not shared [but] I'm more interested in how we can look at connection.'[17]

13 Description by Gwen Morton Spencer, co-editor at Ure Smith Pty Ltd, in a letter to H. Temby, Secretary, Commonwealth Literary Fund, 28 May 1948, accompanying Preston's approach to the Commonwealth Literary Fund to assist with publishing the manuscript. Publishers rejected it in 1949 on the basis that 'unfortunately, Mrs. Preston has deliberately made of her story of Central and Northern Australia a guide-book rather than a personal record'. Beatrice Davis, Angus and Robertson, letter to H.S. Temby, Commonwealth Literary Fund, 16 February 1949, Margaret Preston series, archive, Art Gallery of New South Wales, Sydney.

14 Margaret Preston, 'Painting in Arnhem Land', *Art in Australia*, ser. 3, no. 81, Nov 1940, pp. 58–59, 61–63.

15 Margaret Preston, 'The application of Aboriginal designs', *Art in Australia*, ser. 3, no. 31, Mar 1930, n.p.

16 Hetti Perkins, 'The brown pot', in Edwards, Peel and Mimmocchi, 2005, p. 212.

17 Jonathan Jones quoted in Andrew Frost, 'Jonathan Jones: Afraid of the dark', *Australian Art Collector*, no. 42, Oct–Dec 2007, pp. 132–41.

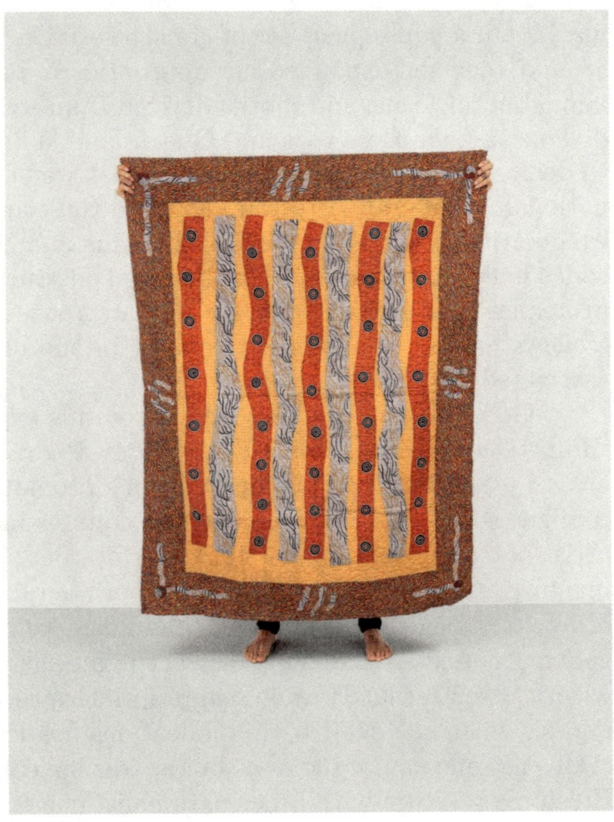

FIG 04
Kate Harding, *Carnarvon underground water* 2020, textile and appliqué, 169 × 128 cm, Courtesy of the artist. Photo: Carl Warner

The experience of Carnarvon Gorge, which is Kate Harding's heritage and a site of Margaret Preston's cultural tourism, casts one radius of connection over the two disparate artists' work. The Carnarvon galleries of rock art, along with other major rock-art sites, catalysed Preston's recognition that Indigenous art was an expression of both concept and place, and taught her lessons concerning palette, symbolic form, and what she called 'mural construction', all of which she applied to her major 1940s landscapes. Connections can also be explored between Preston's and Kate Harding's involvement in the arguably still gendered space of craft and the domestic arts. Both artists have worked in this arena with a shared commitment to reconfiguring its parameters, believing in its power to elicit change.

Preston's 1920s appropriations of Indigenous artworks as blueprint designs for domestic cushions, splash mats, curtains, sofa covers and even bracelets subsequently became a focus for re-readings of the Indigenous and non-Indigenous artistic relationship, and for interrogations of white art history—its universalising mythologies and colonialist appropriations.[18] Hoping craftspeople would succeed 'where the artists have failed', Preston's aim in promoting the domestic arts was, in essence, to create a grassroots movement to modernise Australian culture and to Australianise the modern.[19] In 1924 and 1925 she published the results of her initial studies of Indigenous artworks held in Sydney's Australian Museum as source material for such domestic designs.[20] Her focus on bold colours and flat geometricism conformed to the aesthetic emphasis of modern design, and drew her particularly to works such as a shield from Cairns, North Queensland ('for hanging shades, curtains, cushions'); a Pikan shield from Russell River, North Queensland ('appliqué work'); and a design from a 'taphoglyph' (or dendroglyph),[21] Dubbo ('suitable for a mat').[22] In a subsequent set of gouache studies created around 1927 she expanded her appropriative bases in an 'alphabet' of forms and motifs derived from sources as diverse as Lake Eyre toas and Queensland shields. Aiming to define essential artistic principles that would inform a national art of craft, Preston identified the concepts of irregularity (asymmetry) and of dynamic and complex codes between colour and form as key constructive principles of Indigenous art. By the late 1920s she had eschewed modernism's bright colours for subdued palettes associated with Indigenous work.

Gordon Bennett's late works from his expansive 'Home Décor' series, *Home décor (after M Preston)*, 2012–13, specifically focus on Preston's promotion of an 'Indigenised' home environment. His counter-move, as an artist of Anglo-Celtic and Indigenous descent, was to magnify and reorient Preston's appropriated designs in order to return the 'originals' to the fine art and art gallery context as arresting abstract paintings, carries with it a sense that Preston's appropriative racism was greater when she dealt with applications for domestic craft. Yet one can argue also for the ideological fluidity of Preston's position within her nationalistic agenda. Her unusual admiration for contemporary Indigenous craftwork, and her focus through much of the 1920s on addressing women and the domestic environment, revolved around an identity politics sustained by her sense of the profound capacity of everyday hand-crafted objects to express and transform a cultural vision. She saw these 'decorative arts' as the sub-strata of civilisation: 'Art is not cosmopolitan . . . [it] must come from ourselves and the beginning should come from the home and domestic

18   See Margaret Preston, 'The Indigenous Art of Australia', *Art in Australia*, ser. 3, no. 11, Mar 1925, n.p.

19   Ibid.

20   Margaret Preston, 'Art for crafts. Indigenous art artfully applied', *The Home*, vol. 5, no. 4, Dec 1924, pp. 30–31 and Margaret Preston, 'The Indigenous art of Australia', 1925.

21   Dendroglyphs (or what Preston and others of her time called taphoglyphs) are carved ceremonial trees which were found across large areas of south-east Australia.

22   Preston, 'The Indigenous art of Australia', 1925.

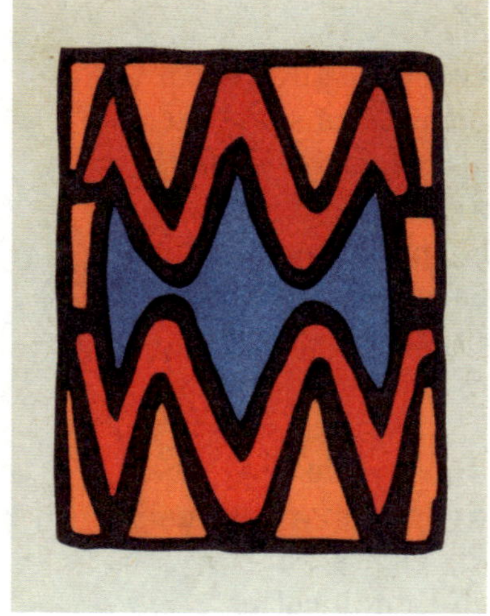

FIG 05
Margaret Preston, *Design from a shield, Cairns, North Queensland* c.1925, reproduced in *Art in Australia*, series 3, no. 11, March 1925. © Margaret Preston/Copyright Agency, 2021

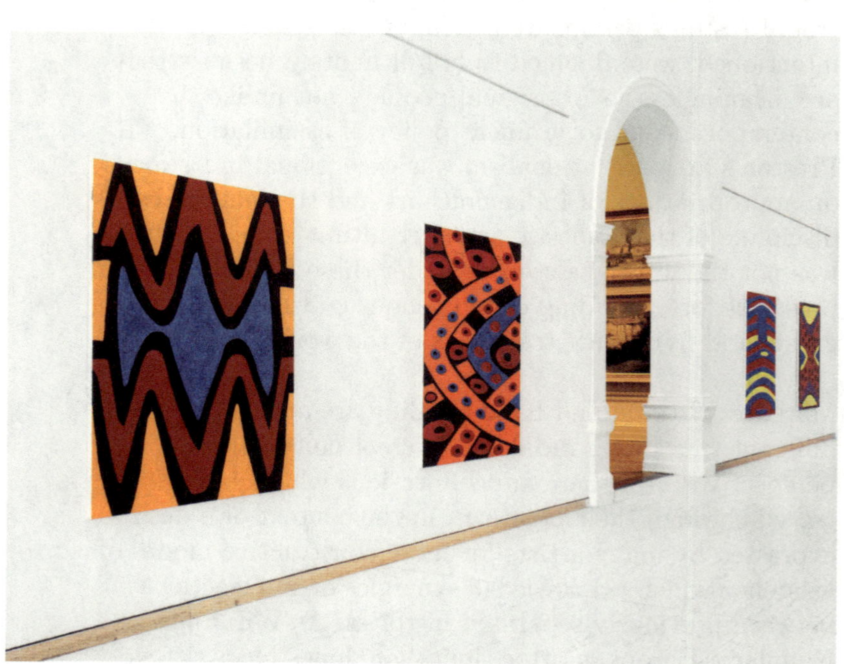

FIG 06
Gordon Bennett, works from the *Home décor (after M Preston)* series 2012-13. Installation view, Art Gallery of New South Wales, Sydney, 2017. Photo: Jenni Carter

arts. This is the reason I have studied the Aboriginal's art and have applied their designs to the simple things of life', she wrote in 1925.[23] In this sense, Preston's modernist desire for the collapse of traditional (Western) hierarchical distinctions between the fine arts and craft establishes a point of contact with Indigenous culture—a culture that resists such demarcations and incorporates such arts into all levels of life.

If her initial explorations in the Australian Museum conformed to an ethnographically organised (and static) concept of Indigenous art, Preston's first trip to Queensland (in 1927) was a revelation. It not only provided direct (and perhaps her first) exposure to Indigenous enculturation of the environment in rock-art sites, but to contemporary Indigenous craftwork such as the feather-flower posies being created by women of the Wik region of Cape York.[24] She acknowledged this work in the painting *Aboriginal flowers*, 1928, which also indicates her sense of craft as a politicised act: a recognition of the historical hierarchical distinctions between the fine arts and crafts as central to the marginalisation of women's work. This work acknowledged contemporary Cape York craft practice in a form highly resonant for her (the still life), at a time when such objects of cultural exchange were largely excluded from the category of art, dismissed instead as examples of the denigration caused by the exigencies of the European tourist trade.[25] Preston's exceptional painterly fusion of the geometrics of Purism and the Indigenous principles of 'austerity, simplicity and unity' subverts the pervasive view of Indigenous art as 'timeless and static'. In the context of her ambitions for domestic craft, this painting suggests that, far from overlooking the issue of authenticity, Preston recognised a contemporary practice which at least mirrored, and perhaps surpassed, her own pursuit of a hand-crafted composite: an authentic art at the intersection between the Indigenous and the Western.

For Kate Harding also, the domestic context is both loaded and productive. Its territory encompasses several generations of domestic work or 'service' on her mother's side, and defines the arena in which she has created artworks for decades. As Dale Harding finds that 'the countless sandstone rock-art galleries and natural spaces out on my grandparent's Countries colour my sensibility as an artist', so too Kate Harding's shift away from creating functional domestic quilts under European (largely Scandinavian and American) traditions has been driven by her connection to the Carnarvon Ranges and Mount Moffatt Country, and her family's history.[26] She now incorporates forms and colours associated with her culture and Country; she has turned to Indigenous traditions of functional making associated with her region; and she has moved away from all printed fabrics (including licensed Indigenous prints), to use ochre dyes from Country in her embroidery and fabric art—as seen in the arresting abstract *Carnarvon*, 2020.

Kate Harding's wall hangings now explicitly deliver meaning, aesthetically and conceptually, through Indigeneity. *Looking at women's influence*, 2019; *Carnarvon underground water*, 2020; *Digging for yams*, 2020; and Harding's recent work *Cloak*, 2020, all deliver embedded content through a form traditionally seen as 'decorative' (and thus contentless), demonstrating Harding's desire to 'put a story into the quilts so people can actually see them . . . our traditional stories . . . the story of our culture and our places.'[27] Kate Harding, like

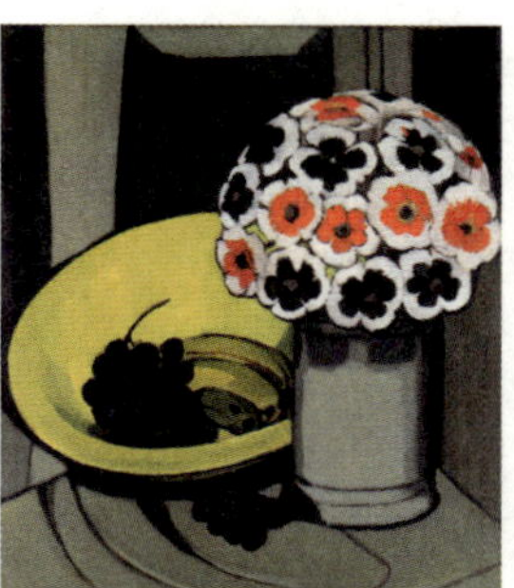

FIG 07
Margaret Preston,
Aboriginal flowers
1928, oil on canvas,
53.6 × 45.8 cm, Art
Gallery of South
Australia, Adelaide,
Gift of the Art
Gallery of South
Australia Foundation
1981, 816P15. ©
Margaret Preston/
Copyright Agency, 2021

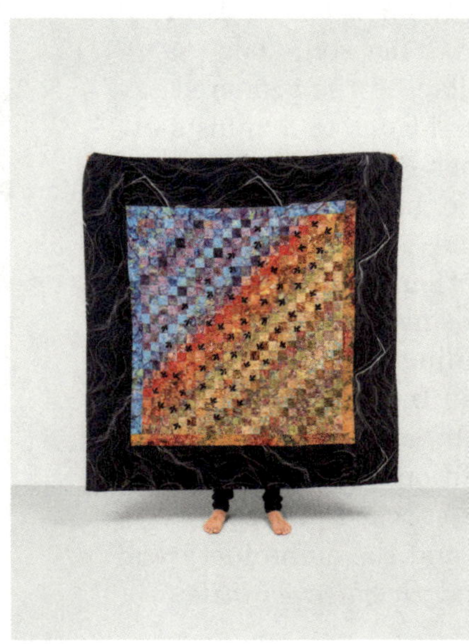

FIG 08
Kate Harding, *Tribute to women—past, present and future* 2019, textile and appliqué, 171 × 160 cm, Courtesy of the artist. Photo: Carl Warner

23 Ibid.

24 The Prestons spent six weeks travelling through North Queensland (including Rockhampton, Cairns, the Atherton Tableland, the Daintree [by boat], Cape York Peninsula, Innisfail, Herberton, Cardwell and the Great Barrier Reef), where it is probable that Margaret Preston first saw the spectacular collection of Queensland shields from the Mitchell River, Cairns district and the South West regions, at the Queensland Museum. The Prestons subsequently moved to Berowra on the outskirts of Sydney (in 1932), where her interest in rock-carving sites intensified during exploration of the Sydney and Hawkesbury region. She later published the article, 'Forming the queue for Queensland. An artist's appreciation of a six weeks tour among the grandeurs of the Northern State', in *The Home*, vol. 8, no. 12, Dec 1927, pp. 37–39.

25 The feather-flowers were acquired by Preston at Kuranda, north of Cairns. Similarly, Preston extended her acknowledgement of contemporary Indigenous women's craft in the shell-worked box from the La Perouse community featured in her painting *NSW everlasting flowers*, 1929.

26 See Dale Harding and Hendrik Folkerts, 'The present continuum: a conversation on Carnarvon Gorge, ambivalent artefacts, and reproduction as artistic method in the work', *Mousse Magazine*, no. 58, Apr–May 2017, quoted in Tess Maunder, 'Honouring cultural continuum with Dale Harding', *4A Papers*, no. 5, Nov 2018, http://www.4a.com.au/4a_papers_article/dale-harding-tess-maunder/.

27 Kate Harding, interview with Dale Harding, n.d., shared with author.

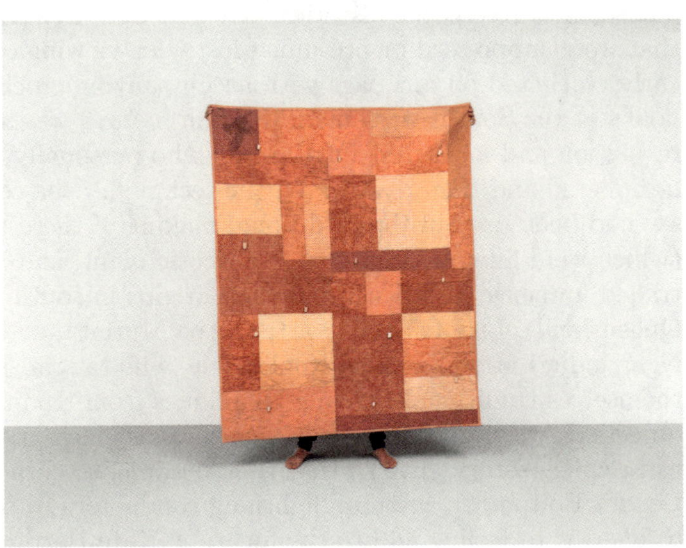

FIG 09
Kate Harding, *Carnarvon* 2020, textile and appliqué, attached thread bags, 188 × 157 cm, Courtesy of the artist. Photo: Carl Warner

Preston, believes that the domestic arts are entirely capable of embodying such narratives, and is now engaged with complex objects that signal the political, cultural, spiritual, aesthetic and (sometimes) utilitarian. Like Preston, she also came to these arts through European traditions, and continues to draw from them. Such traditions, which in part reflect the colonising framework, are now re-shaped by Harding. She creates her work in the space of bi-culturalism, through a set of productive dialogues between Indigenous and non-Indigenous traditions, techniques and motifs.

Embroidery, which Harding has described as a large part of her life, has been closely identified with nature and the feminine over centuries of Western culture, and more specifically, with the relationship of mother and daughter. Kate Harding first learnt sewing at her Catholic primary school in Clermont and by watching, from an early age, the sewing, crocheting and embroidery—'fancywork'—practices of her mother, grandmother and aunts.[28] By her early twenties she was entirely accomplished in these and other crafts in which she is largely self-taught, and she took up quilting in the early 1980s.[29] She has subsequently imparted skills in sewing, embroidery and appliqué to her son, Dale Harding. He has exposed and collapsed the gendered territory of such work in ways analogous to feminists of the 1970s who questioned divisions—between public and private, professional and domestic, intellectual and emotional, masculine and feminine—which rendered craft as 'women's work', and various other artists since the 1960s who have challenged the dismissal of textiles as 'craft' and 'feminine'. Understanding the irrelevance of the (Western) art-craft division in Indigenous histories, Dale Harding acknowledges and broadens what have been specifically matrilineal traditions in the Harding family in works such as the cross-stitched panel *A cock'atwo and a kangaroo*, 2012, and the embroidery and appliqué works *White collared* and *Bright eyed little dormitory girls*, 2013.

Crochet, one of the earliest techniques Kate Harding watched her mother and aunties engage in while making lace on linen doilies, is a practice which also belongs to the history of her people.[30] Within the context of cultural repatriation and her desire to 'leave behind . . . not just my story but the Elders' story too', crochet is one point of bi-cultural resonance.[31] Like many Indigenous artists, particularly those subject to the most corrosive effects of colonisation, Kate Harding has explored archives and museums to rediscover histories, artefacts and artworks that were suppressed or presumed lost. Her viewing of early crocheted pityuri bags with accompanying crochet hooks at the South Australian Museum in 2015 was a revelation and a catalyst for Harding who personally deciphered and then reactivated the techniques she could see had been used in the traditional making of these bags (which were filled with pityuri, a narcotic plant, and traded immense distances from their origins in south-west Queensland). Like Girramay artist, Abe Muriata, and Ngarrindjeri artist, Yvonne Koolmatrie, who taught themselves traditional weaving techniques from traditional objects, Kate Harding sees how museum-collected artworks can render history alive so that they become, as curator Lissant Bolton has written, 'lightning conductors to place, to history, to feeling and to the future'.[32] Kate Harding's miniaturised pityuri bags, which were first exhibited as prefiguring works in Dale Harding's exhibition *The drive home* in 2018, have been spontaneously scattered and then sewn onto the major wall hanging, *Carnarvon*.

28   Kate Harding, conversation with author, 16 September 2020.

29   Ibid.

30   Ibid.

31   Kate Harding, interview with Dale Harding, n.d., shared with author.

32   Lissant Bolton, 'Moving objects: Indigenous Australia in the British Museum', in Therese Osborne and Julie Simplin (eds), *Encounters. Revealing stories of Aboriginal and Torres Strait Islander objects from the British Museum*, National Museum of Australia, Canberra, and the British Museum, London, 2015, p. 30.

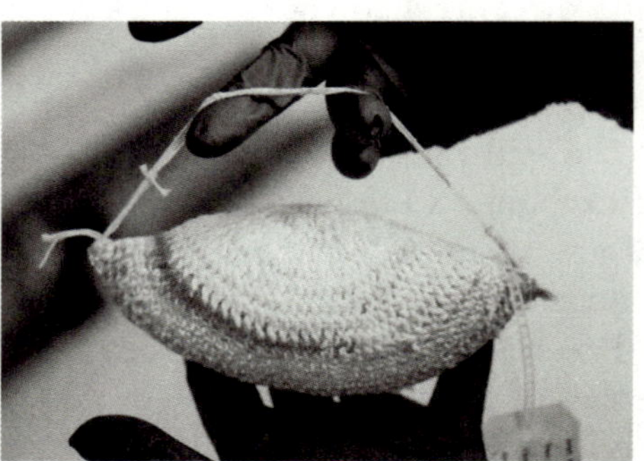

FIG 10
Bag, pituti (pityuri bag), South Australian Museum, Adelaide, 2014. Photo: Dale Harding

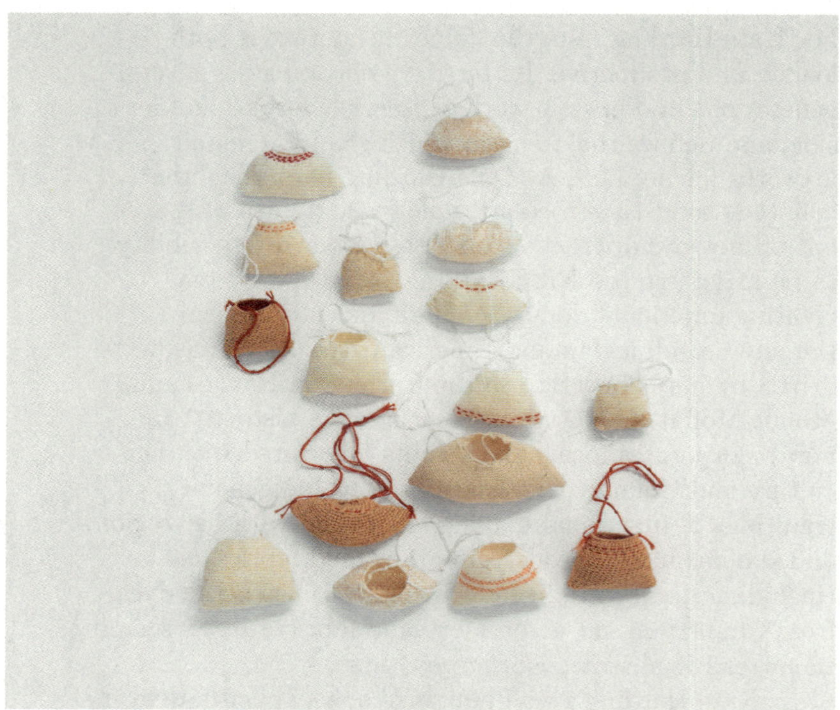

FIG 11
Kate Harding, selection of pityuri bags 2019-20, thread, each approx. 3 cm, Courtesy of the artist. Photo: Carl Warner

In the 1940s Margaret Preston reasserted her commitment to a national art forged through appropriation of Indigenous artforms—one which relied on the relationship between the artist and the wider population, 'without whose thoughts and wishes no national art that is vital and living can be produced'.[33] In doing so she embarked on a new genre in her oeuvre—that of landscape—under artistic revelations prompted by viewing Australian rock-art sites.

In 1937, the Prestons had travelled to the United States, Mexico and South America where, in modern mural paintings, Preston saw what she believed was an ideal of 'constructive nationalism'—a fusion of democratic, national and artistic ideas in a publicly sited communal art. Three years later, viewing the magnificent painting galleries at Injalak Hill and (probably) Carnarvon Gorge, Preston recognised that a more significant model for an intrinsically collective art, based on principles of 'mural construction', and expressing the essence of a people and a country (its geological forms, living organisms, and elemental actions), lay in the Indigenous rock-art sites of the Australian continent. Preston claimed Aboriginal artists to be among the finest 'muralists' in the world and wrote in 1941: 'Australia is the only country . . . that has rock cave painting consistently present. It is the only country in which rock painting still flourishes as the normal expression of Aboriginal people . . . The drawing and rock carvings . . . are realism in a wider sense than is recognised by European art . . . The study of the work of the Australian Aboriginals is nearly exhaustless.'[34]

Understanding rock art as a public communal art, fulfilling art's social function and claiming a synergy between culture and Country was Preston's central revelation, and her responses were poetic: 'The country . . . has gorges which are curiously distinctive' with 'whole walls covered with fine decorations superimposed and superimposed again. None . . . gave the feeling of chaoticness, only massiveness.'[35] Through such viewings, at Carnarvon, Gunbalanya and Groote Eylandt, Preston became convinced that 'the attention of the Australian people must be drawn to the fact that it is a great art', and that to 'be Aboriginal' was to 'know your subject and paint your knowledge'.[36] In landscape paintings created between 1940 and 1949 and monotypes between 1946 and 1948, she sought to emulate the connection to Country, and the simultaneous expression of concept and place that she recognised in rock art, in works which reveal a shifting exchange between flat mural-like composition and the spatial claims of perspectival rendering. In *Aboriginal landscape*, 1941, *Grey day in the ranges*, 1941, monotypes such as *Aboriginal design*, c.1947, and her culminating synthesis of the Western vista and Indigenous land map, *Flying over the Shoalhaven River*, 1942, Preston appropriated the flattened spaces; incipient geometricism; segmented designs; and non-hierarchical, rhythmic dispersal of forms and colours over the surface—all of which she identified as central principles of Indigenous 'mural construction'. She also modulated colours within the earth range of the regions she encountered, highlighting her understanding of the diversity of the 'Aboriginal palette'. Eighteen hues of red ochre were identified in the stencil galleries of Carnarvon for example, and this amalgam is implied in the pink, mauve and brown palette of *Aboriginal landscape*.[37] Thus in a genre (landscape) which has recently been seen as little more than an artistic representation of the processes of colonisation, one can also argue that Preston's radicalisation of this tradition was born out of a recognition of the claims to Country made by Indigenous rock-art sites.

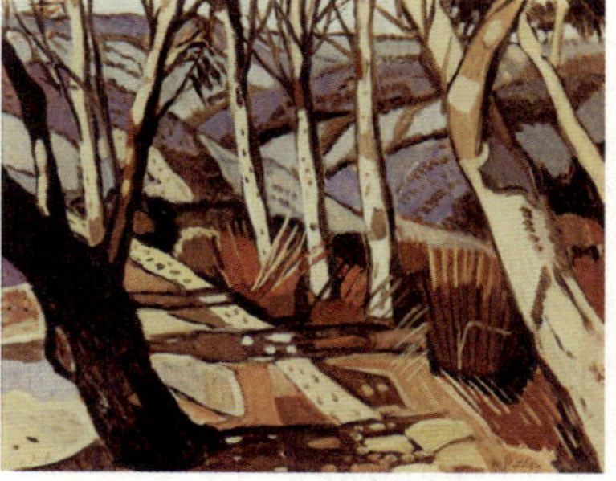

FIG 12
Margaret Preston, *Aboriginal landscape* 1941, oil on canvas, 40 × 52 cm, Art Gallery of South Australia, Adelaide, D. & J.T. Mortlock Bequest Fund 1982, 821P3. © Margaret Preston/Copyright Agency, 2021

33 Margaret Preston, 'American art under the new deal: murals', *Art in Australia*, ser. 3, no. 69, Nov 1937, p. 53.
34 Margaret Preston, 'Paintings in Arnhem Land', 1940, pp. 58–59, and Margaret Preston, 'New development in Australian Art', *Australia National Journal*, 1 May 1941, n.p.
35 Ibid.
36 Margaret Preston, 'Aboriginal art', *Art in Australia*, ser. 4, no. 2, Jun 1941, p. 46; Margaret Preston, text which appeared alongside her 'Aboriginal landscape in Australia', *Australia:National Journal*, 1 May 1941, n.p.
37 See Michael Clifford Quinnell, 'Aboriginal rock art in Carnarvon Gorge, South Central Queensland', Masters thesis, University of Sydney, 1976, p. 3.

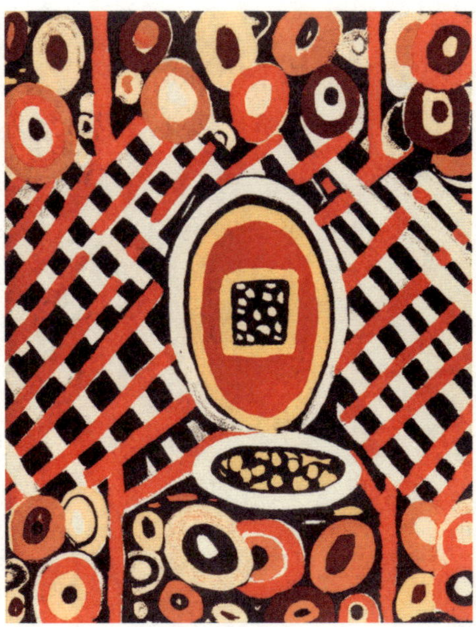

FIG 13
Margaret Preston, *Aboriginal design* c.1947, monotype, reproduced in *Margaret Preston's Monotypes*, Sydney Ure Smith (ed.), Ure Smith Publication, Sydney, 1949, end papers, © Margaret Preston/Copyright Agency, 2021

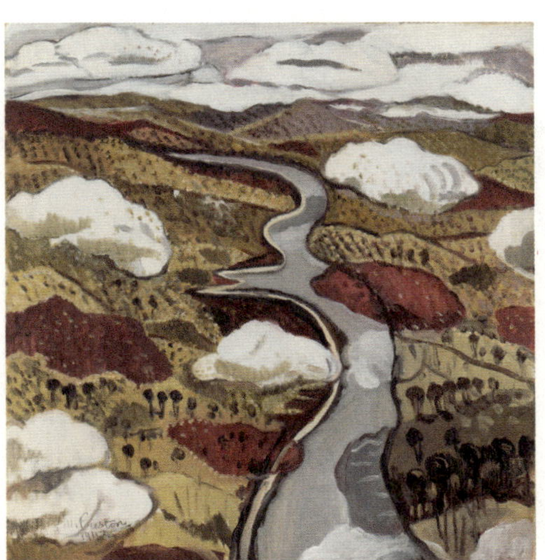

FIG 14
Margaret Preston, *Flying over the Shoalhaven River* 1942, oil on canvas, 68.6 × 68.6 × 6.8 cm framed, National Gallery of Australia, Canberra, Purchased 1973, 1973.21. © Margaret Preston/Copyright Agency, 2021

In hindsight, Preston's landscapes (and the
modernist mythologies of artists such as Russell Drysdale,
Arthur Boyd and Sidney Nolan) were perhaps the last
manifestation of an unknowing white desire for
authenticity through connection to Indigenous art and to
Country, before the paintings of Albert Namatjira and the
Indigenous art movements after him exposed such
impulses as built on borrowed land.

The creative ability to rework traditional principles,
in different media and different contexts, within the
dictates of individual expression, and yet retain the
authenticity of cultural knowledge, has been claimed as
the triumph of contemporary Indigenous art. It is by such
means that Dale Harding and Kate Harding indigenise the
global spaces of contemporary art. Kate Harding now
artistically repossesses and repositions the territories
sought by Preston for her craftwork and her painting over
the early decades of the twentieth century.

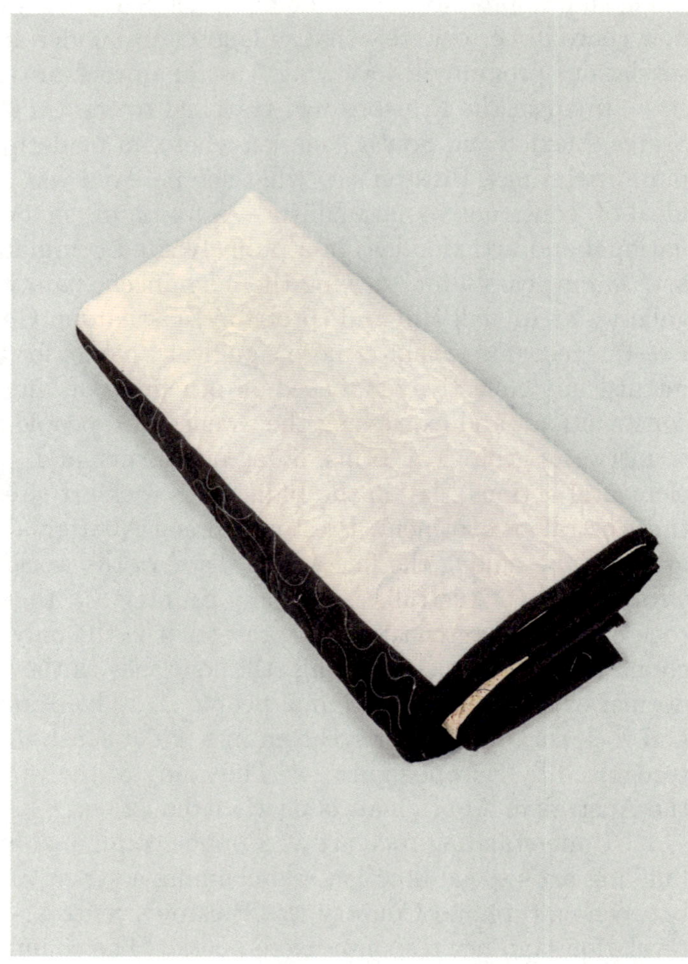

FIG 15
Kate Harding, *Cloak* 2020, textile, 70 × 40 cm, Courtesy
of the artist. Photo: Carl Warner

The ongoing Aboriginal–white Australian entanglements by Nancy Underhill

The cultural custodial obligation Dale Harding holds for the Carnarvon Range in Queensland is the core of his contemporary art practice. This conjunction, to quote Harding, 'forces him to sort out what obviously does not fit together'. The exhibition and book, *Through a lens of visitation*, are structured to assist him with that opportunity.

His approach exposes the differing responses to the Carnarvon Range by three Australian artists: his mother, Kate Harding, as well as Margaret Preston and Sidney Nolan—both of whom made visits to his grandparents' Country in the 1940s. Harding selected senior curators and art historians to provide interpretations of those artists' responses in order to elaborate his own self-exploration. Their interventions engage this exhibition and book with 'the ongoing Aboriginal–white Australian entanglements.[1]

Nolan's Outback landscapes, like Margaret Preston's works such as *Flying over the Shoalhaven River*, 1942, celebrate being modern. Air travel offered a new way of seeing landscape without reference to human achievement or scale. For Nolan and Preston, Indigenous imagery that mapped landscape was a tantalising resource. However, while Nolan's contact with the land was direct, his interaction with Indigenous people was largely second-hand via informed reports or images of the experiences of others. In fact, there is little evidence that Nolan carefully examined the rare artefacts collected by Baldwin Spencer and Leonhard Adam that were available to him in Melbourne.

For Harding the choice to include Sidney Nolan's work in his investigation was obvious.[2] He understood Nolan's short visit to Carnarvon Range in late August 1947 was the source for the imagery he deployed in the

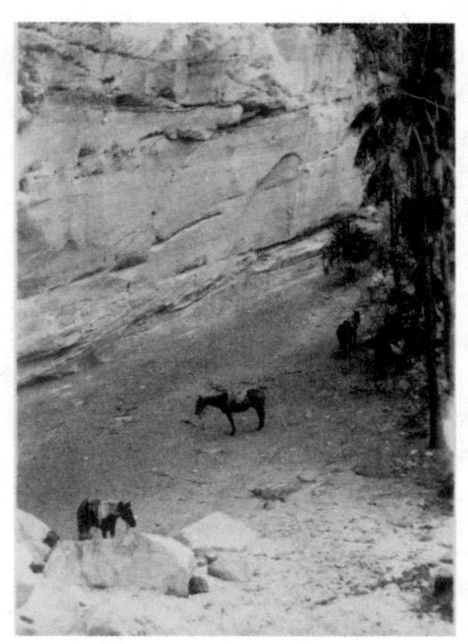

Sidney Nolan, Photograph taken entering the Carnarvon Gorge on his August 1947 visit, Papers of John and Sunday Reed, MS13186/4/PHO20, Australian Manuscripts Collection, State Library of Victoria, Melbourne

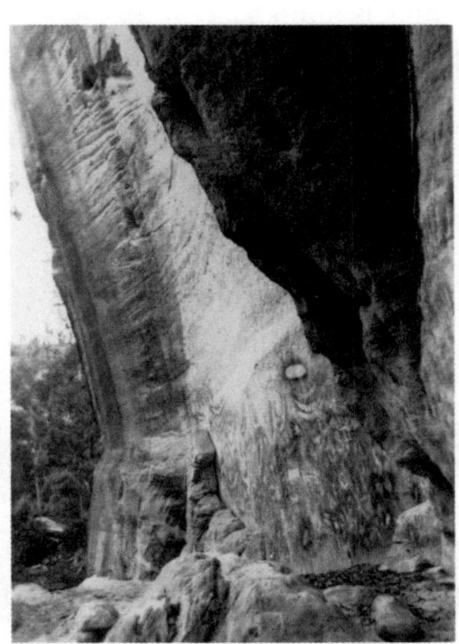

Sidney Nolan, Photograph of a Carnarvon cave taken on his August 1947 visit, Papers of John and Sunday Reed, MS13186/4/PHO17, Australian Manuscripts Collection, State Library of Victoria, Melbourne

1   A phrase used by Roslyn Poignant who was a distinguished anthropologist and wife of the photographer Axel Poignant in conversation with Natalie Wilson in the catalogue for the exhibition, *Indigenous connections*, Art Gallery of New South Wales, Sydney, 2 November 2007 – 3 February 2008.

2   Paula Dredge finds a direct connection between Nolan's 1947 visit and the stencilled hands he incorporated on the dancers' leotards in *The rite of spring* in 1962. Dredge also sees late abstracts Nolan did at The Rodd as 'strongly evocative of the Carnarvon Gorge rock art painting'. See *Sidney Nolan: The Artist's Materials*, Getty Publications, Los Angeles, 2020, pp. 101, 107 and 123. Josh Milani, Dale Harding's dealer, pointed this reference out to him.

sets and costumes for Igor Stravinsky's ballet, *The rite of spring,* chosen and choreographed by Kenneth MacMillan to celebrate Stravinsky's 80th birthday at The Royal Opera House, Covent Garden in 1962.[3] In October 1999 at his London home, Bryan Robertson, a former director of the Whitechapel Gallery, told me that as artistic advisor to The Royal Ballet Covent Garden he had ensured Nolan designed *The rite of spring.*

For many *The rite of spring* remains the greatest ballet and music of the twentieth century, which cast powerful reverence and great expectation over any new production. The aim is inevitably to honour the shock tactics established at the 1913 Paris opening of the ballet when leading radicals Igor Stravinsky, Vaslav Nijinsky and Sergei Diaghilev broke all conventions of music and dance, causing a riot inside the Paris theatre. Shock and newness remained a priority when the Royal Ballet Company decided to stage *The rite of spring* in 1962.

In that tradition, the company hired the relatively unestablished but preciously talented creative team of Kenneth MacMillan as choreographer and Sidney Nolan as designer, with Colin Davis as conductor and Monica Mason as solo dancer.[4] Davis, who conducted the notoriously eccentric music with its frequent jazz beat, was just establishing his career and his conducting of Stravinsky had been praised. Kenneth MacMillan, who had already choreographed two Stravinsky ballets, declared he would break with the conventions of classical ballet and from Stravinsky's Russian peasant setting. Instead, the ballet would explore obsession in ritual. MacMillan also radically rejected prima ballerinas *en pointe* and instead used the entire corps de ballet and selected twenty-year-old Monica Mason to debut in the ballet's solo role as the Chosen One.

In 1962, with Nolan on board, the Australian Outback became an obvious setting for this new production in London. After Robertson's 1957 Nolan retrospective at the Whitechapel Gallery, London society was fascinated by what talented, bold Australians presented. Influential art historian Kenneth Clark and critic John Russell praised Nolan's fresh new approach and subject matter. Oxford Colleges tried to buy his work. Thames & Hudson published a book on him. Nolan was regarded by the critic David Sylvester as one of the six current major world painters, outselling Francis Bacon at Marlborough Galleries. In 1957 Ray Lawler's *Summer of the seventeenth doll* won the Evening Standard Award for best new play. In 1959 Joan Sutherland became the new operatic diva at Covent Garden in *Lucia di Lammermoor.* Then came the 1961 sensational exhibition *Recent Australian painting* at Whitechapel Gallery where Arthur Boyd and Brett Whiteley attracted particular attention. In the early 1960s Barry Humphries introduced Edna Everage to London. Novelist Patrick White's *Voss* was published in 1957 and *Riders in the chariot* in 1961.[5] Of these, only *The rite of spring* featured Indigenous culture and again London was overwhelmed by the 'take no prisoners' approach to its presentation.

When Harding chose Nolan, his focus was directed to hand stencils, caves and Nolan's delight and facility at spray painting. Given Harding's role at Carnarvon and his artistic practice, these specific interests merit consideration within a wider investigation of how Indigenous art fits into Nolan's practice and how this intersection relates to what Roslyn Poignant termed 'the ongoing Aboriginal–white Australian entanglements'. To evaluate how mutually exclusive or direct the link was between Nolan's trip to Carnarvon and his design for the

   DALE HARDING: THROUGH A LENS OF VISITATION

3   The Royal Opera House Covent Garden has produced insightful video interviews about *The rite of spring* with Monica Mason and MacMillan's widow, Debora, in particular those dated 8 June 2011, 7 November 2013, and 9 November 2013. These can be accessed by searching 'Monica Mason *The rite of spring*' on YouTube.

4   As their careers progressed the three men were knighted and Monica Mason was appointed a dame for their services to British culture.

5   White, who was British born but raised in Australia, would win the Nobel Prize for Literature in 1973.

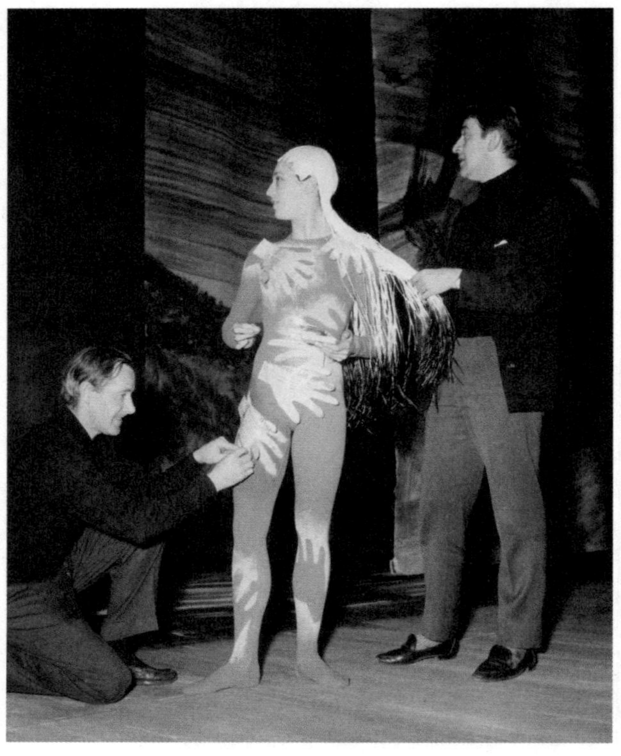

FIG 03
Axel Poignant, Sidney Nolan and Kenneth MacMillan experimenting with the translation of Nolan's design onto the costume of the Chosen Maiden performed by Monica Mason, 1962, printed 1962, gelatin silver photograph, 22.5 × 19.5 cm, Courtesy of Axel Poignant Archive

ballet fifteen years later, Harding sought an understanding of Nolan's broader approach to artmaking. Nolan was a painter who obsessively looked for new subject matter and actively explored technical materials, which for him amounted to subject matter in themselves. He was also capable of obscuring his influences and sources and of creating his own persona.

Nolan's short trip out to Carnarvon in August 1947 involved travelling with a geological expedition run by D.A. O'Brien from the Royal Geographical Society of Australasia and was part of his six-month-long exploration of Queensland and his first experience of the Outback. Nolan claimed it was a break from life with John and Sunday Reed at Heide, their home in outer Melbourne where he was one of several young modernist artists and writers who became known as the 'Heide circle'. By that time Max Harris and Albert Tucker had already left, the Reeds' publishing and artistic patronage had withered and, by July 1947, Nolan had realised his affair with Sunday was also an emotional dead end. Nolan would never live within Heide again.

Queensland's appeal was based on the Reeds' accounts of their own visit to escape Heide life in 1946, and to a large degree Nolan followed their route and advice into Far North Queensland. They did not visit Carnarvon Range. Their trip, like Nolan's, was never an anthropological or site-specific undertaking. While in Brisbane, Nolan stayed with Barrett Reid who became his informative companion on trips to the Tweed River Valley, Tamborine Mountain and Fraser Island. Importantly Reid also introduced Nolan to The State Library of Queensland where he researched accounts of Eliza Fraser's life with Indigenous tribes on Fraser Island (K'gari) and the mainland near Lake Cootharaba, a subject which became a recurring theme in Nolan's work. Nolan's correspondence does not mention researching the Carnarvon Range area.

The letters and assorted photographs sent back home by Nolan privilege landscape rather than Indigenous life. Nolan conveyed his general impressions of the Carnarvon country as well as Fraser Island in a letter of 17 September 1947 to Doris Boyd, matriarch of the Boyd family of artists and mother to Lucy, Arthur, Guy, David and Mary. His description includes:

> the land is rough with great gorges running for miles through mountains flanked on each side by sheer sandstone cliffs that are pure white in the morning sun and have just about every colour in the spectrum running through them. In the cliffs are hundreds of caves, where once the aborigines lived leaving behind them the paintings which they made by placing their hands or a boomerang against the rock and then chewing the powdered ochre in their mouths and blowing it against the object leaving the stencil imprint . . . It is strange country and stays in your mind.

Nolan added that he would like to spend a long time understanding the country.[6]

Again, on 26 July 1950, concerning a later extensive trip with his family through the Outback, Nolan wrote to Albert Tucker:

> One of the main surprises was the strong impact the aborigines made on us. They give you the key to the whole situation. They are not only intelligent but superlatively so, skilled in relations and gentle to a degree. Apart from these human factors they inform the land in an extraordinary way. They show you that the

6 Extract from a letter to Doris Boyd from Chermside, 17 September 1947, in Nancy Underhill (ed.), *Nolan on Nolan*, Viking, Melbourne, 2007, p. 146.

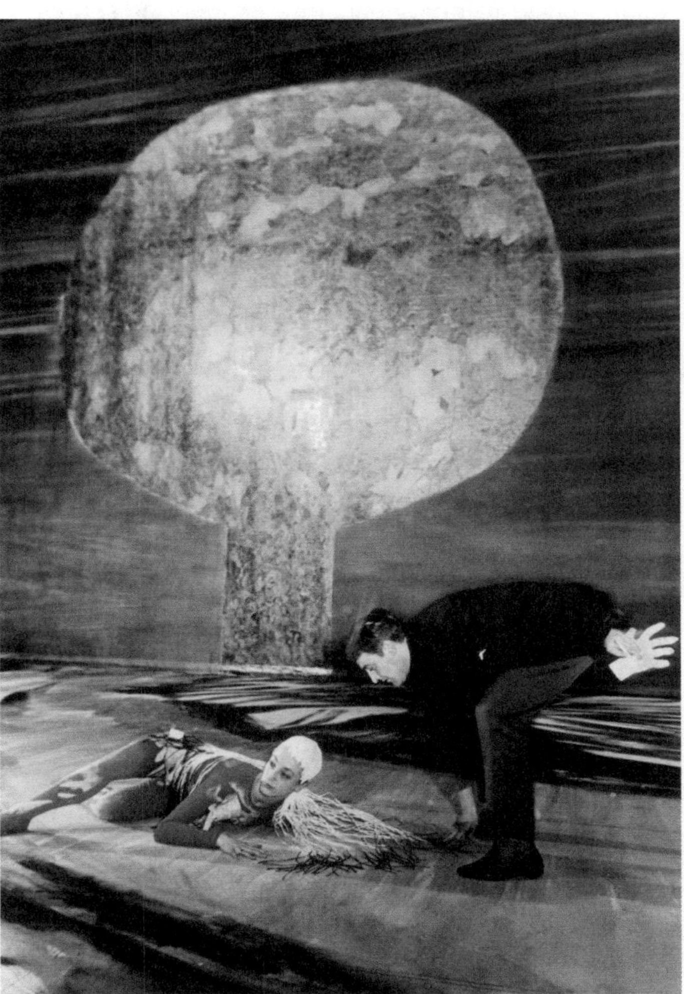

FIG 04
Axel Poignant, Kenneth MacMillan in rehearsal with Monica Mason as the Chosen Maiden, 1962, printed 1962, gelatin silver photograph, 24.5 × 16.3 cm, Courtesy of Axel Poignant Archive

7   Extract from letter to Albert
     Tucker from Wahroonga, 26
     January 1950, ibid., pp. 159–60.
8   Interview from *A current affair*,
     Australian Broadcasting
     Commission, 1 June 1987.

*country is a gentle declaiming one, the
barrenness and harshness is all in our
European eyes and demands.*[7]

In 1950 when interviewed to promote his exhibition
at David Jones Gallery, Sydney, Nolan reiterated what he
had written to Doris Boyd about Carnarvon:

> *I was fascinated by the objectivity of the arid
> endless land. The land stated its terms and left
> you to your own adjustment. Only the
> Aborigines were relaxed in an environment
> which rejected the white man . . . the rules of
> European paintings don't seem to apply out
> there.*[8]

Nolan's generalised *Landscape Carnarvon Range
Queensland*, now in the University of Western Australia
Collection, was painted in early 1948 in Sydney and
reflects his 1947 Queensland visit along with other
paintings of wildflowers, buildings and Fraser Island.

In 1947 Nolan was not an innocent and certainly
possessed the required components for being modern. To
shock and be talked about was his skilful tactic. He was
very familiar with the modernist literary cohort, which
included Charles Baudelaire, Arthur Rimbaud, Rainer
Maria Rilke, D.H. Lawrence, T.S. Eliot and Herbert Read.
Robert Lowell, Stephen Spender and Patrick White
became his close friends sharing in varying measure what
became known as 'confessional' content. Australia's most
infamous bushranger Ned Kelly, who wrote the Jerilderie
Letter, and the fictitious creation Ern Malley, for whom
two Sydney poets wrote surrealist poems, became alter
egos of fascination for Nolan. Despite mundane results,
Nolan longed to be a poet. Interestingly he shared few
close friendships with visual artists compared to musicians
and writers.

Nolan's singular training was at commercial art
firms and they acquainted him with the vibrant changes in
advertising in the 1930s and artists who purposely
featured styles and techniques which eroded the formal art
school and academy traditions of oil paint, life drawing
and single point perspective. Instead, his trade training
featured spray paint, enamels, work on glass, simplified
shapes imposed on a flat background, high key colours,
large-scale imagery and photography, and magazines
ranging from the esoteric surrealist *Vevre* to the graphic
arts journal, *Penrose Annual*. Everything was game for
adaptation. To be modern involved breaking down the
conventional through shock.

Thanks to literature, occasional exhibitions,
expansive holdings at the Victorian State Museum and
Library, and people he met and articles he read via the
Reed-supported 'little magazine' *Angry Penguins*, Nolan
could connect with a like-minded diaspora active in New
York, London, Paris and elsewhere.

At the core of this Modernist position was a
fascination with The Primitive which for Nolan was more
about inhospitable landscape than its inhabitants. Put
simply, there was a view that European individuals and
their culture had become stale, too intellectualised and
even corrupt, at the expense of an instinctive emotional
response. This is of course the thesis of Edward Gibbon's
six volume *The decline and fall of the Roman Empire*
published in the late eighteenth century and the two-
volume tome by the German thinker, Oswald Spengler
The decline of the West (1918 and 1922) which became the
authority to read—though often not completely. Spengler
argued that a need for rebalance was vital if European
culture was to become healthy. Nolan tackled that text
during war duty in the Wimmera in the early 1940s.

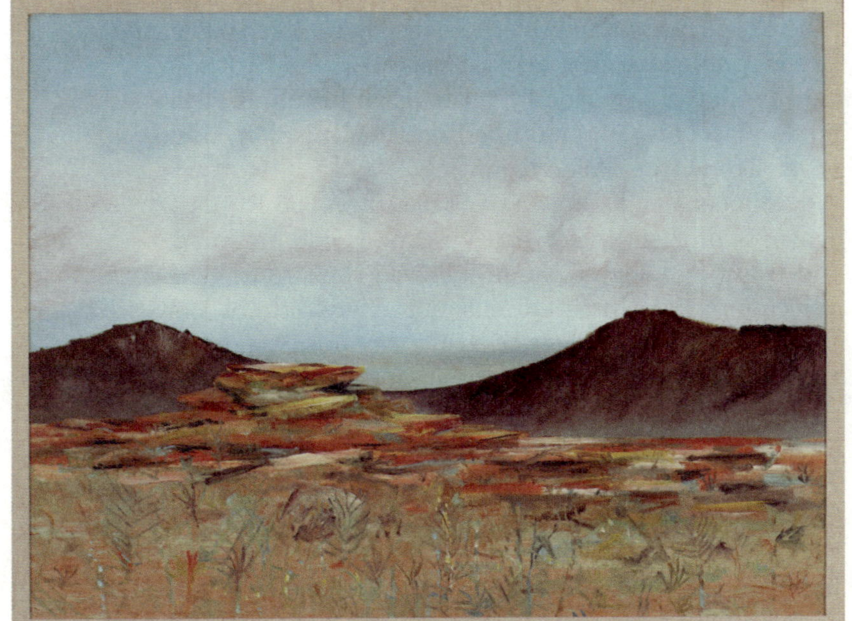

FIG 05
Sidney Nolan, *Landscape Carnarvon Range, Queensland* 1948, ripolin on
board, 91 × 121 cm, The University of Western Australia Art
Collection, Perth, Tom Collins Memorial Fund, 1953. © The Sidney
Nolan Trust. All rights reserved. DACS/Copyright Agency, 2020

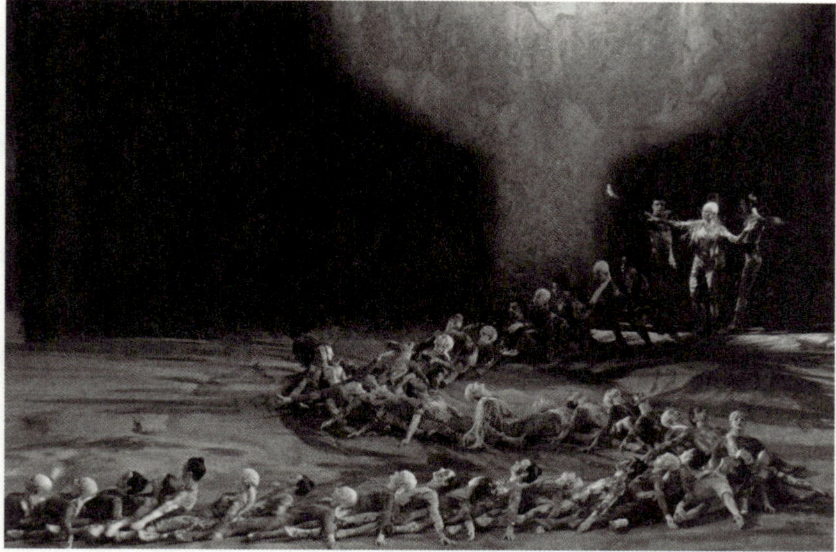

FIG 06
Axel Poignant, Dress rehearsal of Part 2, 'The Sacrifice': Rapidly, the interlocked bodies of the dancers formed a spectacular serpentine and uncoiled again, 1962, printed 1962, gelatin silver photograph, 20 × 30.3 cm, Courtesy of Axel Poignant Archive

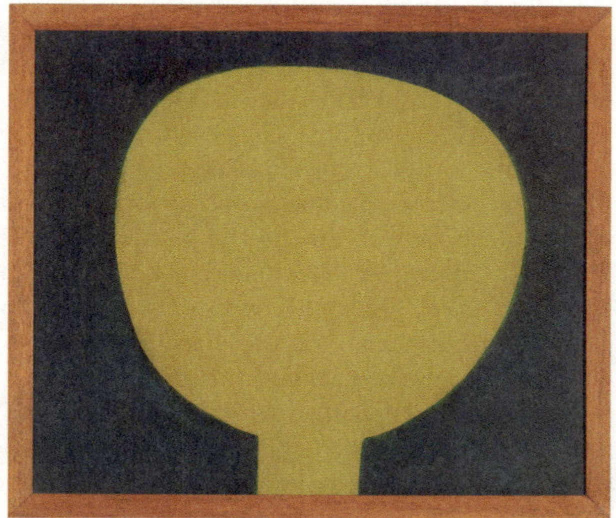

FIG 07
Sidney Nolan, *Boy and the Moon* c.1939–40, oil on canvas, mounted on composition board, 80.1 × 95 × 3 cm framed, National Gallery of Australia, Canberra, Purchased 1976, 1976.560. © The Sidney Nolan Trust. All rights reserved. DACS/Copyright Agency, 2020

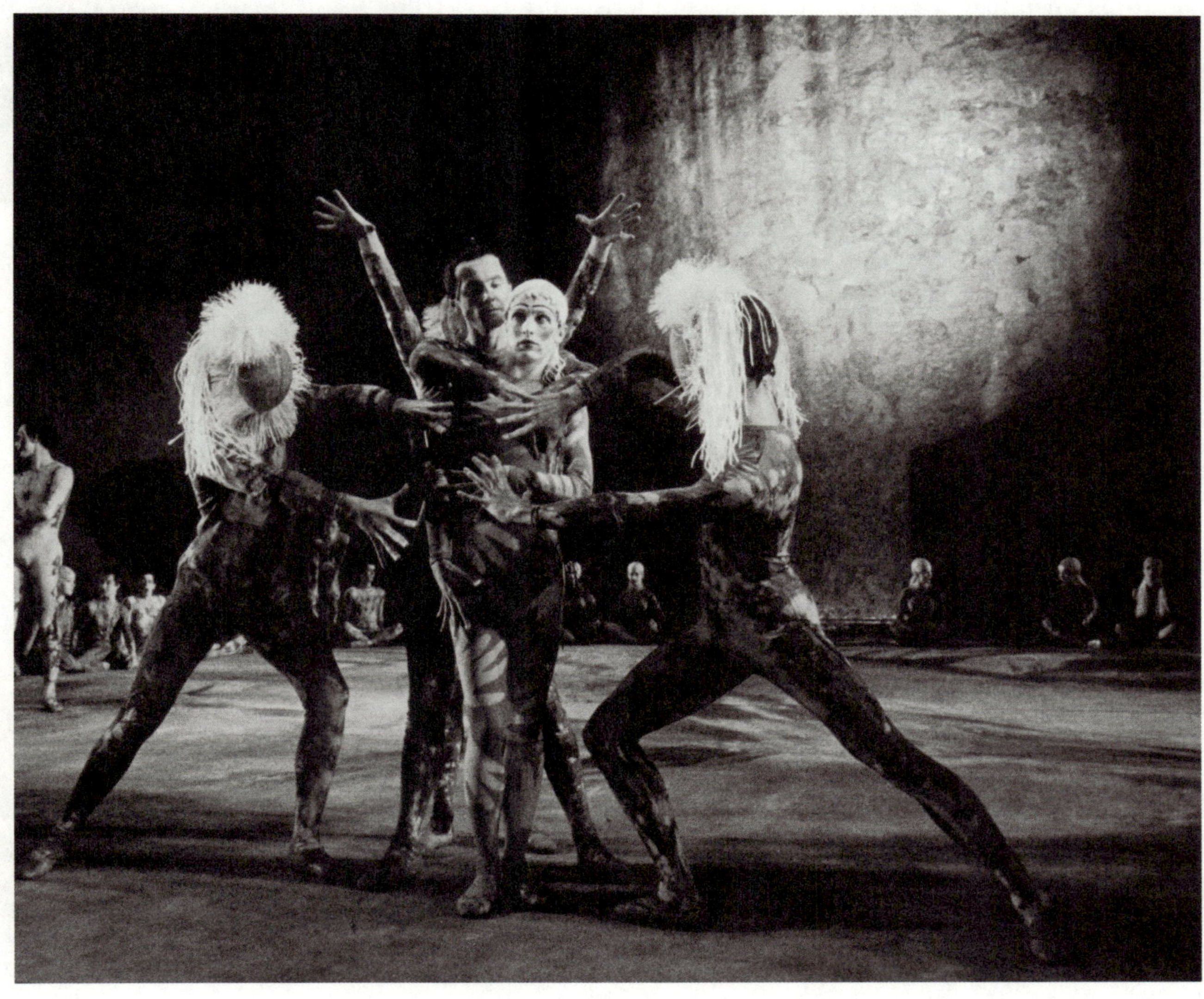

FIG 08
Axel Poignant, The Chosen One seized by the Elders, 1962, printed 1962, gelatin silver photograph, 19.5 × 24.5 cm, Courtesy of Axel Poignant Archive

Advances in psychology, anthropology and empire-building coincided to energise the theory of Social Darwinism. It found childhood to be a period of innocence when life is in accord with pristine nature. Its proponents believed that as civilisations progress out of collective childhoods their spontaneity and emotional health degenerates. The antidote involved recapturing that state of innocence and reconstruction.

Via ritual, Indigenous cultures including American, African, Australian, Tahitian and Maori were assumed to be examples of that innocent state, unfettered by decline and therefore positioned as remnants of the human stage of childhood. In nations such as Germany and Russia what passed for simplicity in peasant life and folk art offered memories of such innocence.

For cultures deemed to be advanced, the efficient way to spiritually recapture the lost primeval was via Myth. To paraphrase Baudelaire, Myth fills gaps which History cannot. Fairytales and sagas, such as those reworked by Richard Wagner, became powerful and dangerous tools for national refreshment. Nolan and many others believed that until Australia could identify and image a primitive past and laud a folk culture, the country lacked the platform on which to become a mature civilisation. In Nolan's case Ned Kelly riding away to nowhere, the doomed explorers Burke and Wills and shipwrecked Eliza Fraser were historical characters he depicted so powerfully that those images still move between History and Myth.

To image the primal landscape Nolan repeated that same incredible feat with his Outback aerialscapes and the cattle carcass series, some of which allude to the Australian map and enclose Outback landscapes. During the 1950s when they were painted, organised tourism was some years away, images came via magazines like *Walkabout*, the watercolours of Albert Namatjira, Russell Drysdale's paintings and films such as *The overlanders*, *The back of beyond* and *Jedda*.

Through anthropological studies by Baldwin Spencer, Frank Gillen and Leonhard Adam, Indigenous art forms such as Oenpelli x-ray bark painting became valued as art. Nolan knew Adam and had read his Pelican book *Primitive Art* (1940) and his article 'Has Australian Aboriginal Art a Future?' in the Ern Malley edition of *Angry Penguins*.[9]

Nolan's aerialscapes remove all reference to European landscape typology. Humans no longer establish the relative scale, and should one be present, they would be less than a pinpoint viewed from that height. Nolan had succeeded in providing images of Australian legends and a uniquely mysterious landscape free of European convention. But he had not yet inhabited that land. *The rite of spring* allowed him to venture there.

The initial impetus for the aerialscapes exhibited by Nolan in April 1950 came from the photographer Axel Poignant, who would become a key participant in *The rite of spring*. They met in 1948 at the Journalists' Club in George Street, Sydney where Poignant gave Nolan sage advice about his forthcoming family trip through the Northern Territory in 1950. Poignant had done extensive aerial photography there from Eddie Connellan's airplane on his thirteen thousand kilometre mail delivery circuit between Alice Springs and Milingimbi at the mouth of the Liverpool River. He had also filmed ballet in Perth and had shot footage for *The overlanders* and *Namatjira the painter*. In 1952 he spent about six months in Arnhem Land where, with their permission, he extensively filmed the Kunibidgi and neighbouring tribes for six weeks.

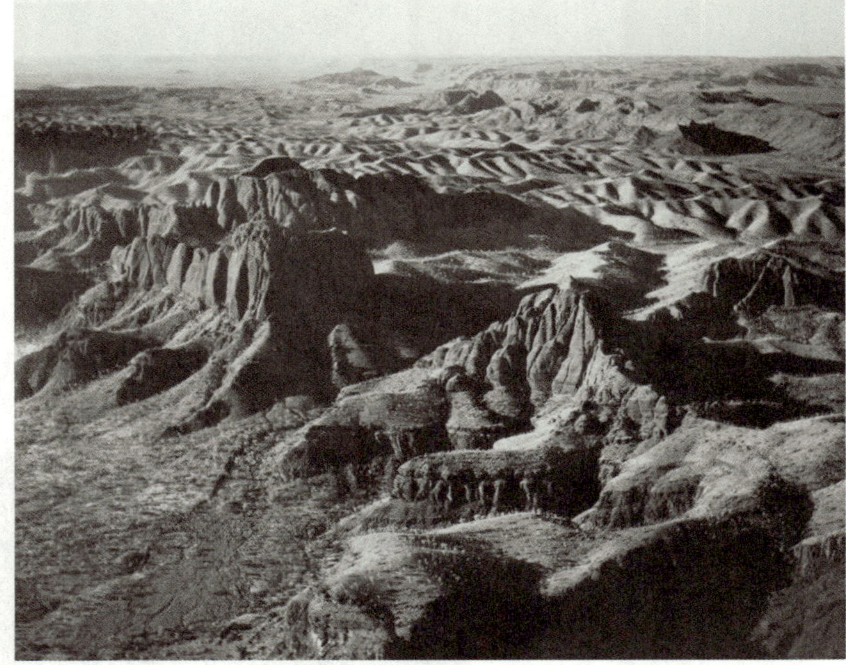

FIG 09
Axel Poignant, Aerial view of the MacDonnell Ranges, Central Australia, c.1947, printed by Ros Poignant 1988, gelatin silver photograph, 41 × 51 cm, National Library of Australia, Canberra, nla.obj-133499141

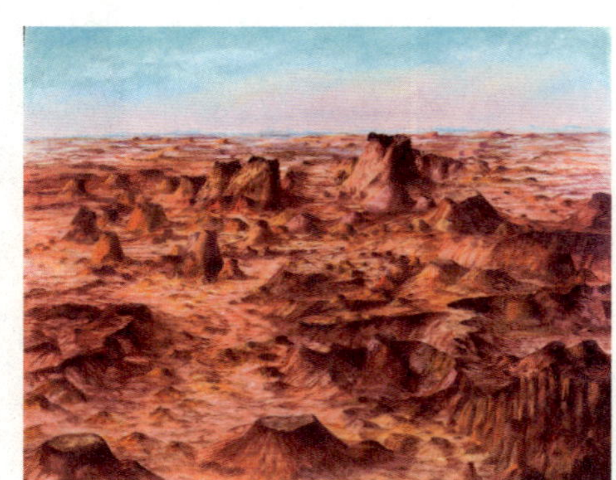

FIG 10
Sidney Nolan, *Inland Australia* 1950, oil on hardboard, 121.9 × 152.4 cm, Tate, London, Purchased 1951. © The Sidney Nolan Trust. All rights reserved. DACS/Copyright Agency, 2020. Photo © Tate

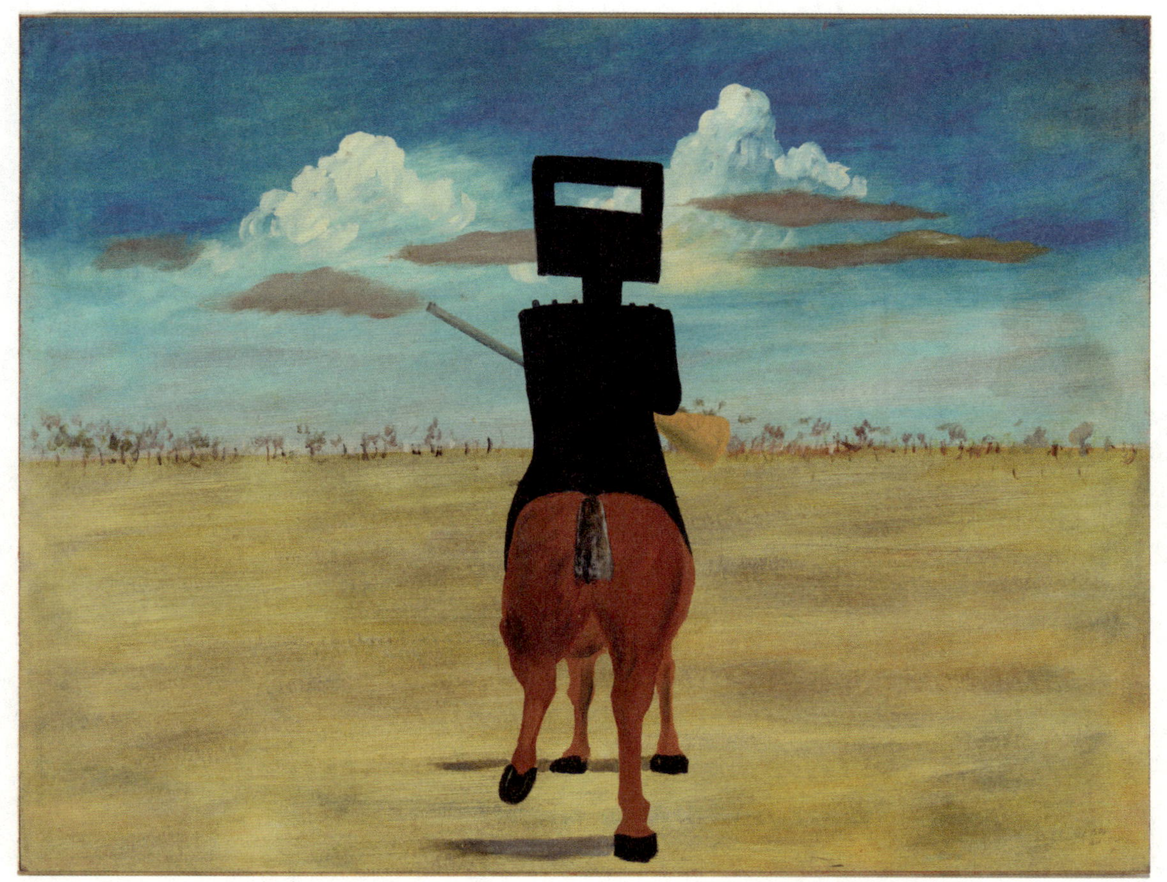

FIG 11

Sidney Nolan, *Ned Kelly* 1946, enamel on composition board, 90.8 × 121.5 cm, National Gallery of Australia, Canberra, Gift of Sunday Reed 1977, 1976.277. © The Sidney Nolan Trust. All rights reserved. DACS/Copyright Agency, 2020

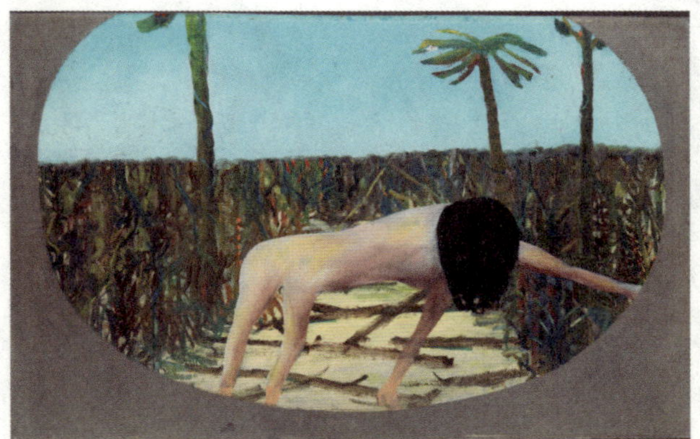

FIG 13

Sidney Nolan, *Mrs Fraser* 1947, ripolin enamel on hardboard, 66.2 × 107 cm, Queensland Art Gallery | Gallery of Modern Art, Purchased 1995 with a special allocation from the Queensland Government, celebrating the Queensland Art Gallery's Centenary 1895–1995. © The Sidney Nolan Trust. All rights reserved. DACS/Copyright Agency, 2020. Photo: Natasha Harth, QAGOMA

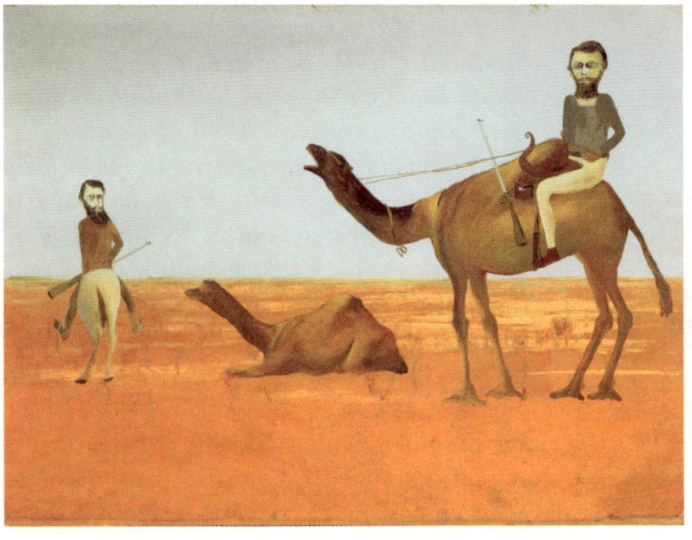

FIG 12

Sidney Nolan, *Burke and Wills Expedition* 1948, enamel on board, 91.3 × 122.2 cm, Nolan Collection, managed by the Canberra Museum and Gallery on behalf of the Australian Government. © The Sidney Nolan Trust. All rights reserved. DACS/Copyright Agency, 2020

In London during 2006 his widow, Roslyn Poignant, showed me a selection of the aerialscapes available to Nolan in Sydney. These photographs and Nolan's paintings virtually match. *Inland Australia*, 1950, bought in 1951 by The Tate Gallery, documents Axel Poignant's mail delivery flight. She also showed me Poignant's photographs of Indigenous life, mainly in the community of Milingimbi, which were available to Nolan and MacMillan in London.

These 2,500 visual documents that Poignant created of Indigenous life are the key reference for the set, costumes and dance of *The rite of spring*. Of those who created the ballet, Poignant alone had directly experienced and recorded Indigenous life. Specific images by him attest to their connection with the ballet. Monica Mason found the white headdresses from the Marndialla (Dupi) initiation ceremony especially dramatic because when the ballet dancers' bodies froze those headdresses kept sweeping across the dark stage. Weaving lines reminiscent of the great snake marked in the Milingimbi earth became patterns for the corps de ballet.[10] And while Harding found possible synergy between hand stencils in the Carnarvon caves and those Nolan placed on the performers' leotards, hands also cover the male dancers in the Marndialla (Dupi) ceremony. For Nolan these hands represent the first human markings, the primitive beginnings of art.

Poignant's engagement with the ballet went further. As the Royal Ballet's photographer for *The rite of spring*, his documentation included the design planning, six weeks of preparation and the dress rehearsal. These are publicity shots of carefully posed key people in clean street clothes, as well as the dancers and the totemic 'Moonboy' set of Part Two: The Sacrifice, but fewer of Part One: Adoration of the Earth.

Nolan airbrushed Axel Poignant from accounts of *The rite of spring*, including in his 1988 Reynolds Lecture given at the Royal Academy:

> He [MacMillan] analysed the music and produced the dance forms. I made some suggestions as to what I could do—which was basically to produce a kind of Central Australian landscape. Kenneth quite properly thought this was wrong. He suggested I try to produce a more elemental scene which primitive people could worship, and then I thought of Moonboy which I painted in 1940. I burnt some gold foil then stuck it on the back curtain and made it enormous, about forty feet high.[11]

By using *Moonboy* Nolan transferred his own totem, the work that had advanced his position as *enfant terrible* of Australian art, from the private to the universal. For some, including Deborah Williams, Kenneth MacMillan's widow, it represents renewing spring energy pouring from the sun; for others it is a terrible destructive atomic mushroom cloud explosion. Either reading informs the ballet's climax when the frenzied Chosen One dances to death and is hurled upwards by tribal elders.[12]

While Poignant's imagery dominates *The rite of spring*, the cave setting in Part One: Adoration of the Earth was likely stimulated by Nolan's visual recall of the sites at Carnarvon: the deep vast Art Gallery (62 metres long) and the larger Cathedral Cave. Ever since the mid 1940s Nolan had wanted to create what are now termed 'installations'. Nolan's design for *Icare*, performed in Sydney by the Ballet Russes in 1940, had included bringing the backdrop down across the floor creating a

10 *Indigenous connections*, exh. cat., Art Gallery of New South Wales, Sydney, 2007, pp. 21, 22.

11 Sidney Nolan, 'Painting and the stage', Reynolds Lecture, Royal Academy, London, 1988.

12 See video interview of Deborah MacMillan and Monica Mason discussing *The rite of spring* filmed at Royal Opera House Covent Garden, 7 November 2013, YouTube, Royal Opera House, https://www.youtube.com/watch?v=RfGrZZX_ndo.

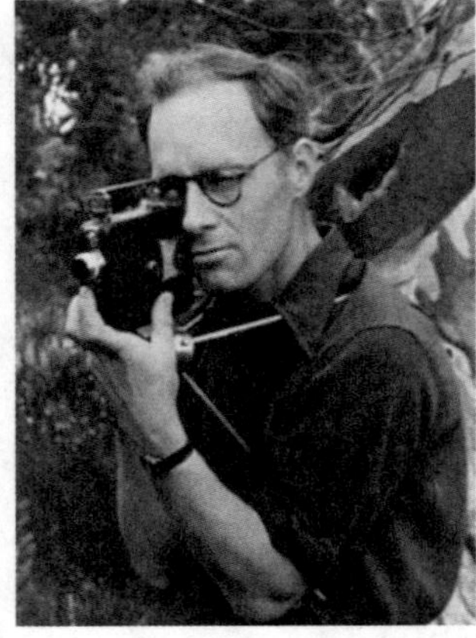

FIG 14
Axel Poignant, Self-portrait with first movie camera, Perth, 1933–34, Courtesy of Axel Poignant Archive

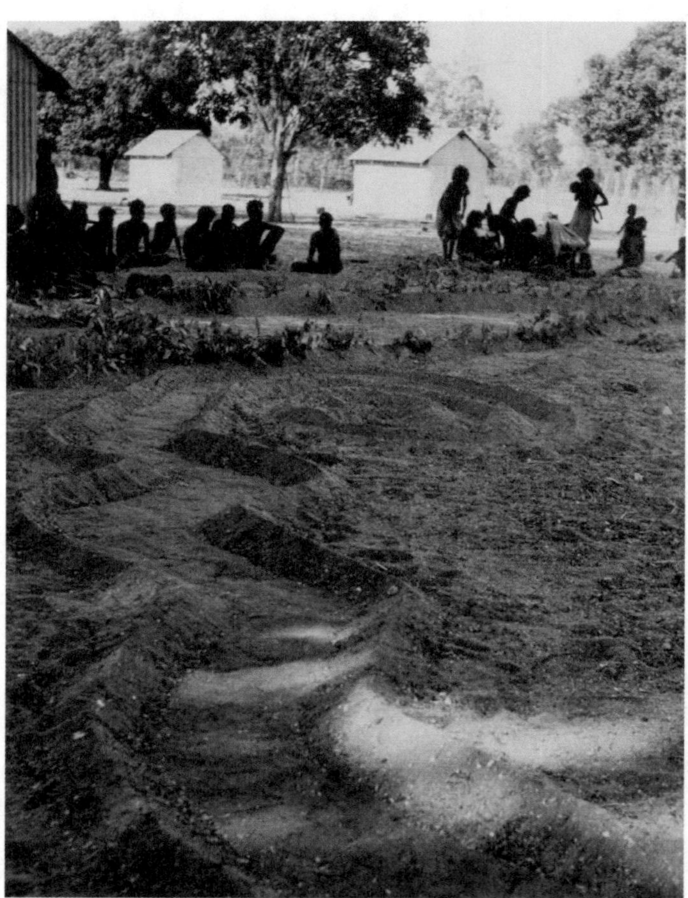

FIG 15
Axel Poignant, The great snake ground pattern, Milingimbi, Arnhem Land, 1952, printed c.1960–64, gelatin silver photograph, 37.5 × 29 cm, Courtesy of Axel Poignant Archive

unified environment. This break in convention was not tolerated by dancer Serge Lifar, but provided *The rite of spring* with a cave-like environment where ritual could take place.

While American contemporary art featured very large installations, Nolan's *Riverbend 1*, 1964–65, and *Riverbend 2*, 1965–66, made soon after *The rite of spring* are inspired by panoramas of his father's country near the Goulburn River at Shepparton. Their sense of mapping memory, their vast size (nine panels making up 1.5 × 10 metres) and their curved installation, suggest a subconscious affinity with the Carnarvon caves.

After *The rite of spring* Nolan planned three projects that directly referred to Indigenous culture before his death in 1992. While he still painted for gallery sales, his personality and acceptance in London's cultural elite as 'Australia's most famous artist' meant his projects veered towards a much grander scale for specific places and events. A few seemed almost plausible thanks to the unflinching patronage and friendship of British businessman and philanthropist Alistair McAlpine over nine years.

These projects include the vast *Snake* originally titled *The Rainbow Serpent*, 1970–72, and two pipe dreams that in the 1980s would have been found culturally offensive thanks to the growing concern for attention to Indigenous traditions.

Serpent, based on an Indigenous creation myth, is a monumental multi-panel wall work composed of 1,620 panels (measuring 9.14 × 45.72 metres in total) that depicts the snake embedded among flowers and Indigenous faces. The 1969 working diagram for *Serpent* has handwritten notes including 'Wagner Fire (Ring)', 'Spiral Galaxy M 101 in Ursa Major', 'Rainbow Serpent' and 'Purgatory' similar to jottings in Nolan's diaries. He intended it as the upper of three bands that together would form the *Oceania* installation, with *Serpent* at the top and two almost half-sized works *Shark* in the middle and *Paradise Garden* at the bottom.

This metaphorical wall was never permanently sited and sections are now spread over various collections. *Serpent* is dramatically displayed at the Museum of Old and New Art in Hobart and is best viewed from above, looking down and across at the complete work. When *Oceania* proved impossible to realise, Nolan and McAlpine intended this section of the original work to mimic how one walks along a large decorated cave. Imagine *Serpent* curling its way under a sheltered walkway through Perth ending at the Old Court House and a huge fountain designed by Nolan with some hundreds of cast metal budgerigars. In December 1983, when Nolan offered *Serpent* to the West Australian Government, the Premier approved the idea based on McAlpine's varied investments throughout Western Australia. When McAlpine's company went broke and the government got cold feet, Australia was deprived of an important totem and tale of genesis.

The two other proposed projects involved Nolan's intrigue with opera and ballet.[13] During his 1970 trip to the Olgas and Uluru with composer Benjamin Britten, who was performing at the Adelaide Festival, the two men thought to create a ballet based on Indigenous initiation rites for the commission offered Britten by The Royal Opera House. Apparently they were unaware that many of these cultural ceremonies were considered highly secret. Furthermore it is likely their choice would have struck London audiences as an inferior sequel to the contentious but acclaimed *The rite of spring* and once Britten became very ill the idea went no further.

13   Robert Helpmann's ballet *The display*, 1964, Saint-Saens' *Samson and Delilah*, 1981, Verdi's *Il Trovatore*, 1983, and Mozart's *Entführung aus dem Serail*, 1987, were designed by Nolan.

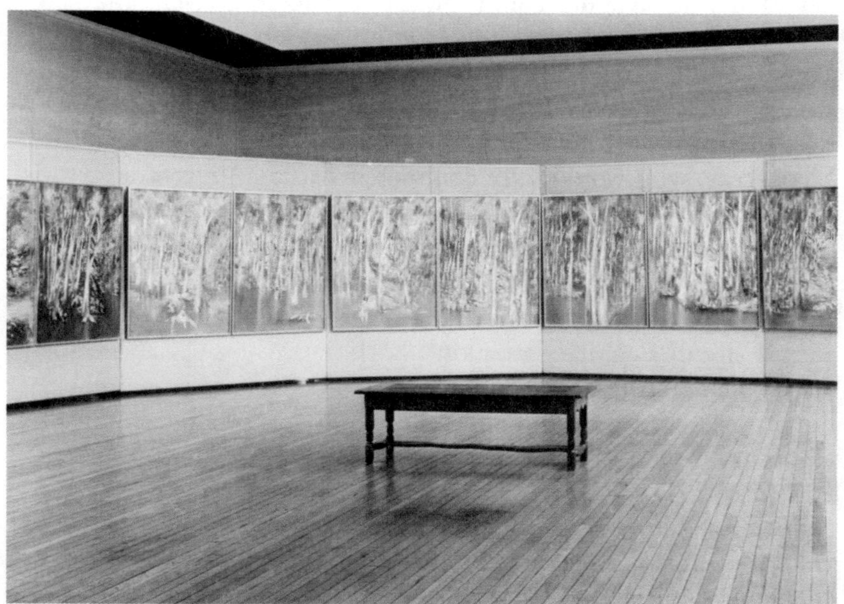

FIG 16

Sidney Nolan, *Riverbend 1* 1964–65, as displayed in David Jones, Sydney, 1965. © The Sidney Nolan Trust. All rights reserved. DACS/ Copyright Agency, 2020

Nolan's other project stalled after missing out on
Parsifal which he had hoped to design, with Elijah
Moshinsky as director, at the Royal Opera House. Later,
designer Peter Hall and conductor Bernard Haitink also
blocked Nolan's proposal for a production of Wagner's
'Ring Cycle' there. For Nolan, an admirer of Wagner's
grandeur, the 'Ring Cycle' offered greater memorial than
Oceania. Indeed, the grandest achievement any Australian
besotted with Wagner could undertake was an Australian
'Ring Cycle' with Brunnhilde atop a fiery Uluru as
Valhalla and Indigenous people in the cast. In March 1980
Nolan's idea was supported by Richard Divall, Director of
the Victorian State Opera and conductor Charles
Mackerras, who would only conduct if Austrian director,
Wolfgang Weber, was appointed as the producer. That
mega dream was scrapped in June 1991. It is fair to
conclude that Nolan saw a 'Ring Cycle' on Uluru as fusing
the most potent expression of Western Myth with a very
sacred site of Primitive mankind.

Dale Harding was initially drawn to Nolan as part of
his project because the hands, caves and spray paint
technique Nolan saw at Carnarvon in 1947 appeared in his
1962 designs for *The rite of spring*. A singular direct
connection between these two events has not been
validated. Instead, less visually obvious links now
challenge Harding to 'sort out what does not obviously
come together'. For example, Nolan's debt to Carnarvon
for working on an expansive horizontal scale and using
walls as a flat surface on which to place multiple repetitive
imagery and the memory of one's country.

Harding's biggest challenge could be to assess the
sincerity of Nolan's indirect and infrequent engagement
with Indigenous culture and how that jibes with Nolan's
singular obsession to create the modernist vision of
Australia.

*I would like to thank Dale Harding for taking
me on this cultural and art historical journey.*
Nancy Underhill

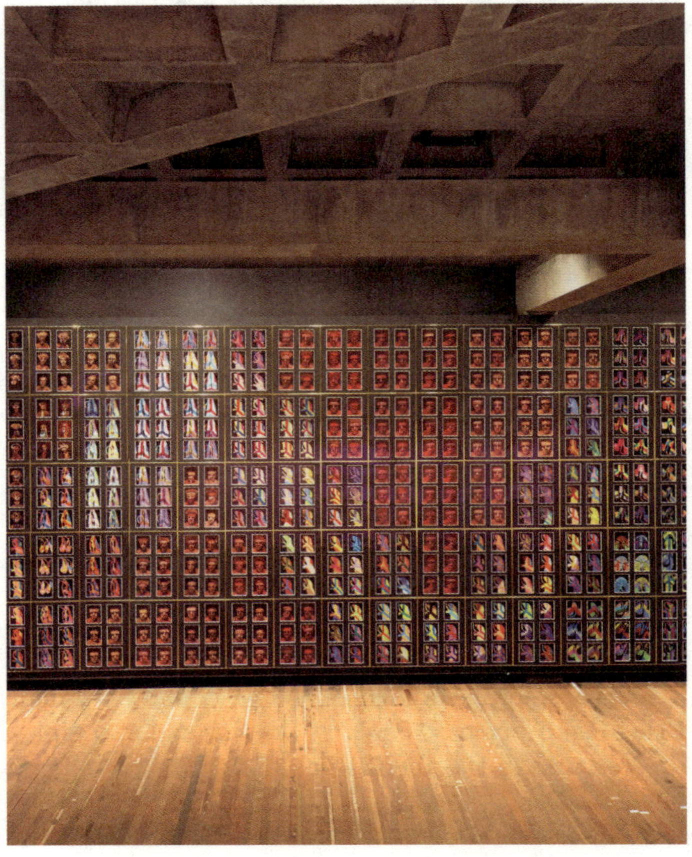

FIG 17
Sidney Nolan, *Snake* 1970–72 (detail), wax crayon,
water-based dyes, paper, Museum of Old and New Art
(Mona), Hobart, 2006.021. © The Sidney Nolan Trust. All
rights reserved. DACS/Copyright Agency, 2020

Beyond trauma narratives
by Ann Stephen

Dale Harding works with two inheritances, one grounded in the ancestral lore of his Bidjara/Ghungalu/Garingbal Country, the other plundered from the Eurocentric canon of cosmopolitan modernism. His achievement lies in making visible, as *abstraction*, the intertwined practices and histories of these conflicting and disparate worlds. He takes nothing for granted—neither pigment, nor place, nor partners—in seeking what he describes as 'the potential for cultural practice as a mode of resistance . . . to colonising hegemonies . . . [and to] building visual literacy'.[1] The following account of Harding's more recent works—which culminated in a major public commission, *Spine*, 2018, for the University of Sydney—traces a critical reorientation towards a reparative and abstract aesthetic. This tectonic shift came about as a result of intense debates within his extended family as to how cultural forms might safely deal with the colonial legacy of violence, anger and defiance. The outcome of these extended deliberations was a decisive move to create works that, in Harding's words, allow 'the opportunity to move beyond trauma narratives'.[2]

ON COUNTRY AND PIGMENT

Harding looks to the rock art of his ancestors as a guiding force in his practice. He cross-references familial and community perspectives with academic research on 'the positive and negative ochre stencil artworks; and positive drawn and painted imagery and petroglyphs on the sandstone walls, overhangs and caves that constitute rock-art galleries in the Carnarvon Range'.[3] His art is premised upon extensive field work on family languages, oral histories, botanical and material cultures spanning the precolonial and colonial histories of the country now known as Central Queensland. The implications of such

1   Dale Harding, 'The language of space', PhD thesis, Queensland College of Art, Griffith University, 2019, pp. 50, 40. I am indebted to the artist for many conversations during the commission and construction of *Spine* at the University of Sydney. I am also grateful for insights about Dale's work that I have gained from Tim Bass, Nick Croggon, Susan Best and Josh Milani.

2   Ibid., p. 39.

3   Ibid., p. 17.

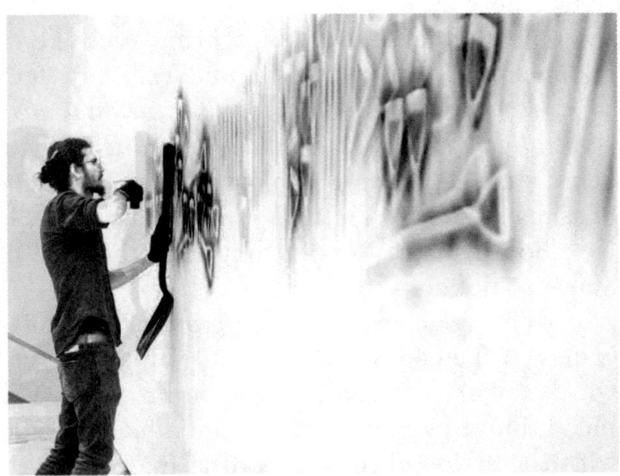

Dale Harding working on his commission *Wall composition in Reckitt's Blue*, 2017, onsite at the Queensland Art Gallery, Brisbane. Photo: Chloe Callistemon © QAGOMA

research convinced him that 'this process of colonisation is one that is ongoing and will continue unless conscious efforts are made to disrupt and to destabilise it'.[4]

When he began making monochrome stencils in 2014, he sourced colour from the local plants, clays and ochres from Carnarvon Gorge. These colours were not mixed but used as pure pigments to outline repeated sequences of cultural artefacts, like digging sticks and boomerangs. The stencils made directly onto the museum wall possess a grand scale to 'interact with white-walled galleries as landscapes . . . [to] recall sensibilities of being in and with landscape'.[5] To imagine the white cube as landscape is a radical Indigenous inversion of the strategies developed by the Land Art movement of the late sixties; instead of Robert Smithson's dialectical concept of site and non-site, which brought the non-site (rocks, earth, etc.) into the gallery, Harding imagines the white walls as Country.

To link his stencils to those of rock-art galleries, Harding blows pigment directly from his mouth or through an atomiser onto canvas, glass or plaster walls. Unlike the impersonal sprayed surfaces of 1960s Pop and Lyrical Abstraction, his process is both an intimate performance, and an act of reappropriation taken from the Australian primitivism of Sidney Nolan. As Harding explains:

> *The paintings are literally illustrations of my breath. I use a little atomiser to blow the pigment onto the wall. I appropriated the atomiser from Sidney Nolan. Nolan had been to see the rock art at Carnarvon Gorge in 1948, he rode in on horseback, then went onto the Royal Ballet in London and appropriated rock-art techniques using an atomiser spray with negative stencils to blow paint onto the costumes.*[6]

In 2015, in what looks like a modernist monochrome (with perhaps a nod to Yves Klein blue and Ian Burn's *Blue reflex*), Harding began to use an intense blue powder, Reckitt's Blue. However, as he subsequently revealed, the choice of this nineteenth-century laundry bleach powder was driven by a decolonising impulse representing 'a symbol of the forced domestic labour that generations of my female members endured . . . to keep the "whites" of colonials "white".'[7] In this way he traces powerful undercurrents of colonial violence, whether represented by the burnt black walls of *Their little black slaves, perished in isolation*, 2015; the gouged lines in *Wall composition in Reckitt's Blue*, 2017, at Queensland Art Gallery and Gallery of Modern Art (QAGOMA); or the repeated ochre frieze of fighting sticks he made with his uncle and cousins Milton and Will Lawton for *Know them in correct judgement* in *The national 2017: New Australian art* survey. For the latter, in addition to the ochre stencils, ochre was blown across the names of missionaries carved into the walls of the Art Gallery of New South Wales, condemning these historic figures of abuse to oblivion.[8]

The single canvas, *Blue ground/dissociative*, 2017, comes at the end of the Reckitt's Blue cycle of works which the artist initially made on his knees, rubbing the blue ground pigment into the linen like a washerwoman, with the action of his arm still visible on the surface. Once the all-over blue field had hung overnight in the studio, he completed the work by chewing Carnarvon white ochre and then spitting it onto the canvas, creating a volatile cluster of intense white pigment. Harding's act spoke to communal dispossession of 'family Elders who were forced to live under Queensland government control', 'of the

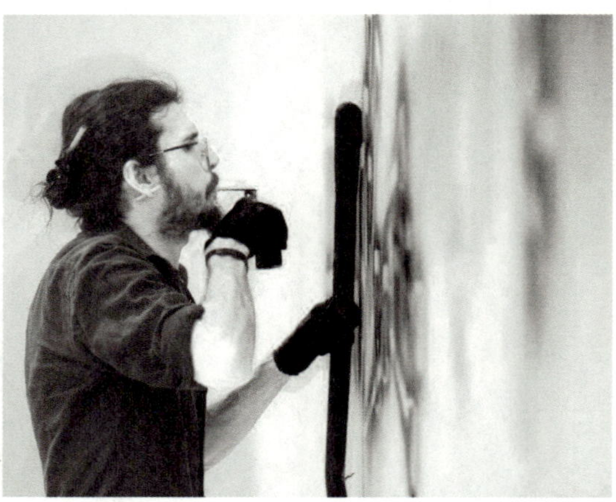

FIG 02
Dale Harding working on his commission *Wall Composition in Reckitt's Blue*, 2017, onsite at the Queensland Art Gallery, Brisbane. Photo: Chloe Callistemon © QAGOMA

FIG 03
Dale Harding, *Blue ground/dissociative* 2017, Reckitt's Blue and white ochre on linen, 180 × 240 cm, Private collection, Brisbane. Photo: Carl Warner

4   Ibid., p. 4.
5   Ibid., p. 45.
6   Dale Harding, conversation with author, August 2018, as are all further quotations by the artist, unless otherwise indicated.
7   Harding, 2019, p. 44. Harding made several cycles of Reckitt's Blue paintings, including for QAGOMA, Brisbane, 2015; the 11th Gwangju Biennale, Korea, 2016; and documenta 14, Athens and Kassel, 2017.
8   Harding's matrilineal family were removed from their Country and confined on Woorabinda Aboriginal Settlement when it was established in 1926.

forced domestic labour that generations of my female members endured' and, more generally, to 'the diaspora of my people in Central Queensland'.[9] His cathartic performance imagines liberating Indigenous art and cultural practices from the toxicity of colonial relations.

It was during his time in Europe, including a residence in Stockholm in 2018, that, remote from family and country, he turned primarily to abstract painting. An abstract diptych, whose title indicates his new receptivity, *What is theirs is ours now (I do not claim to own)*, 2018, enacts that shift. Reading from left to right, the two abutted canvases—from the forbidding Rothko-like cloud of Reckitt's Blue, to the wild and exuberant ultramarine blue spray that speckles at the edges—are joined by a band of blown ochre. The work enacts a highly charged emotional state. But unlike an abstract expressionist painting, the pigments are coded—colonial (Reckitt's Blue), European (ultramarine), Indigenous (ochre)—each applied with an appropriate tool: 'Reckitt's with a bannister brush, ultramarine with a large finely crafted artist brush.'

For another work, *As I remember it*, 2018, he borrowed the format of Robert Hunter's minimal grid *Untitled*, 1970, consisting of six dropped sheets of paper.[10] Harding blew by mouth some outlines of Bidjara cultural objects on each sheet and painted with a yellow pigment ground from a Chinese ink stick. He then concealed these marks with a radiant yellow, sourced in Sweden, which he applied with a small paint roller in a method also derived from Hunter's methodical minimal painting. The underpainting hovers on the edge of visibility.

ON COLLABORATION AND CONCEALMENT

As his focus began to shift Harding started to study his Indigenous languages. 'I personally inherit Bidjara language from my matrilineal grandfather. This paradigm continues where my mother is Bidjara and my father is non-Aboriginal. As is a common contemporary protocol in Murri culture, I also acknowledge the Ghungalu and Garingbal language groups of which my matrilineal grandmother and her Elders are traditional custodians.'[11] He started 'listening to oral recordings of ancestral family . . . drawing out the multiple meanings of language, understanding individual words and phrases, comprehending and consolidating lived philosophical concepts held within the languages, and repairing and mending knowledge gaps'.[12] Being Brisbane-based since 2012, and studying for a decade at Griffith University's renowned centre for contemporary Indigenous art, he knew firsthand the earlier generation of Aboriginal artists including people such as Judy Watson, Tracey Moffatt, Gordon Bennett and Richard Bell. Significantly, the process of immersion in linguistics began to distance him from the prevailing 'identity politics' of contemporary Indigenous art that exposes oppression and trauma to shame the (Western) viewer.[13]

Harding's collaborations take many different forms— assisting his extended family and other artists, as well as incorporating amateur and skilled trades, from needlework and carving to plastering. Such a collaborative practice recalls a focus on communal projects and performances by artists in the late sixties and seventies. He acknowledges the productive role played by his immediate community: 'My making art has gathered intent and opened up to further readings and framings the more I bring my family's artistic traditions into my contemporary practice.'[14] However, such collaboration comes with profound ethical obligations. Harding has wrestled with how best to translate knowledge of Country and kin into art.

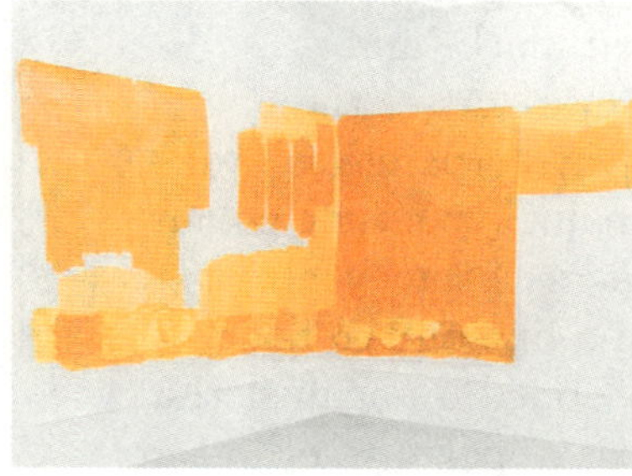

FIG 04
Dale Harding, *As I remember it* 2018, Chinese ink, dry pigment and gum arabic on fabriano paper, 9 parts: each 200 × 150 cm, Private collection, Brisbane. Installation view, *The drive home*, Milani Gallery, Brisbane, 2018. Photo: Charlie Hillhouse

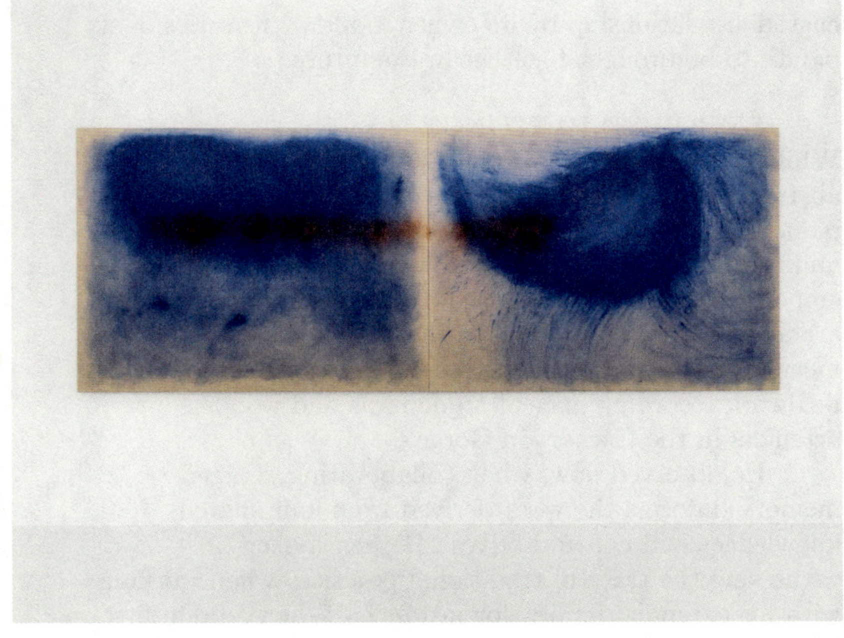

FIG 05
Dale Harding, *What is theirs is ours now (I do not claim to own)* 2018, Reckitt's Blue, ochre, dry pigment and binder on linen, 2 parts, each 180 × 240 cm; 180 × 480 cm overall, Queensland Art Gallery | Gallery of Modern Art, Brisbane, Purchased 2019, Queensland Art Gallery | Gallery of Modern Art Foundation. Photo: Charlie Hillhouse

9   Harding, 2019, pp. 4, 44.

10 Robert Hunter held an exhibition in 2011 at Milani Gallery, where he reconstructed his 1970 stencilled wall paintings. While still an undergraduate student, Harding assisted Hunter, which proved to be a formative experience. Harding has elsewhere written about his interest in the work of Anne Truitt and 'her contribution to minimalism in the context of male-dominated minimalism'. Harding, 2019, p. 36.

11 Ibid., pp. 7–8. Murri is the name of Indigenous people from Queensland and north-western New South Wales.

12 Ibid., p. 8.

13 It is no coincidence that this shift coincides with the final years of Harding's PhD at Griffith University, supervised by the art historian, Susan Best who had recently published her study, *Reparative aesthetics: Witnessing in contemporary art photography*, Bloomsbury, London and New York, 2016.

14 Dale Harding and Hendrik Folkerts, 'The present continuum: A conversation on Carnarvon Gorge, ambivalent artefacts, and reproduction as artistic method', *Mousse Magazine*, no. 58, Apr–May 2017, reproduced in *Dale Harding: Body of objects*, Griffith University, Brisbane, and documenta 14, Kassel, 2017, p. 10.

A strategy of partial concealment was adopted when working with his maternal cousin, Hayley Matthew on *Untitled (private painting H1)*, 2019, at Sharjah Art Foundation in the United Arab Emirates. In an unusual role for an Indigenous male, Harding had previously been given responsibility by his matrilineal grandmother, Margaret Lawton, to know private women's histories within his community. In preparation for their residency in Sharjah, Harding and Matthew 'spoke to my mother and that's how the private painting came about—how to make it culturally safe by veiling . . . to enter into a conversation in an Arabic culture . . . as outsiders at Sharjah.'[15] Over a week they drew and occasionally blew yellow pigment onto stencils of cultural artefacts across six un-primed canvas stretchers creating a series of repeated marks and silhouettes while sharing ancestral stories. After the ritually charged performance these 'private paintings' were subsequently rolled over with white paint (the same colour as the walls), leaving only certain traces of the event on the panels. They were then placed in a line on the floor, except for the final panel that was propped up against the wall. The adoption of a horizontal axis appears to echo the serial floor sculptures of Anne Truitt, a minimalist artist of an earlier generation who Harding admires. Each panel has a subdued glow, with uneven off-white patches covering underlying pale yellow signs in between long, repeated, vertical roller-strokes of white. The uninitiated viewer can only witness a residue of the passing of knowledge that has taken place, which is materialised but not known, recorded but foreclosed. In this way, when not on Country, Harding both reprises and protects aspects of traditional secret/sacred ceremonial practices in collaboration with his extended family who have not had his own exposure to Western, tertiary art education, and who would otherwise be dismissed as amateurs. In acknowledgement of the cultural significance of *Untitled (private painting H1)*, Harding has required that each panel be held in a custodial relationship by its owner to allow the series of six panels to be brought together in the future.

EMBODIED PAINTING
While Harding's paintings have become increasingly abstract—with signs or objects concealed under layers of paint—a bodily trace is ubiquitous in the paint handling and the intangible breath of blown pigment. Such embodied painting suggests how ritual and performance are at the heart of Harding's practice. He also employs the measure of the body through his work, informed by much fieldwork recording ancient stone tools and wooden artefacts in the Carnarvon Gorge.

He observed how, when collaborating, 'epigenetic memory' informs the work derived from 'our shared knowledges and cultural selves'. He has spoken of witnessing the trace of traditional practices when working with his extended family, for instance: 'When Jordon first painted with me, he immediately demonstrated a muscle memory in how to apply and spray paints in stencil form. I also observed that at first application, Will sounded just like his father when mouth spraying, and that Hayley demonstrated muscle memory the first time she used a hatchet for carving.'[16] By celebrating a shared, social memory, Harding marks a significant cultural difference from the individualistic practices of European modernism.

In some of Harding's work, the artist's body is specified as Aboriginal, male and queer. It is the titles that are explicit in works like *Repression cloak (ceremony for a gay wedding)*, 2018. In this work a protective cloak—a blanket painted in pigment and ochre—is a

15   A conversation with his grandmother, Margaret Lawton, appears in the program on Dale Harding in *Colour Theory with Richard Bell*, which first aired nationally in Australia on NITV in March 2014. See also Angela Goddard's recorded interview with Dale Harding, Sharjah Art Foundation, 2019.
16   Harding, 2019, pp. 23–24.

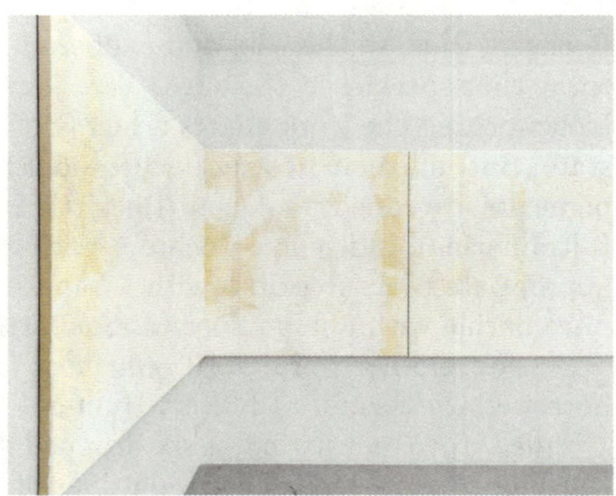

FIG 06
Dale Harding with Hayley Matthew, *Untitled (private painting H1)* 2019 (detail), dry pigment, acrylic and gum arabic on linen, 6 parts, overall dimensions variable. Installation view, *Iterative work*, Milani Gallery, Brisbane, 2019. Photo: Charlie Hillhouse

FIG 07
Dale Harding with Hayley Matthew, *Untitled (private painting H1)* 2019 (panel 2), dry pigment, acrylic and gum arabic on linen, 150 × 150 cm, Private collection, Brisbane. Photo: Charlie Hillhouse

          DALE HARDING: THROUGH A LENS OF VISITATION

response to the homophobic campaigns provoked by the 2018 referendum on gay marriage. When exhibited, it was folded and nailed closed, out of sight. Such a strategy of withdrawal recalls the acts of concealment of complex, secret rituals that inform the social relations within all Indigenous Australian cultures.

Another of Harding's related non-objective works, *Moonda and The Shame Fella*, 2018, has a sheet of glass, the height of the artist, covered in dark yellow resin from the Xanthorrhoea grass tree, formerly known by the racist tag 'black boy'. Harding's colloquial Indigenous title redeems the negative connotations for a minimal self-portrait. The combination of semi-transparent glass with its layer of glowing sticky resin laid horizontally on a pedestal has a delicate precariousness, hypersensitive to materiality and signifier. Harding's abstraction is never purely aesthetic, being socially invested in Indigenous culture and history.

SPINE

In 2018 Harding began a major commission for a new entrance site at the University of Sydney, which marks a crucial nexus in his oeuvre. The work, his first permanent public art work, was on Gadigal Country, which caused him to articulate the distinction between cultural practice on his own country and art made elsewhere, as he explained:

> *I've brought different histories and new materials into my work. It's not separate from cultural practice, but it's culturally safe, in a new way . . . For instance, the interior wall painting at the Lees Building entrance is a departure from my previous use of locally sourced ochres. Instead, I'm using lapis lazuli, that's the blue pigment; vivianite pigment which is bluey-green; hematite, a blood-red ochre and a pure lemon ochre from Italy which is a commercial pigment.*

Harding began by watching how students moved across the site, noting 'the flow of the line of sight from the entrance off City Road and up and down Eastern Avenue. The form of the avenue offers compression and release. The slight elevation rising to the north allows the work to reveal itself as you move through the space.' In an imaginative leap, he linked Gadigal land to his own Country, observing that 'the approach mirrors for me how the Great Dividing Range has those planes before the kick-ups of the cliffs'.

The project evolved from a single monument to a sequence of three works called *Spine*, 2018. It alludes to the ancient ranges running down the Eastern Seaboard that were formed over three hundred million years ago when the continent collided with what are now parts of South America and New Zealand. For tens of thousands of years Indigenous communities, like Harding's ancestors, occupied and painted these caves and rock platforms.

> *You could walk north up the Great Divide all the way from Victoria to the Carnarvon Gorge and beyond to Grandad Bidjara's country, and a bit further up to Townsville. The sandstone of my country leads all the way to Sydney . . . and many of the university buildings here have been built from that sandstone. My works will make a connection between the university campus on Gadigal territory and the culture that my ancestors have passed on.*

The most visible element of *Spine* is starkly minimal: two large sandstone cubes balanced on one end

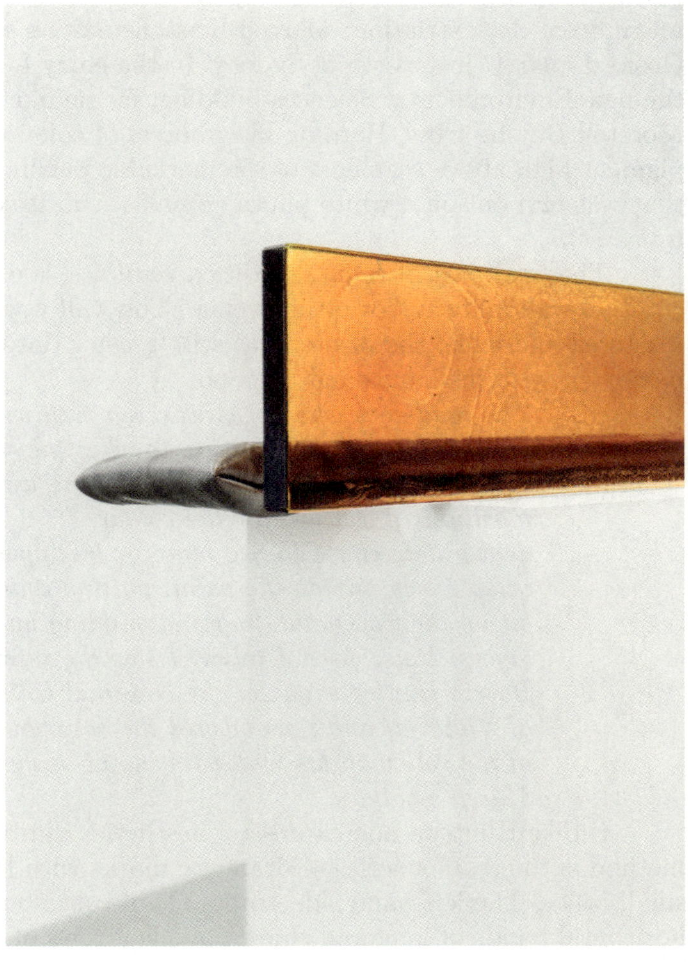

FIG 08
Dale Harding, *Moonda and The Shame Fella* 2018 (detail), glass, xanthorrhoea resin and lead, 3 parts: glass 12 × 210 × 2 cm; lead 5 × 215 × 15 cm; plinth 200 × 120 × 20 cm, Courtesy of the artist and Milani Gallery, Brisbane. Photo: Charlie Hillhouse

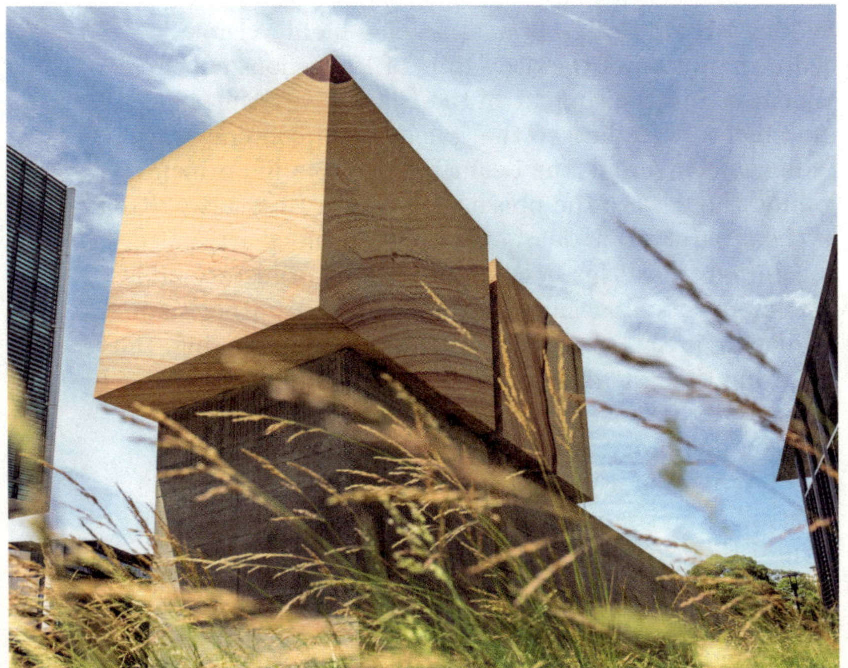

FIG 09
Dale Harding, *Spine 2* 2018, Gosford sandstone, off-form concrete, hematite oxide, 3 parts: wedge-shaped plinth, 113 (to 200) × 1200 × 130 cm; front block 139 × 150 × 150 cm; back block 150 × 150 × 150 cm, The University Art Collection, The University of Sydney, UA2018.25.2. Photo: David Jones

of a concrete wedge aligned to the north/south axis of
Eastern Avenue. As Harding noted, they sit 'side-by-side
with no hierarchy'. At the far end, one block overlaps the
plinth, the other has an uneven edge that reveals a
magnificent dark striation, sourced by stonemasons at
Gosford quarry, just north of Sydney. In the entry foyer of
the new Environmental Sciences building, facing old
Moreton Bay fig trees, Harding blew bursts of coloured
pigment high above segments of a remarkable petrified log
that was laid out on a white plinth (*Spine 1*, subtitled
universe).

The final part of *Spine*, subtitled *radiance*, is on an
external wall midway down the avenue. The wall was
plastered and while the plaster was still 'green', Harding
marked it with his hands and a spoon:

> The renderers who I was working with were
> amused, as it's the opposite to what they do
> with their trowels when smoothing the wall. I
> mostly used a brush for the colour, I
> deliberately chose to use more or less opacity
> when I was mixing the paint, putting a little
> bit on then accumulating and building up the
> layers. I also used a roller. I saw the recent
> Robert Hunter show [at the National Gallery
> of Victoria] and remembered the contribution
> of the roller on his wall painting at Josh
> Milani's gallery.

Unlike Hunter's non-expressive aesthetic, Harding's
method is to create a series of dramatic marks with the
small roller. The left-hand side erupts like a volcano above
horizontal bands of long and short 'spooned' rows of
indentations. Its deep monochrome colour, derived from
hematite oxide, an ancient pigment of rock art, gives
emphasis to the passages of scored plaster and links the
mural to a primal creation landscape. Its two rectangular
earth-red panels, over four metres high and twelve metres
long, command the otherwise grey surroundings.

JOINING THE PAST TO THE PRESENT

Harding's turn to public art coincides with a moment of
world-wide militancy that has targeted symbols of colonial
power. As if in dialectical motion, while police stood guard
on the nineteenth-century sculpture of James Cook in
Sydney's Hyde Park, *Spine* arose as a highly visible
commemoration of the deep time of Indigenous cultures.
When seen in the context of the Black Lives Matter
movement, it testifies to the timeliness of contemporary
Indigenous art, and 'the beautiful idea of a life principle
joining the past to the present', as Susan Best has written
of the reparative mode of another Indigenous artist. Her
conclusion, that 'this new understanding of history and
patrimony sits alongside the colonial legacy rather than
displacing it', is true of Harding's sensitive restaging, thus
'ensuring that the damage of the past is not forgotten'.[17] In
this way Indigenous visual languages claim a sovereignty
and contemporary presence in the public realm.

As part of a new generation of Indigenous
Australian artists who have been exposed to the global
turn of the art market with all its hyped-up visibility,
Harding has adopted modernist erasure and Indigenous
concealment as aesthetic and political strategies to protect
sacred and familial knowledge. To borrow a phrase from
the art historian Darby English, writing on an earlier
generation of Afro-American abstractionists, the act of
'productive deformation of canonical modernism' has
created conditions of possibility for an Indigenous art that
is both contemporary and deeply invested in the recovery
of ancient living cultures.[18]

17   Susan Best, *Reparative
     aesthetics: Witnessing in
     contemporary art photography*,
     Bloomsbury, London, 2016, p.
     98. These quotations are drawn
     from her commentary on the
     series *The pressure of sunlight
     falling*, 2010, by Maori artist
     Fiona Pardington.

18   Darby English, *1971: A year in
     the life of colour*, The
     University of Chicago Press,
     Chicago, 2016, p. 5.

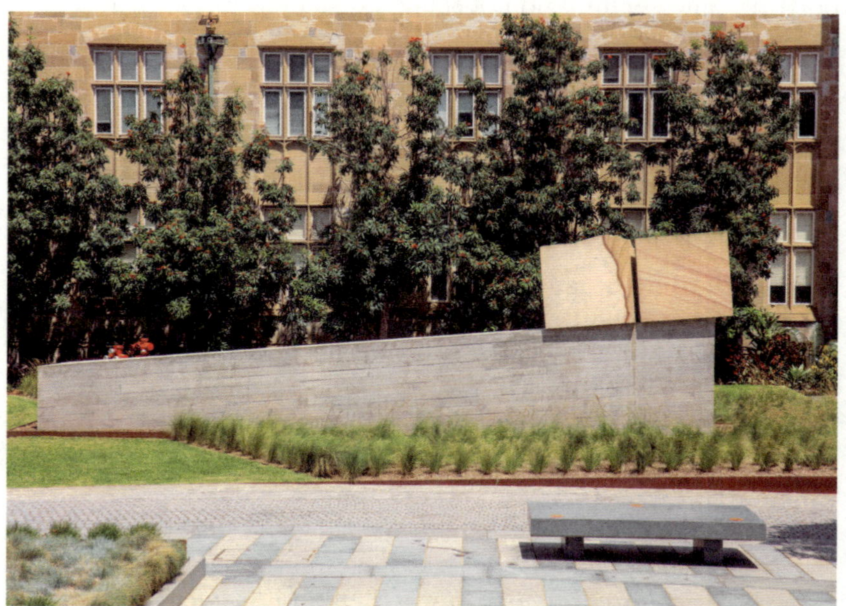

FIG 10
Dale Harding, *Spine 2* 2018, Gosford sandstone, off-form concrete,
hematite oxide, 3 parts: wedge-shaped plinth, 113 (to 200) × 1200
× 130 cm; front block 139 × 150 × 150 cm; back block 150 × 150 × 150
cm, The University Art Collection, The University of Sydney,
UA2018.25.2. Photo: David Jones

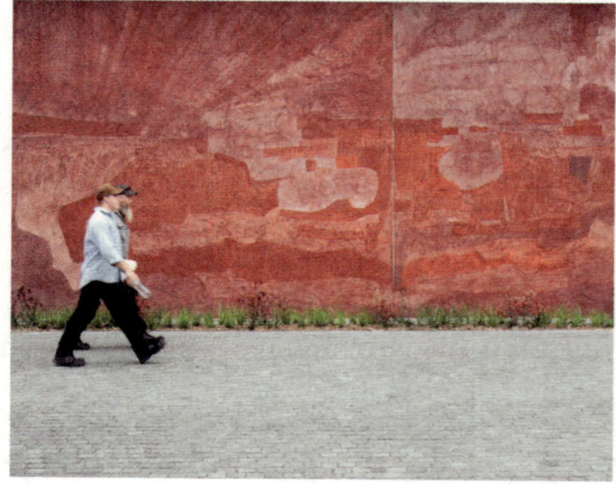

FIG 11
Dale Harding, *Spine 3 (radiance)* 2018
(detail), plaster, hematite oxide, 4.45 × 12
m, The University Art Collection, The
University of Sydney, UA2018.25.3. Photo:
David Jones

Emetic painting
What is theirs is ours now (I do not claim to own)
Blue ground/dissociative
Untitled (private painting H1)
As I remember it
Moonda and The Shame Fella
Untitled
Site Surveys / International Standard
Spine 2
Repression cloak (ceremony for a gay wedding)
Untitled cloak
Cloaks (mortua and mortuus)
Death did not hurt you
Carnarvon underground water
Tribute to women—past, present and future
Cylinders
Carnarvon
White Hill—looking for food at Clermont
Cloak
F1 (Saddler's contract)
F2 (Mt Hetty fire viewed from Bandanna)
Extractive painting 2
Emetic painting (International Rock Art Red and white)

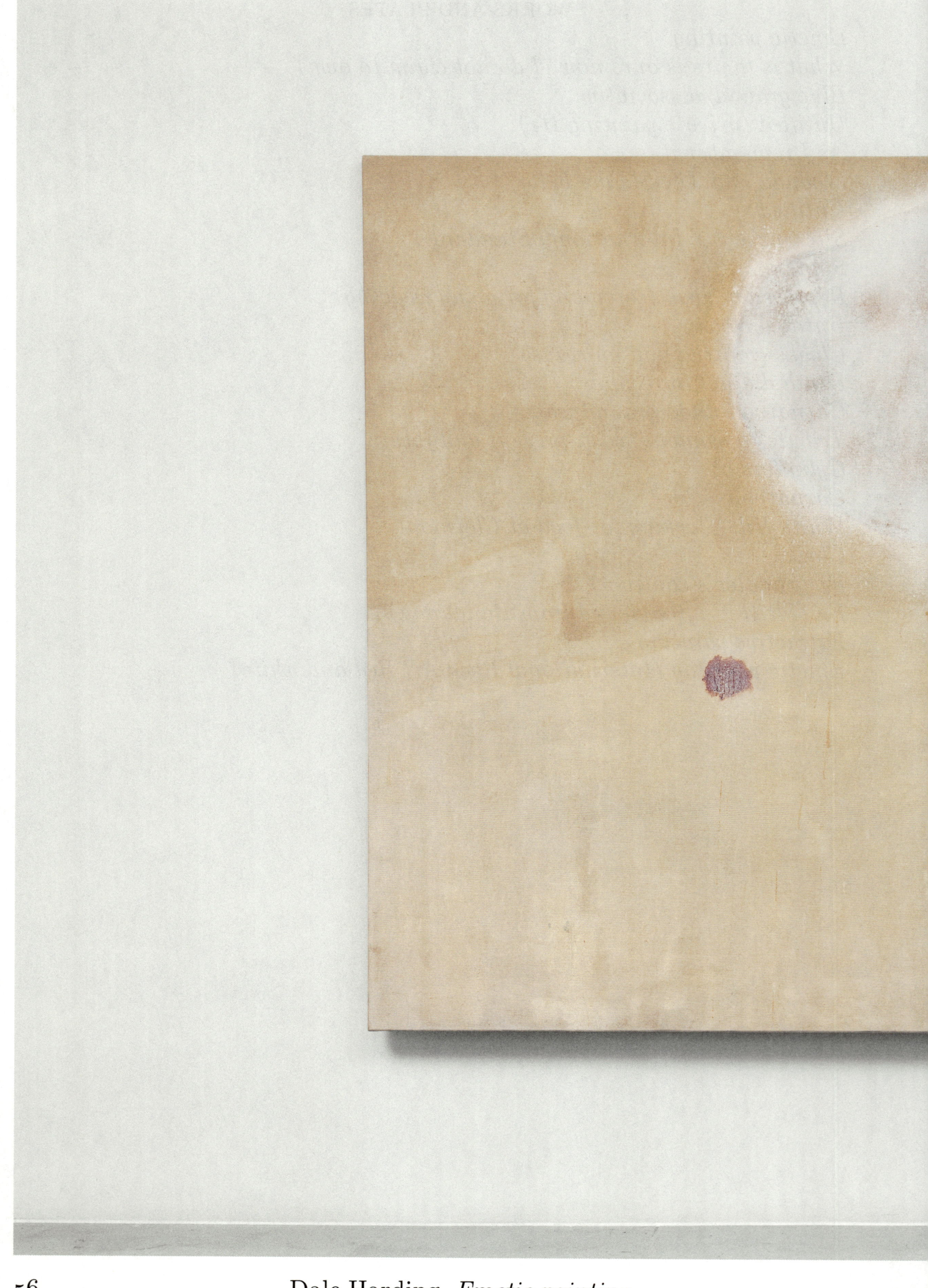

 Dale Harding, *Emetic painting*

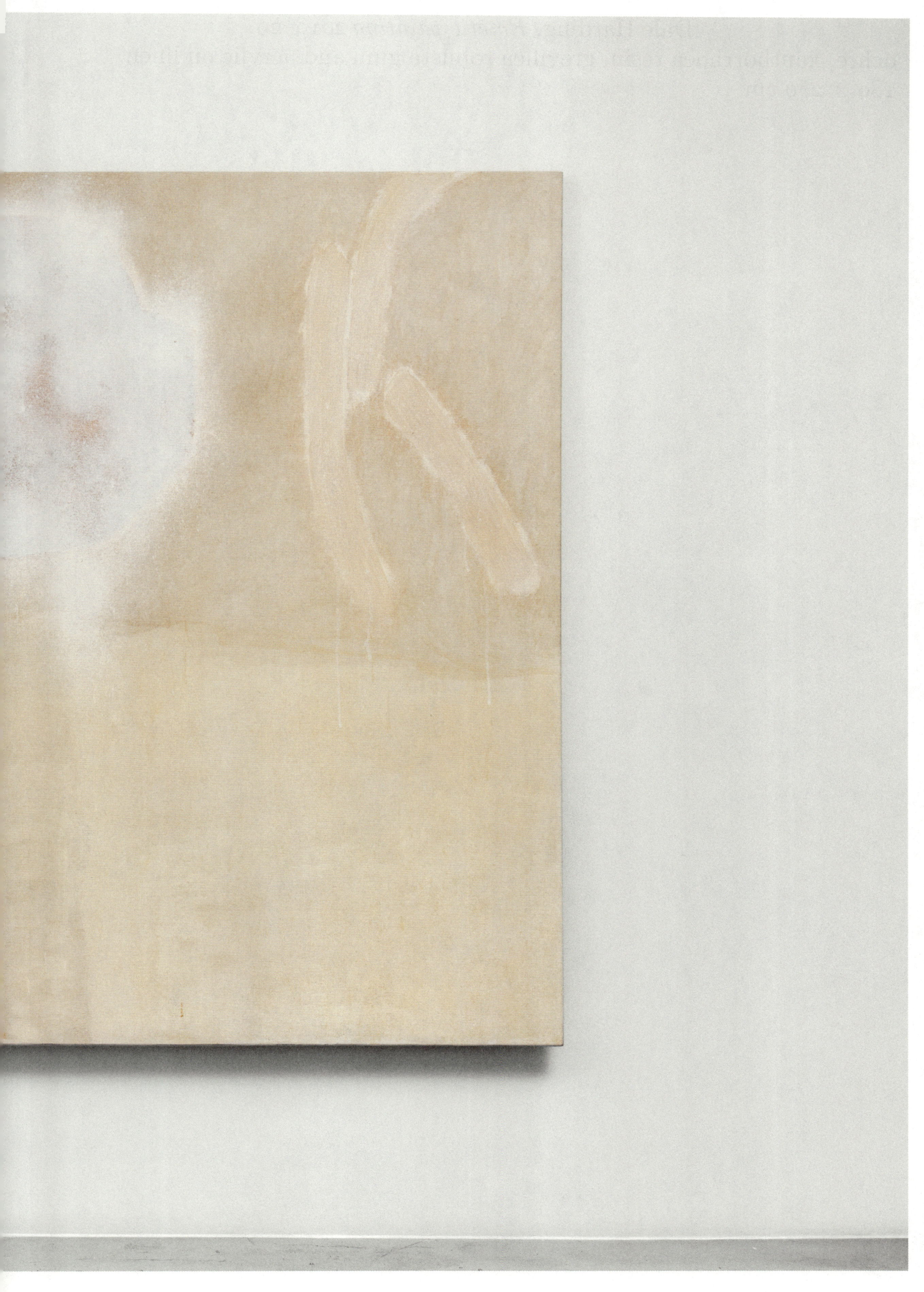

Dale Harding, *Emetic painting* 2019–20,
ochre, xanthorrhoea resin, grevillea robusta gum and acrylic on linen,
180 × 240 cm

(detail)

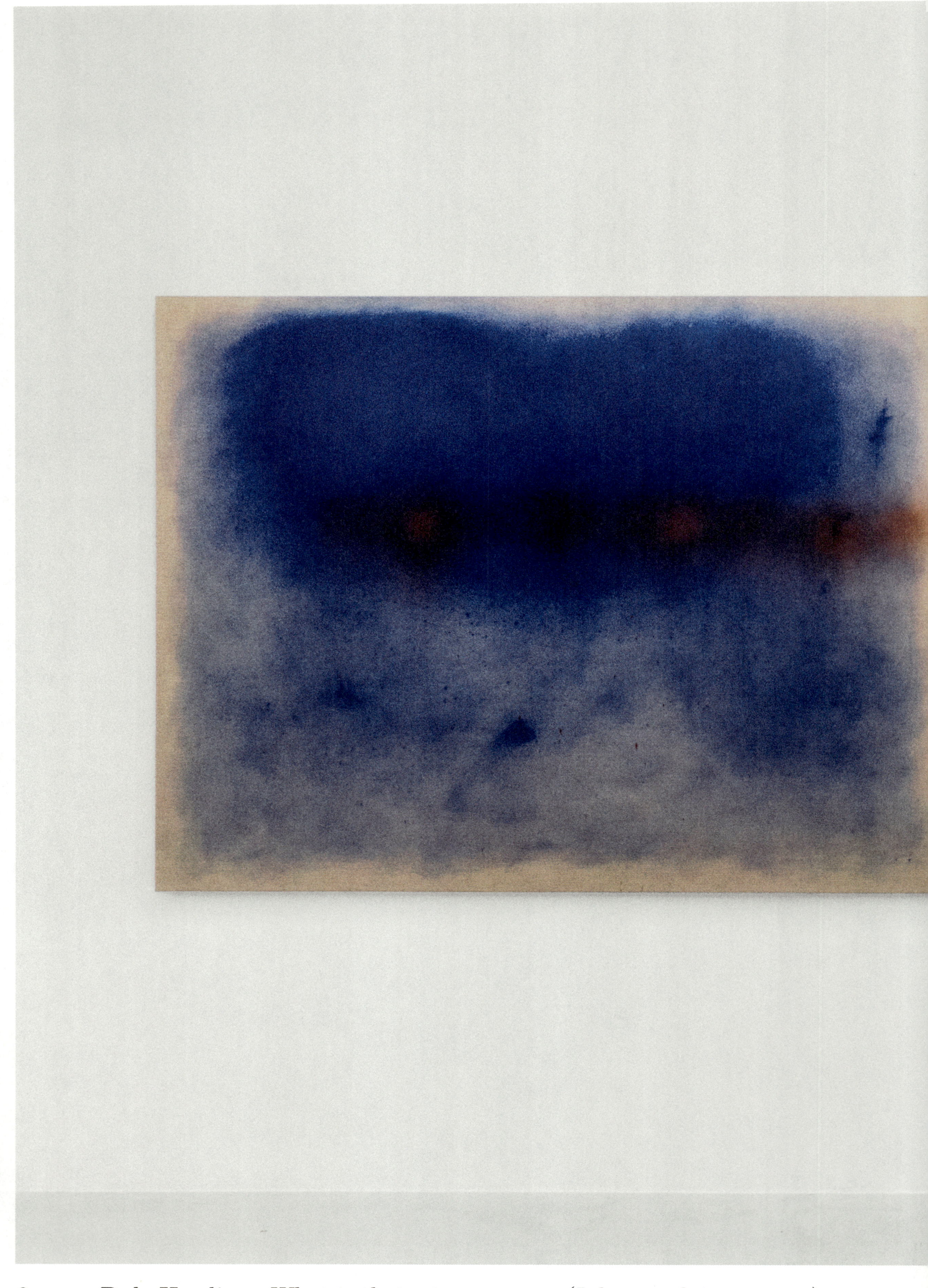

60   Dale Harding, *What is theirs is ours now (I do not claim to own)*

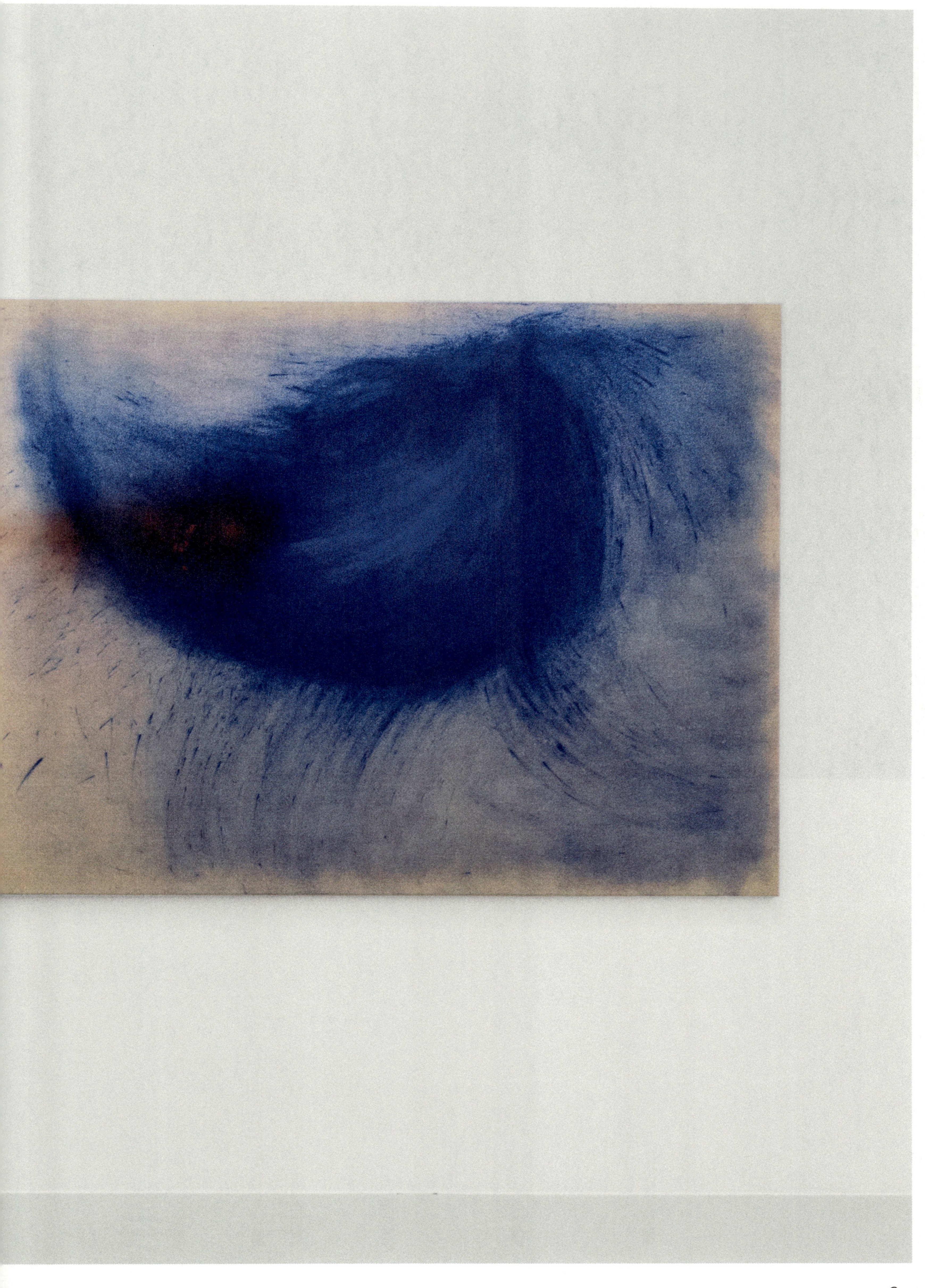

(detail)

Dale Harding, *What is theirs is ours now
(I do not claim to own)* 2018,
Reckitt's Blue, ochre, dry pigment and binder on linen, 2 parts, each 180 ×
240 cm; 180 × 480 cm overall. Photo: Charlie Hillhouse

 Dale Harding, *Blue ground/dissociative*

(detail)

Dale Harding, *Blue ground/dissociative* 2017,
Reckitt's Blue and white ochre on linen, 180 × 240 cm

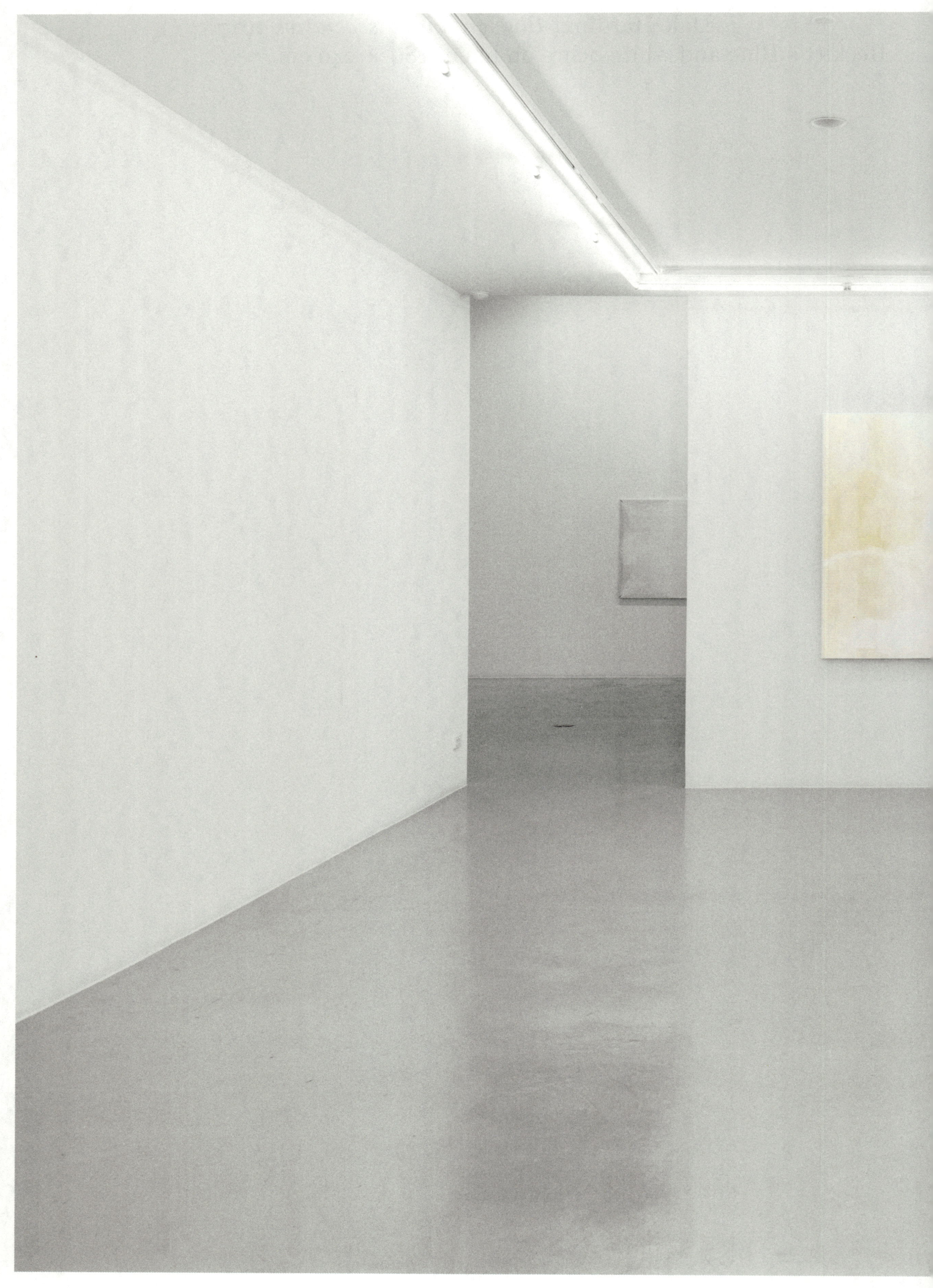

 Robert Hunter, *Untitled no. 4* (detail)

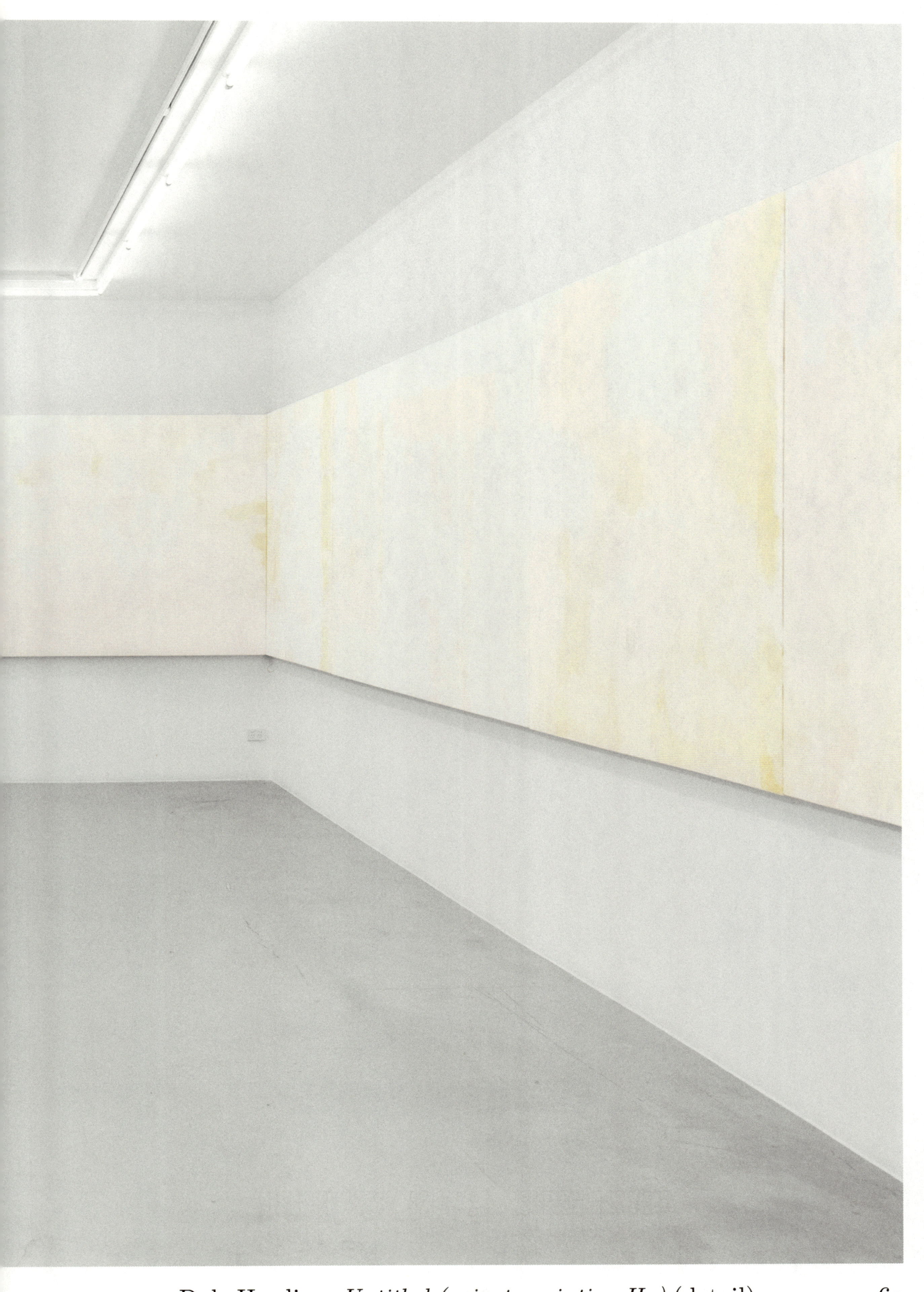

Dale Harding, *Untitled (private painting H1)* (detail)   69

Dale Harding, *Untitled (private painting H1)*, panel 1

Dale Harding with Hayley Matthew, *Untitled*
(private painting H1) 2019
dry pigment, acrylic and gum arabic on linen, 6 parts, overall dimensions
variable

COMPRISING

PANEL 1
(pp. 70–71, 73 TOP), 150 × 250 cm
PANEL 2
(p. 73 BOTTOM), 150 × 150 cm
PANEL 3
(p. 74 TOP), 150 × 250 cm
PANEL 4
(p. 74 BOTTOM), 150 × 150 cm
PANEL 5
(p. 75 TOP), 150 × 250 cm
PANEL 6
(p. 75 BOTTOM), 150 × 150 cm
Photos: Charlie Hillhouse

(pp. 68–69)

Installation view, *Iterative work*, Milani Gallery, Brisbane, 2019. Pictured
with Robert Hunter, *Untitled no. 4* 2003 (detail), synthetic polymer paint
on plywood, 122 × 224 cm. Photo: Charlie Hillhouse

(pp. 76–77)

Installation view, *Surface tension*, Sharjah Art Foundation, Sharjah, 2019.
Photo: Sharjah Art Foundation

Untitled (private painting H1), panels 1 and 2

   Untitled (private painting H1), panels 3 and 4

Untitled (private painting H1), panels 5 and 6

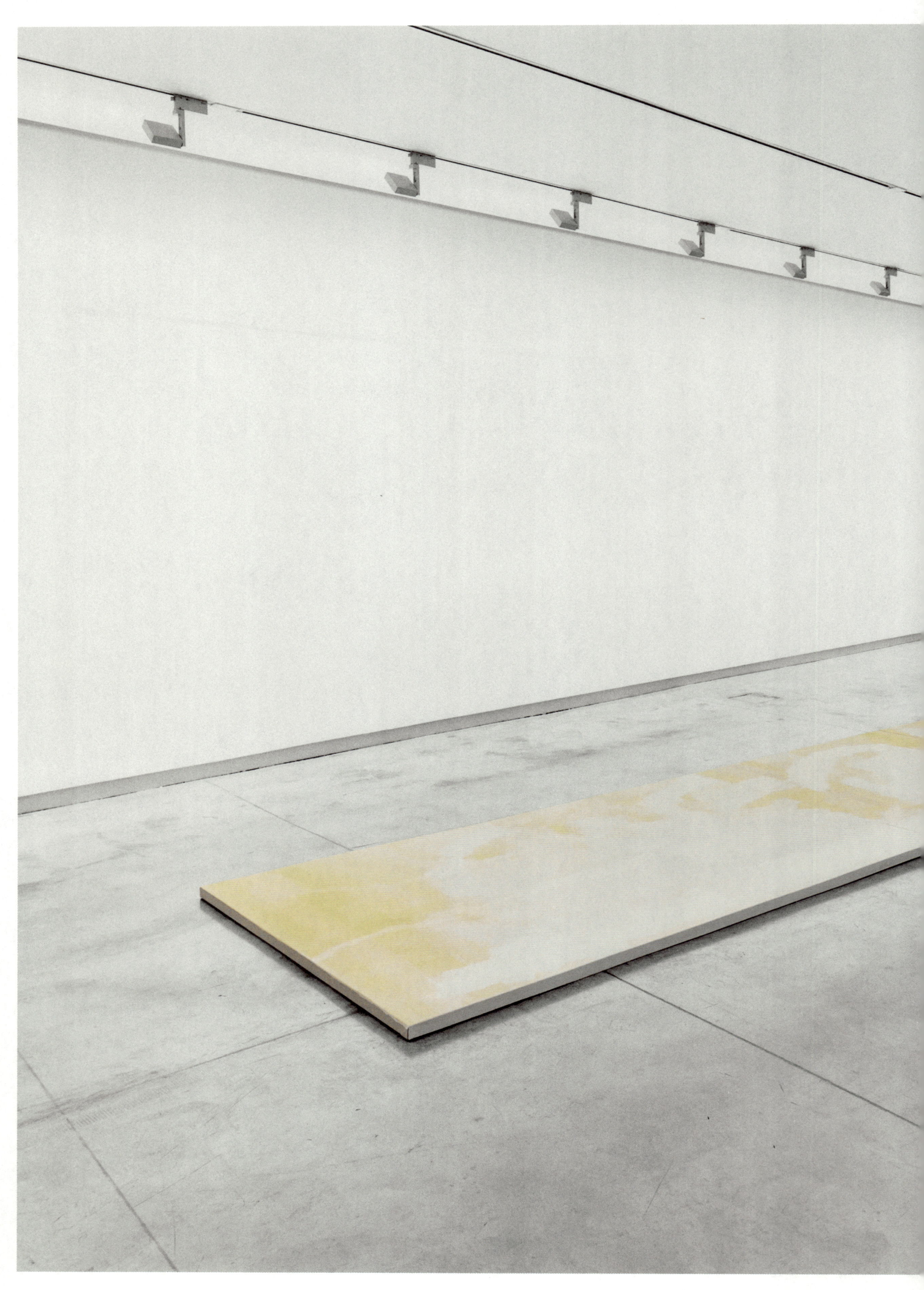

76   Dale Harding with Hayley Matthew, *Untitled (private painting H1)*

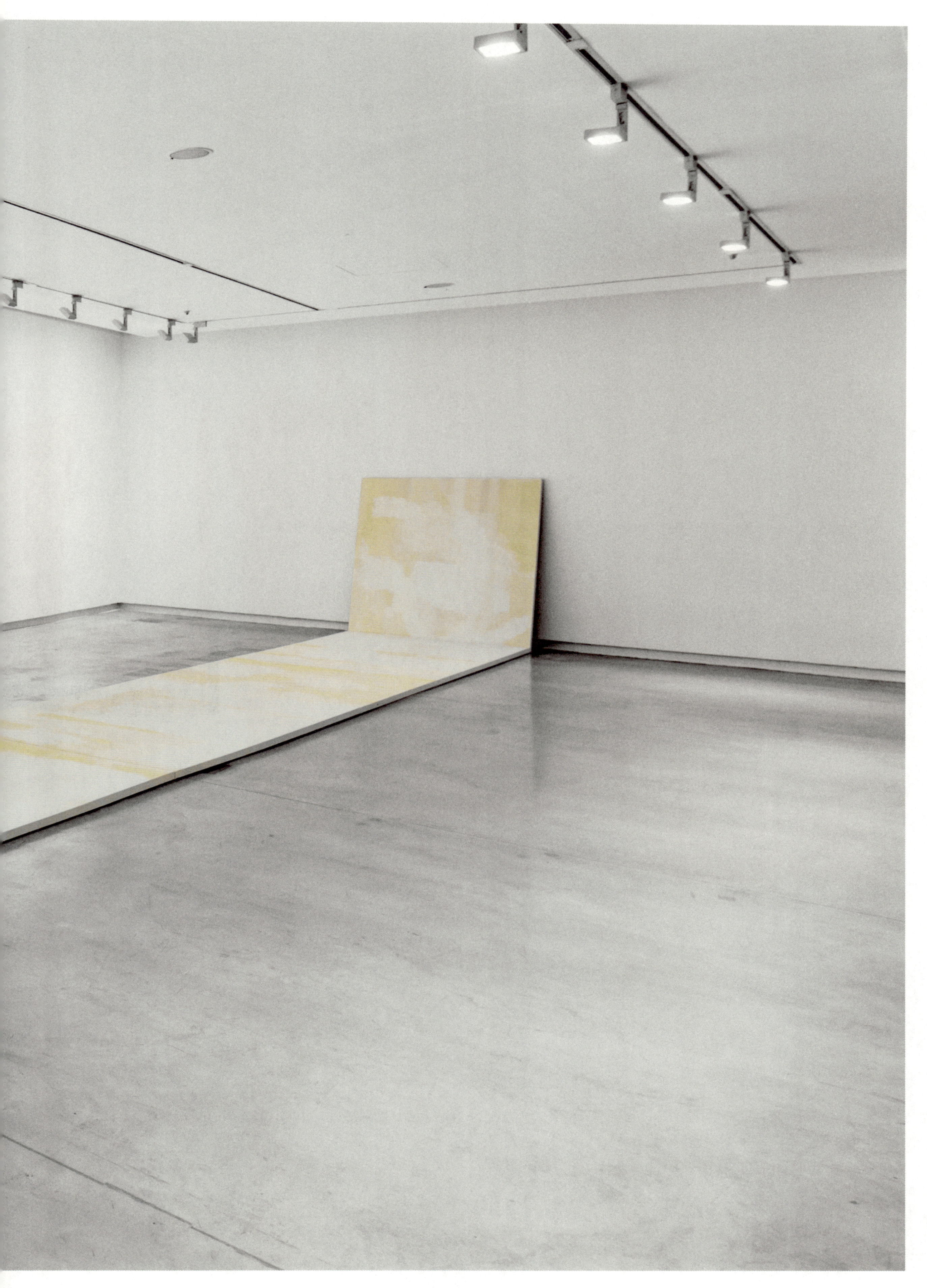

(installation view)

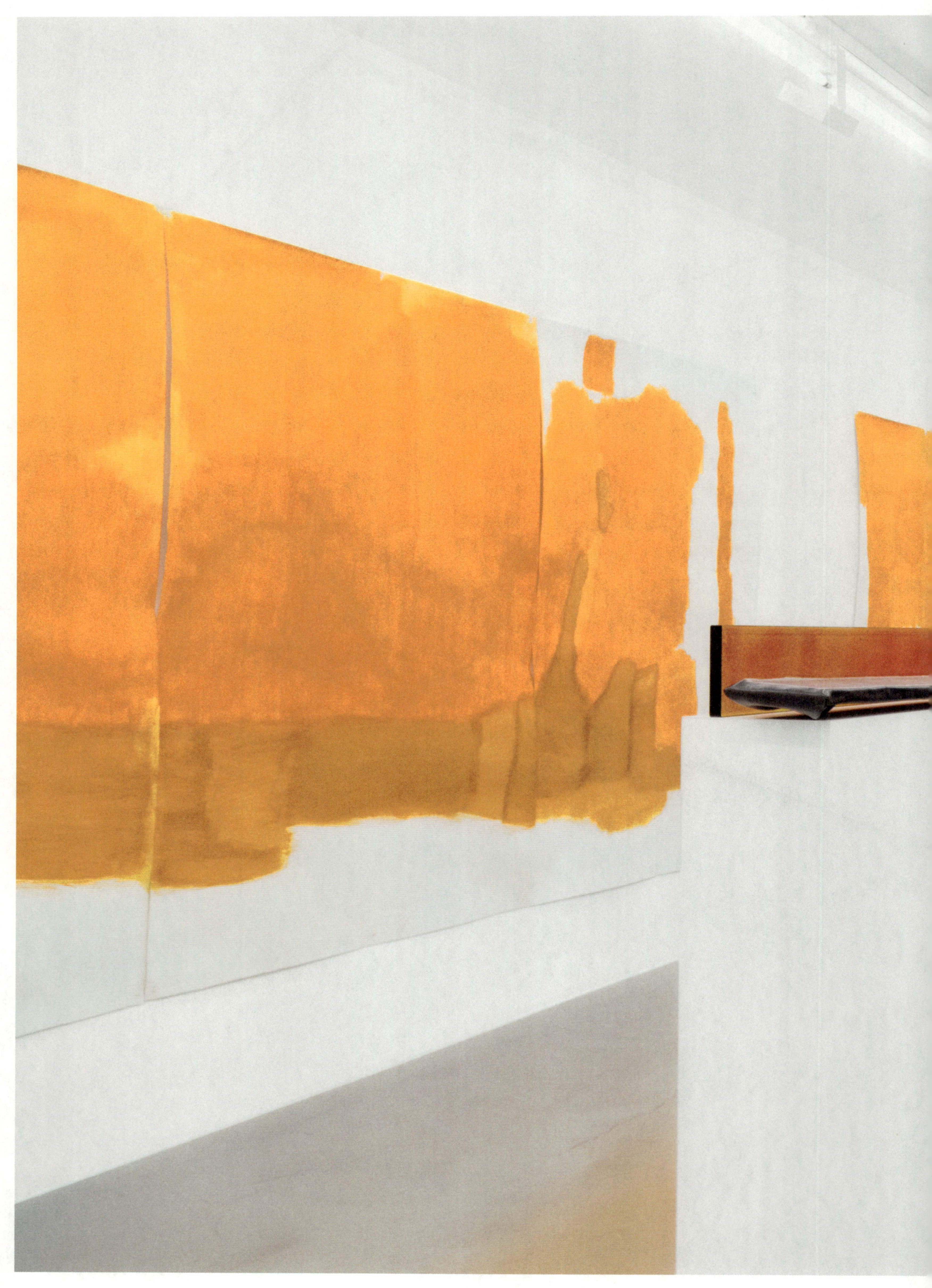

Dale Harding, *As I remember it* (detail)

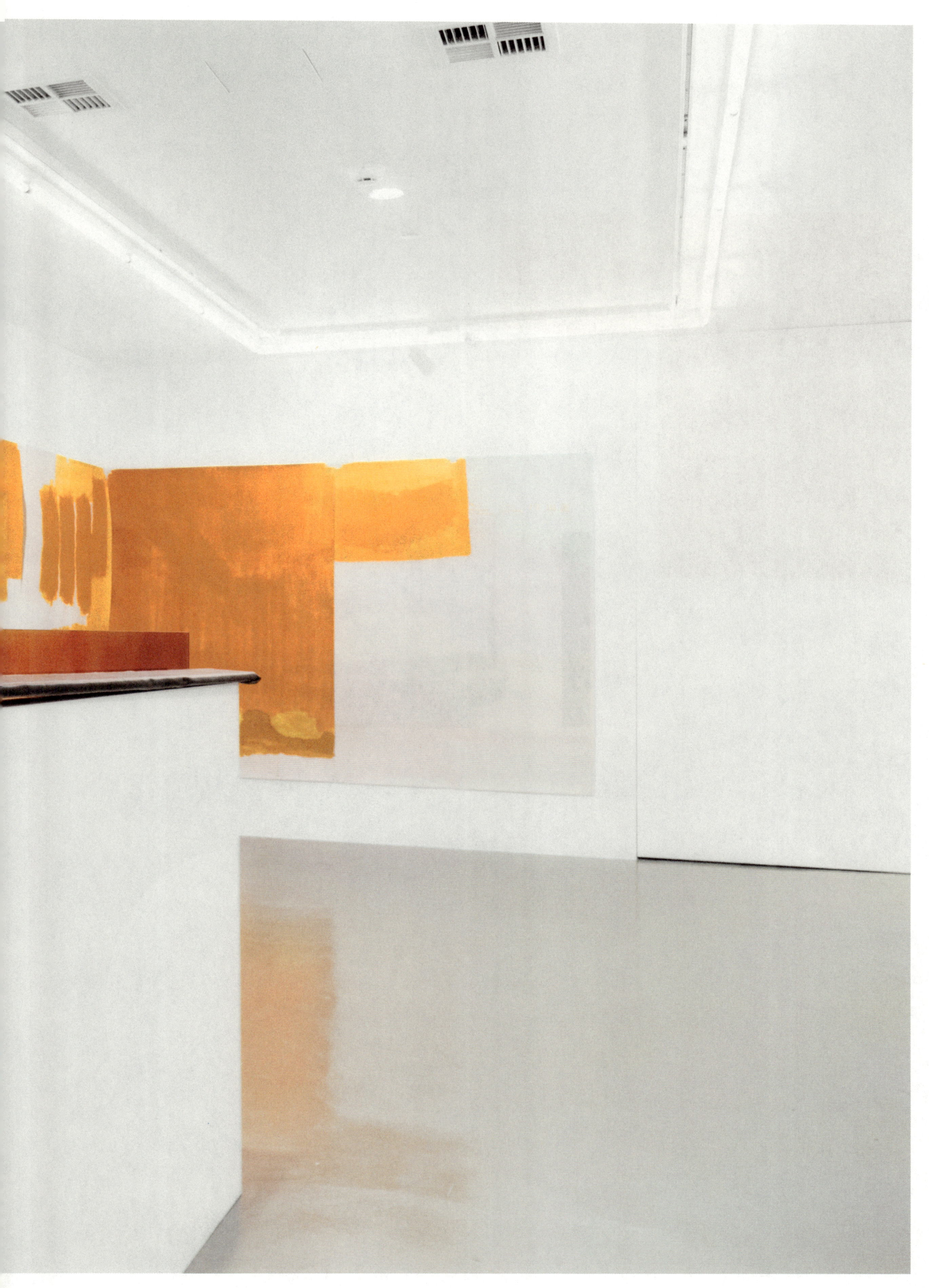

Dale Harding, *Moonda and The Shame Fella*

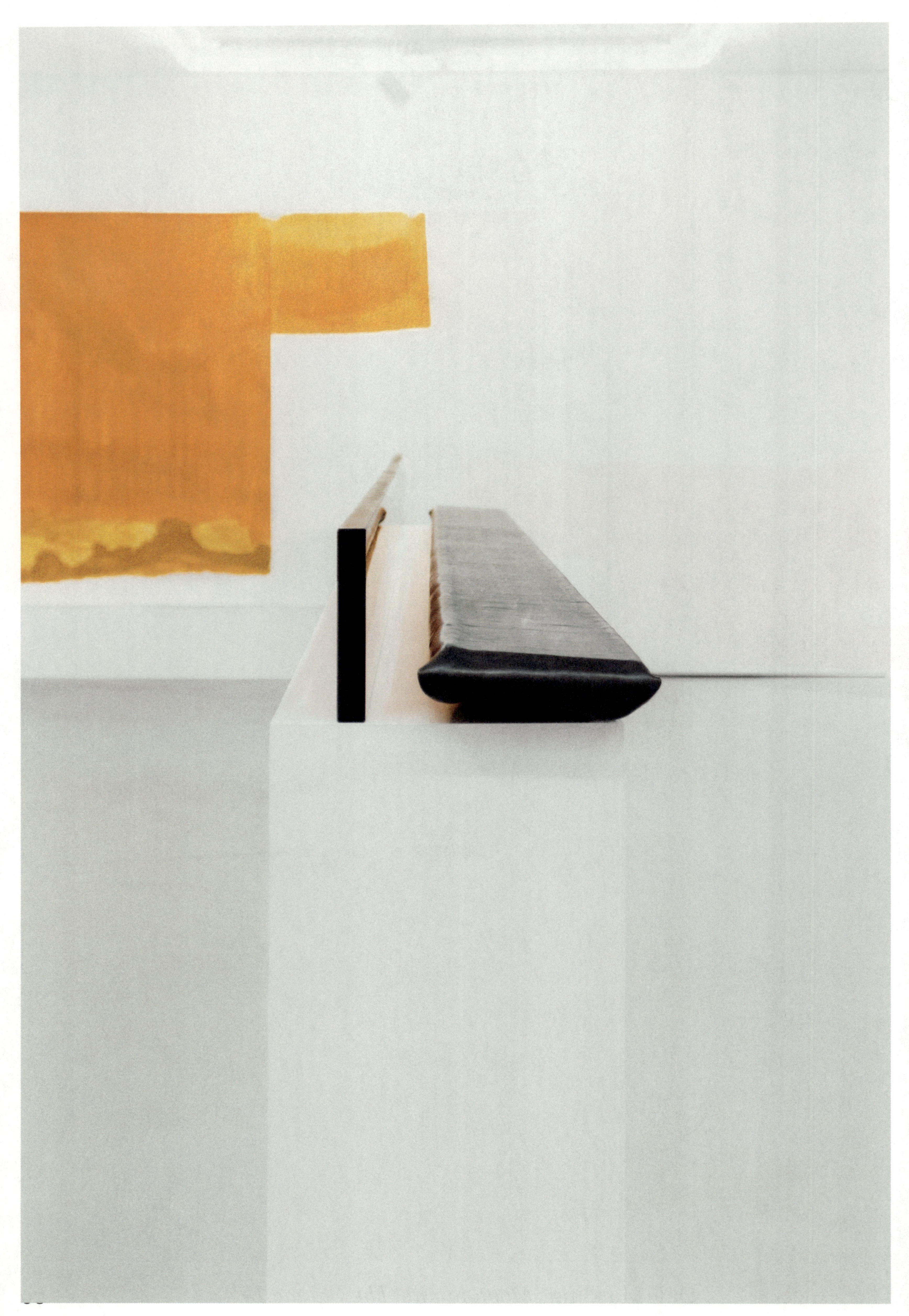

Dale Harding, *Moonda and The Shame Fella* 2018, glass, xanthorrhoea resin and lead, 3 parts: glass 12 × 210 × 2 cm; lead 5 × 215 × 15 cm; plinth 200 × 120 × 20 cm. Pictured with *As I remember it* 2018, Chinese ink, dry pigment and gum arabic on fabriano paper, 9 parts: each 200 × 150 cm. Installation view, *The drive home*, Milani Gallery, Brisbane, 2018. Photos: Charlie Hillhouse

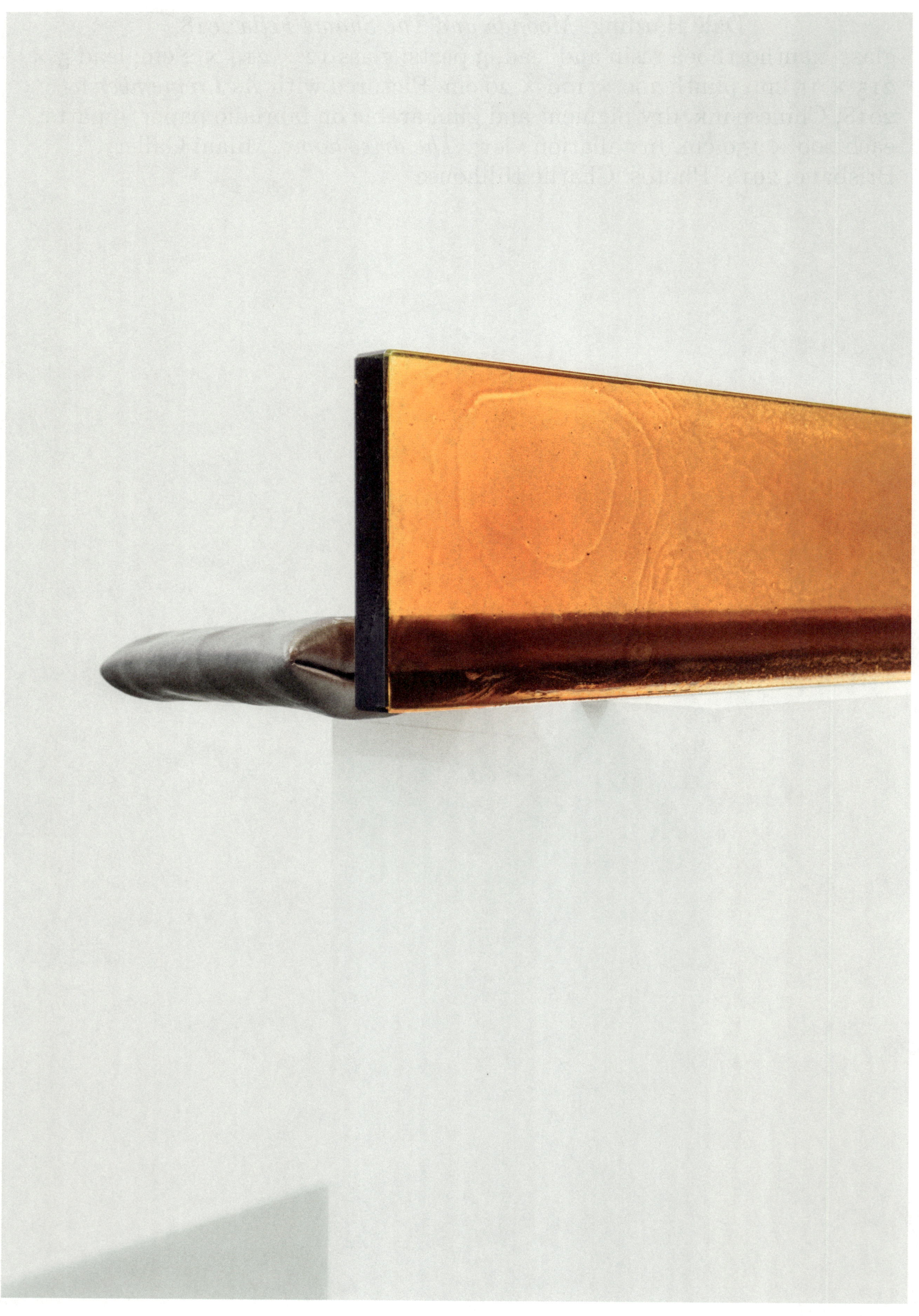

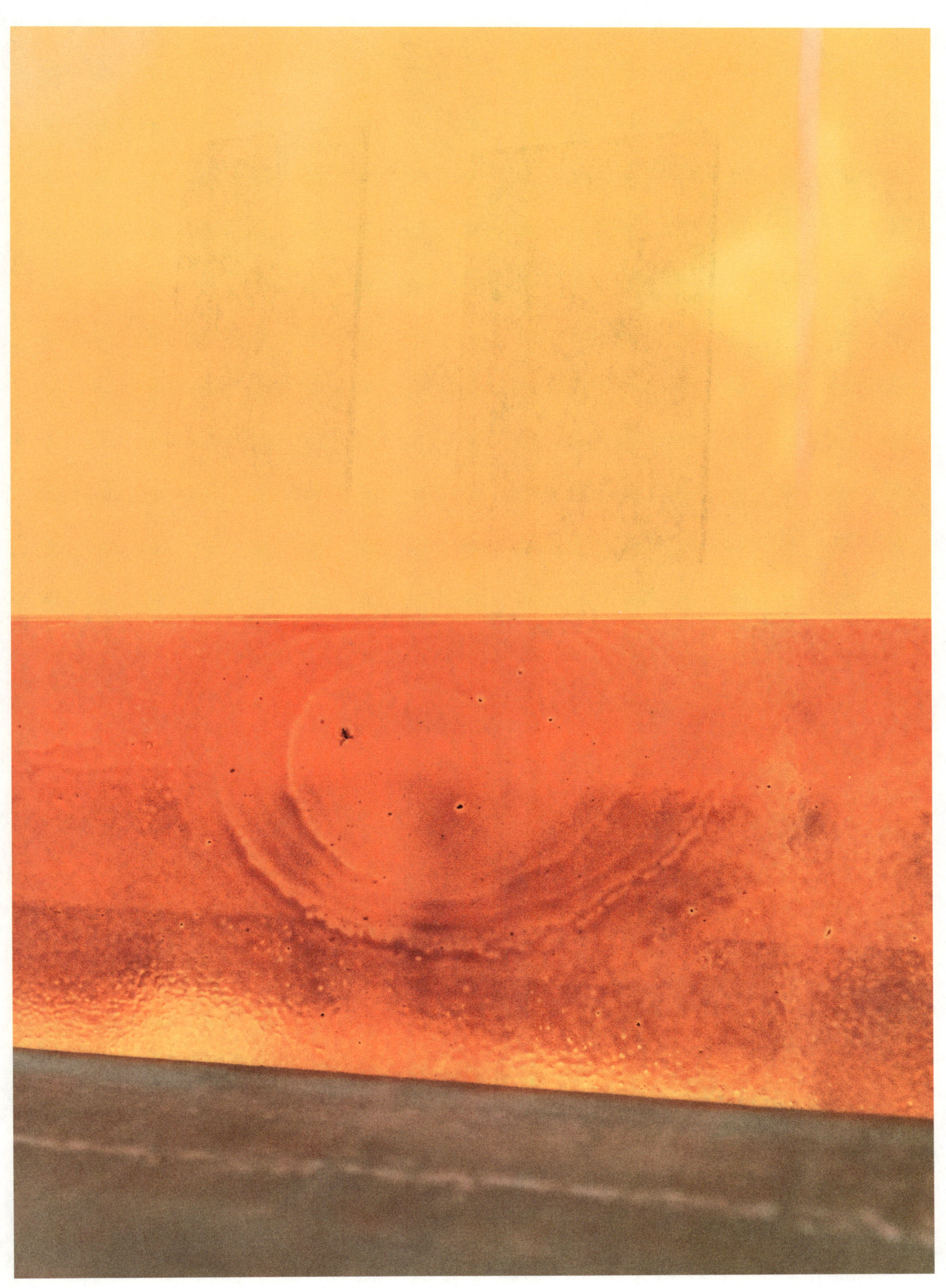

Moonda and The Shame Fella (details)

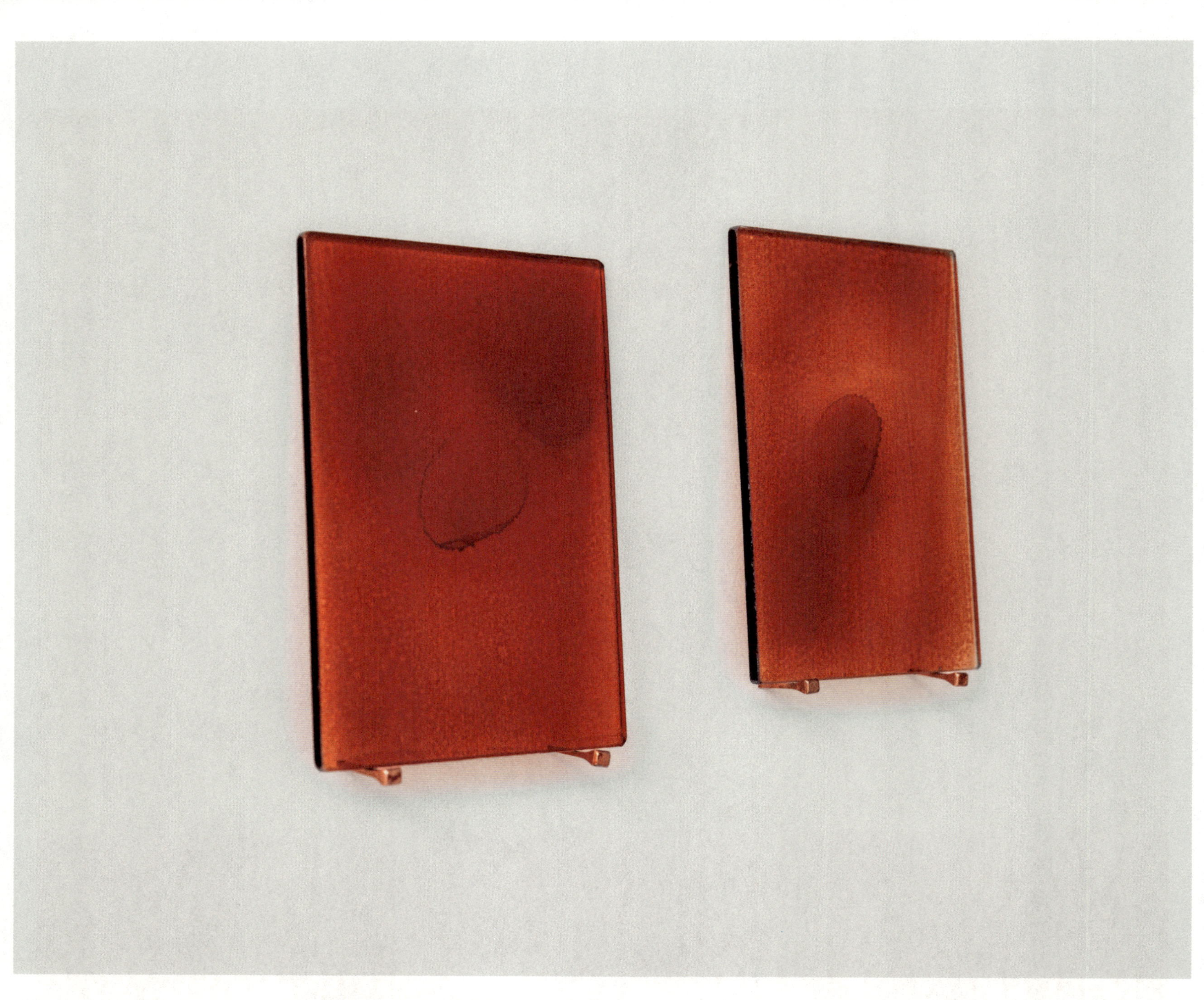

Dale Harding, *Untitled* 2020,
xanthorrhoea resin on glass, 2 parts, each 18 × 14 cm

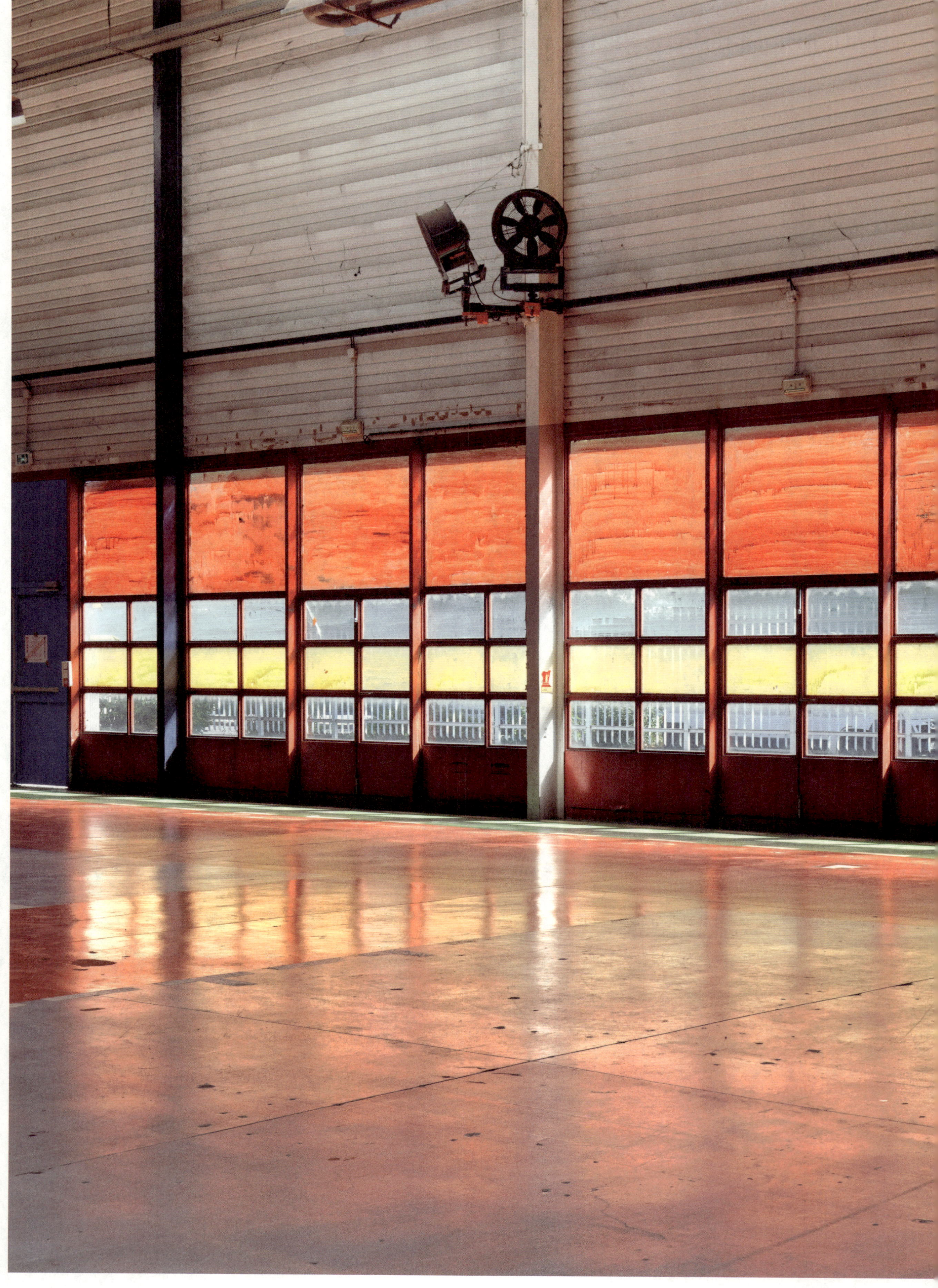

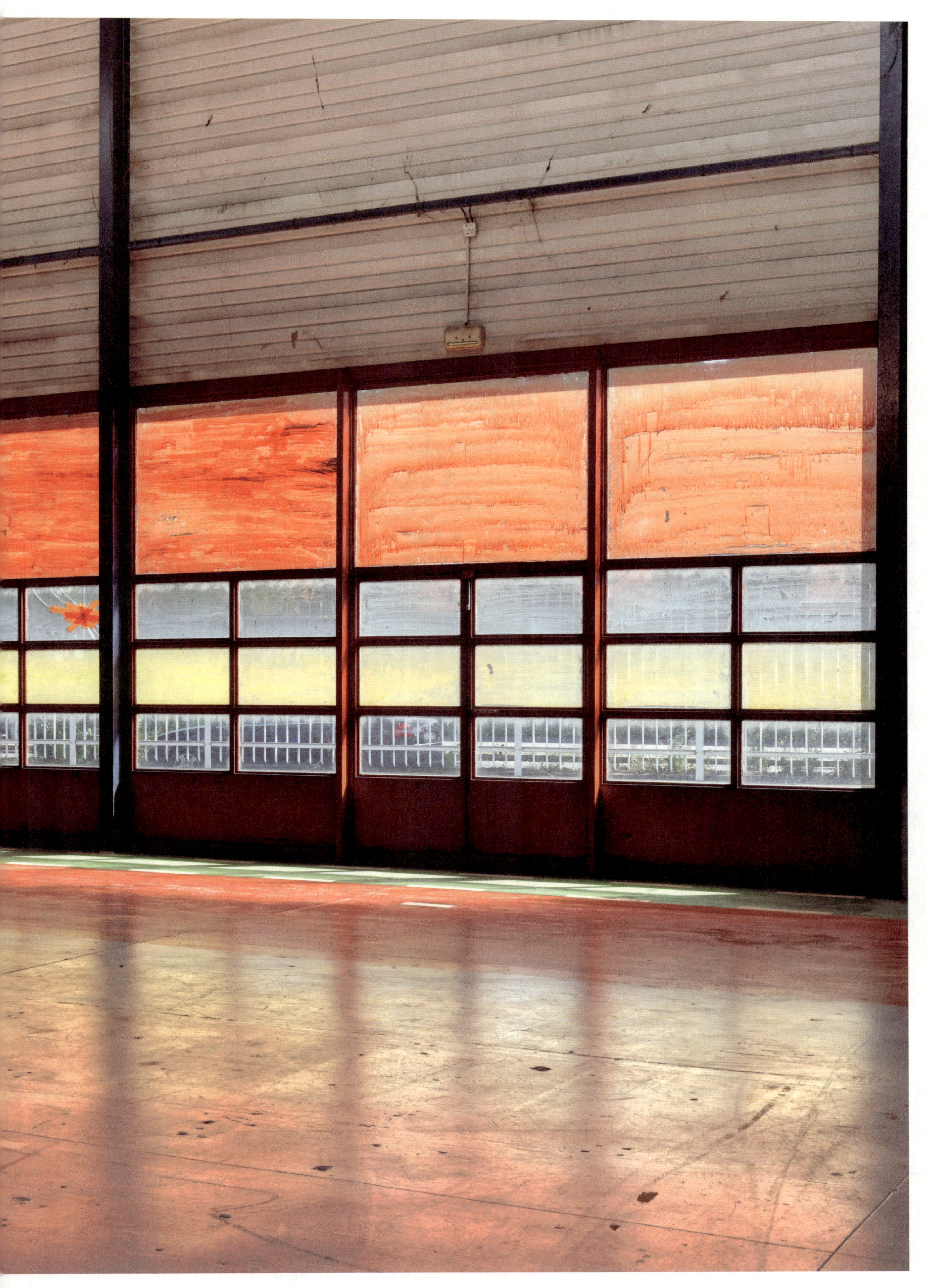

Dale Harding, *Site Surveys / International Standard*

Dale Harding, *Site Surveys / International Standard* 2019, acrylics, dried pigments, gum arabic and glass, dimensions variable. Installation view, 15th Lyon Contemporary Art Biennale, Fagor Factory, Lyon, 2019. Photos: Lyon Biennale .

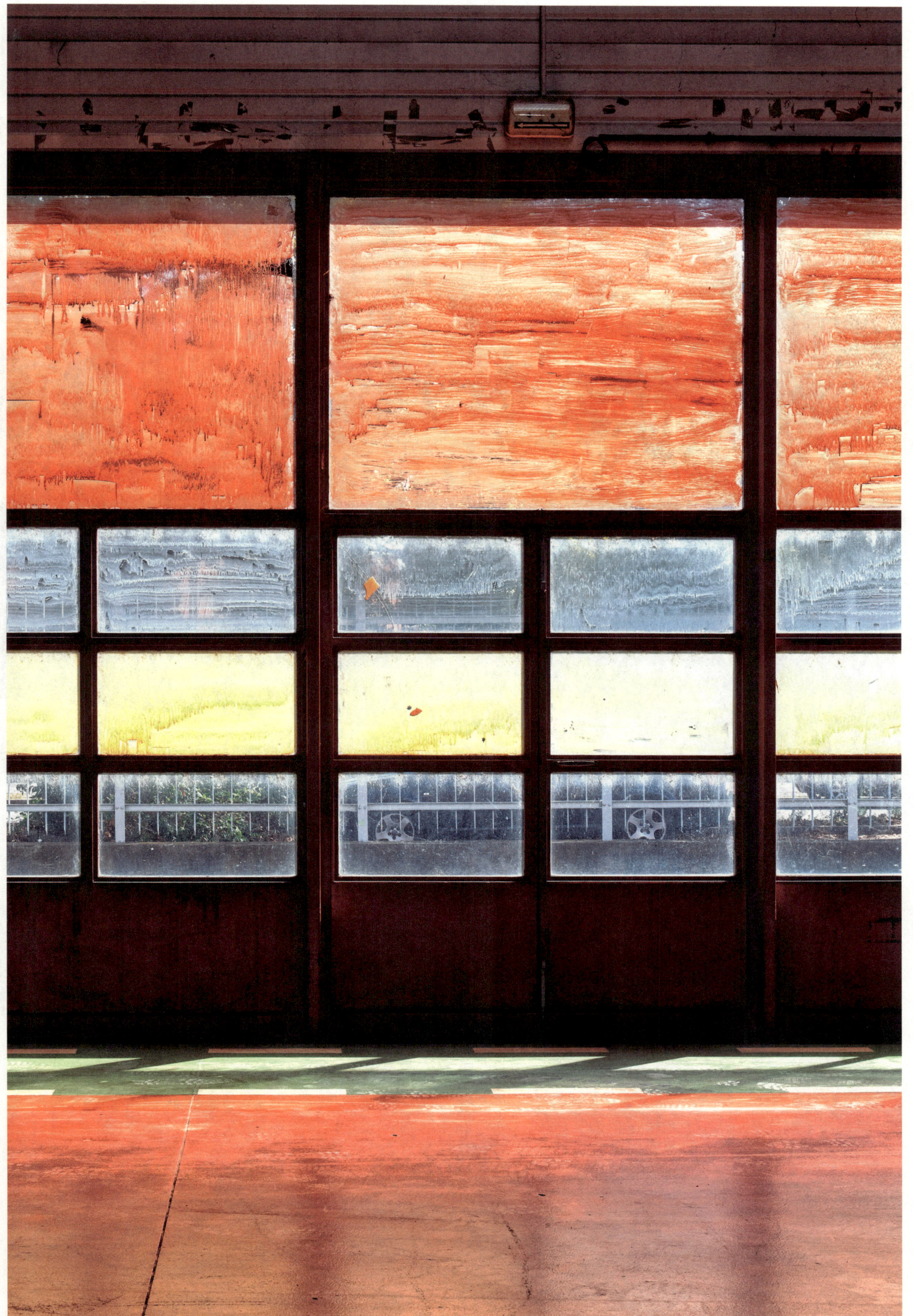

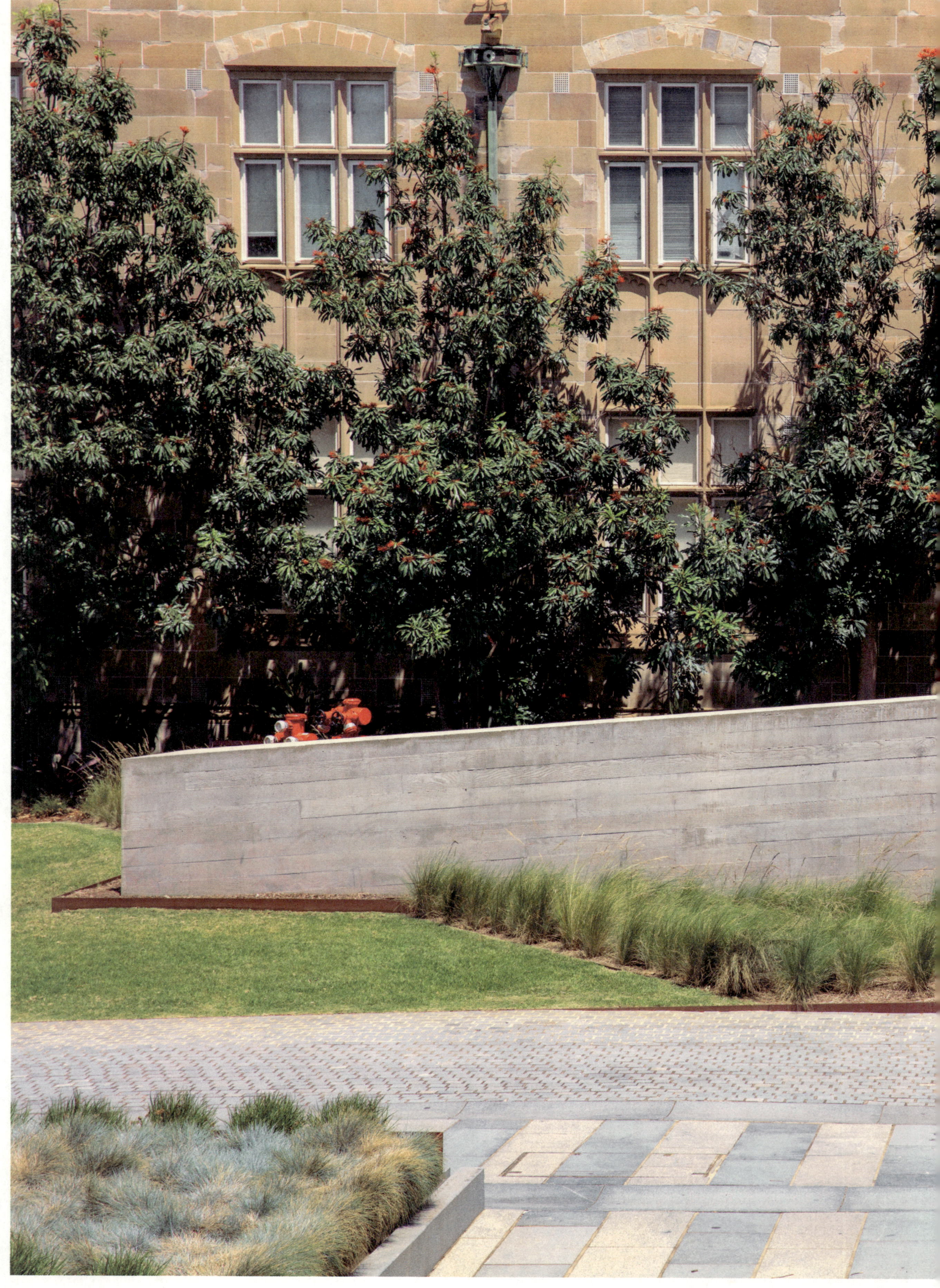

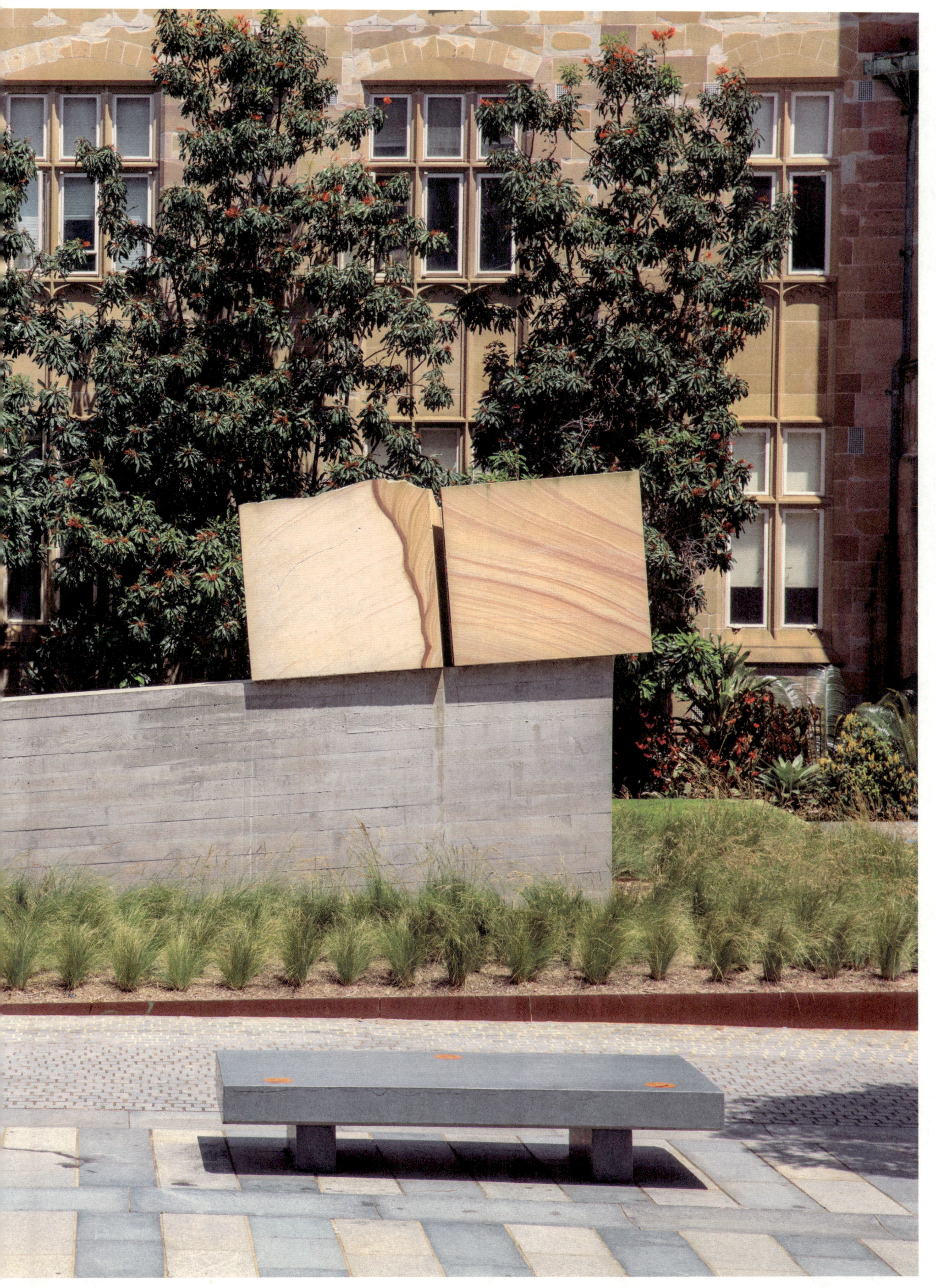

Dale Harding, *Spine 2*

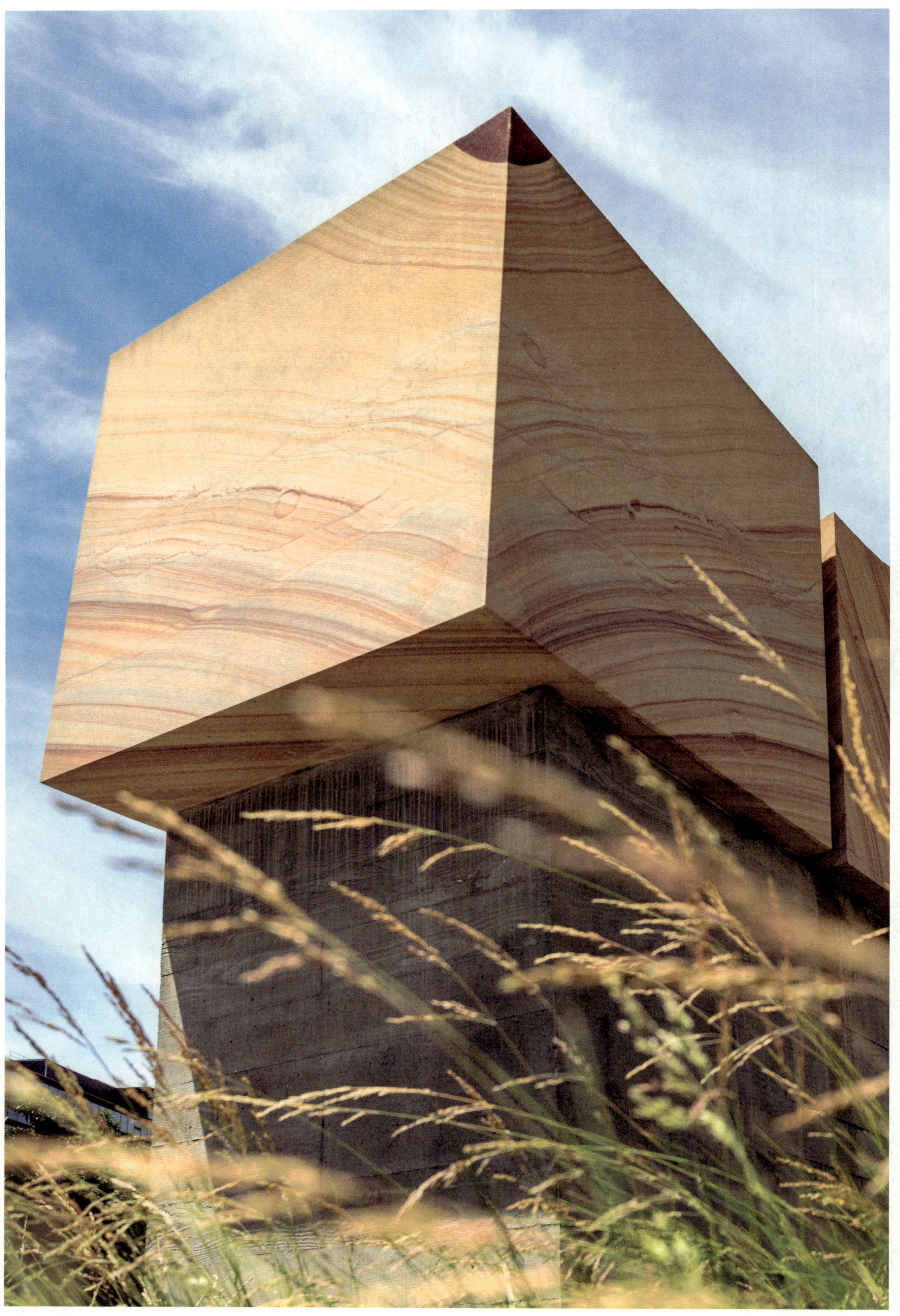

Dale Harding, *Spine 2* 2018,
Gosford sandstone, off-form concrete, hematite oxide, 3 parts: wedge-shaped plinth 113 (to 200) × 1200 × 130 cm; front block 139 × 150 × 150 cm; back block 150 × 150 × 150 cm, Eastern Avenue, The University of Sydney. Photos: David Jones

Dale Harding, *Repression cloak (ceremony for a gay wedding)* 2018, *Untitled cloak* 2018, *Cloaks (mortua and mortuus)* 2018, cotton blanketing, gum arabic and powdered pigment, dimensions variable, displayed folded. Right: Dale Harding, *Death did not hurt you* 2018, glass, cotton blanketing and acrylic, 2 parts: 181 × 12.5 cm, 151 × 12.5 cm. Photos: Charlie Hillhouse

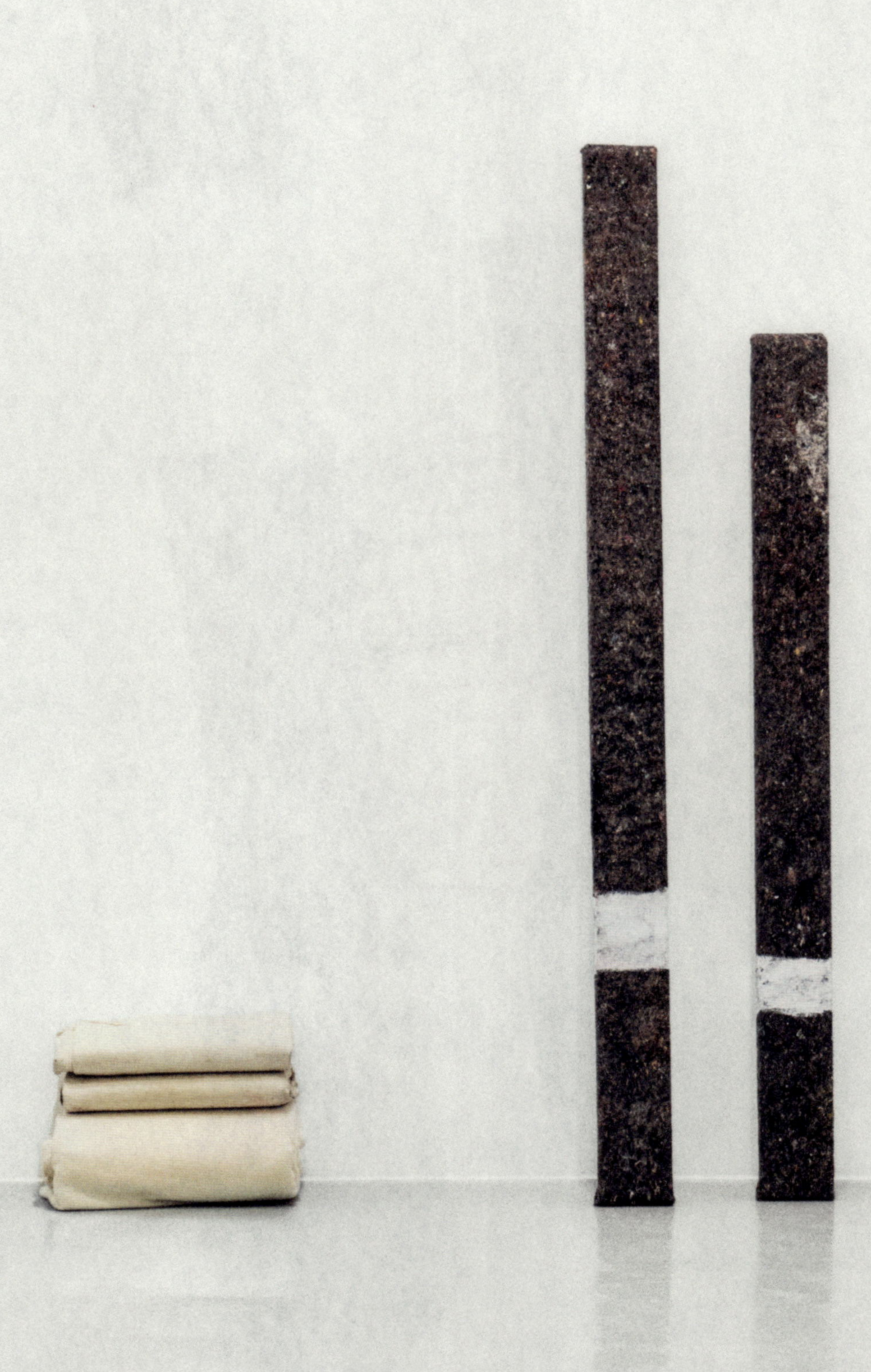

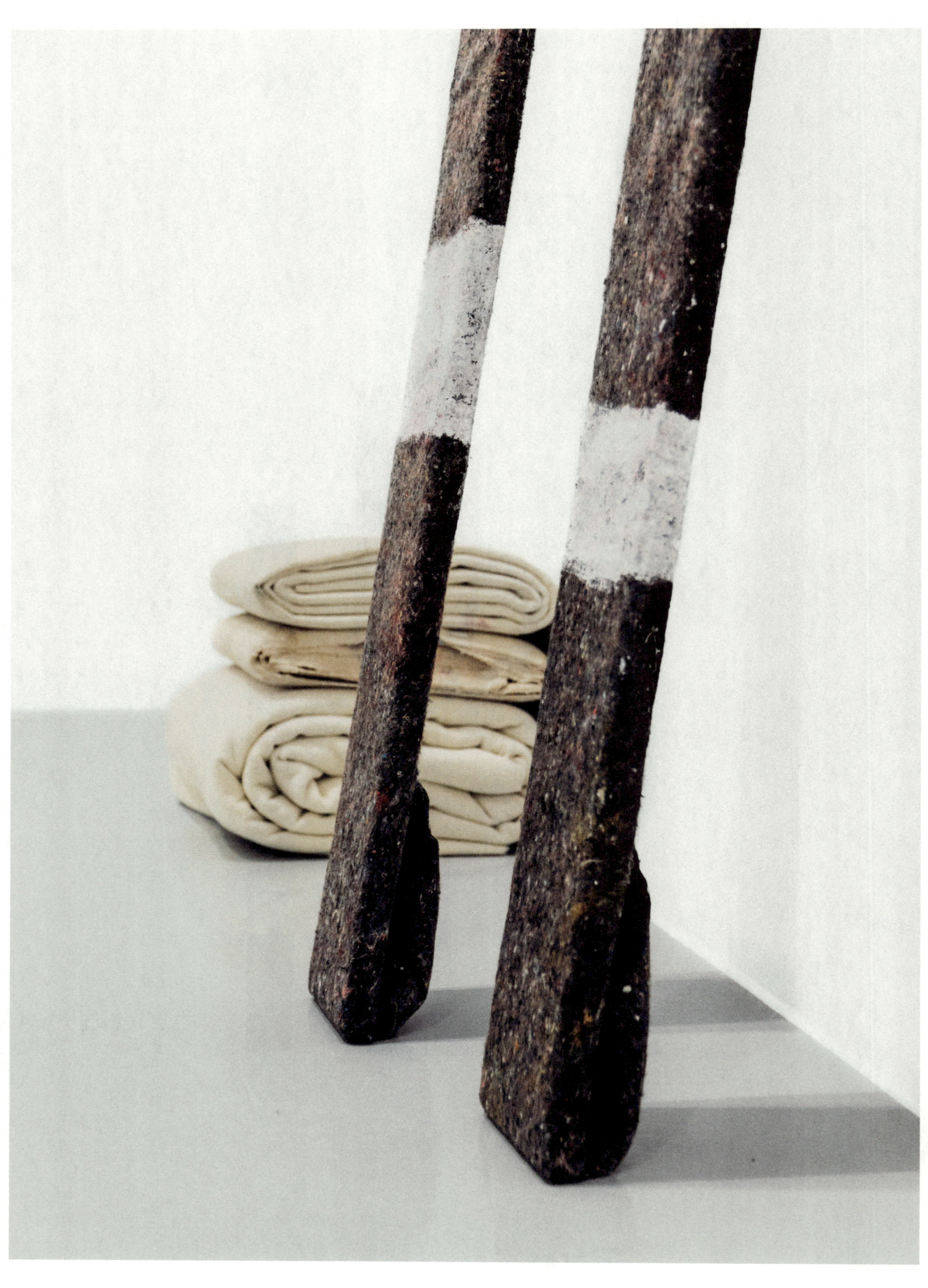

 Dale Harding, *Death did not hurt you* (front, detail)

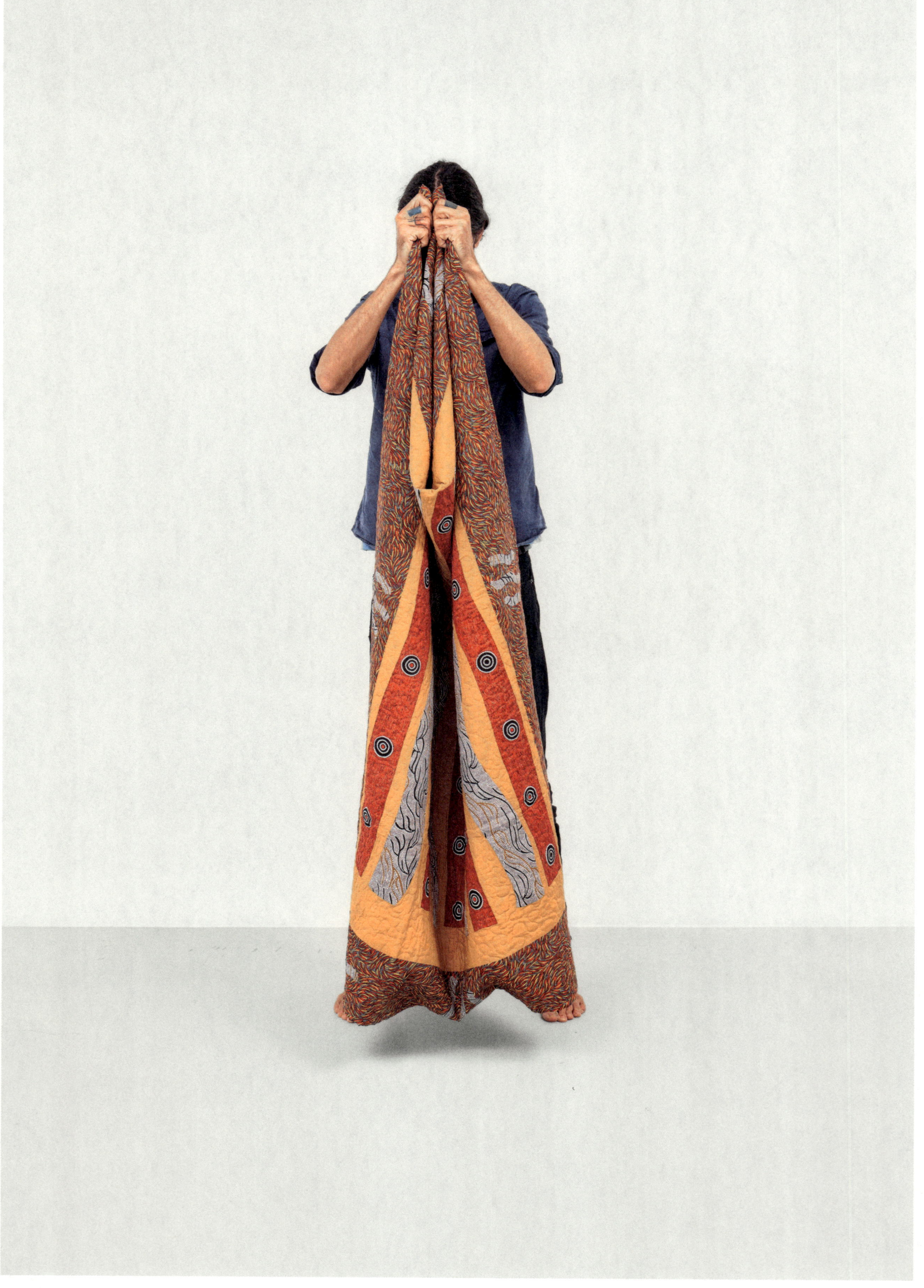

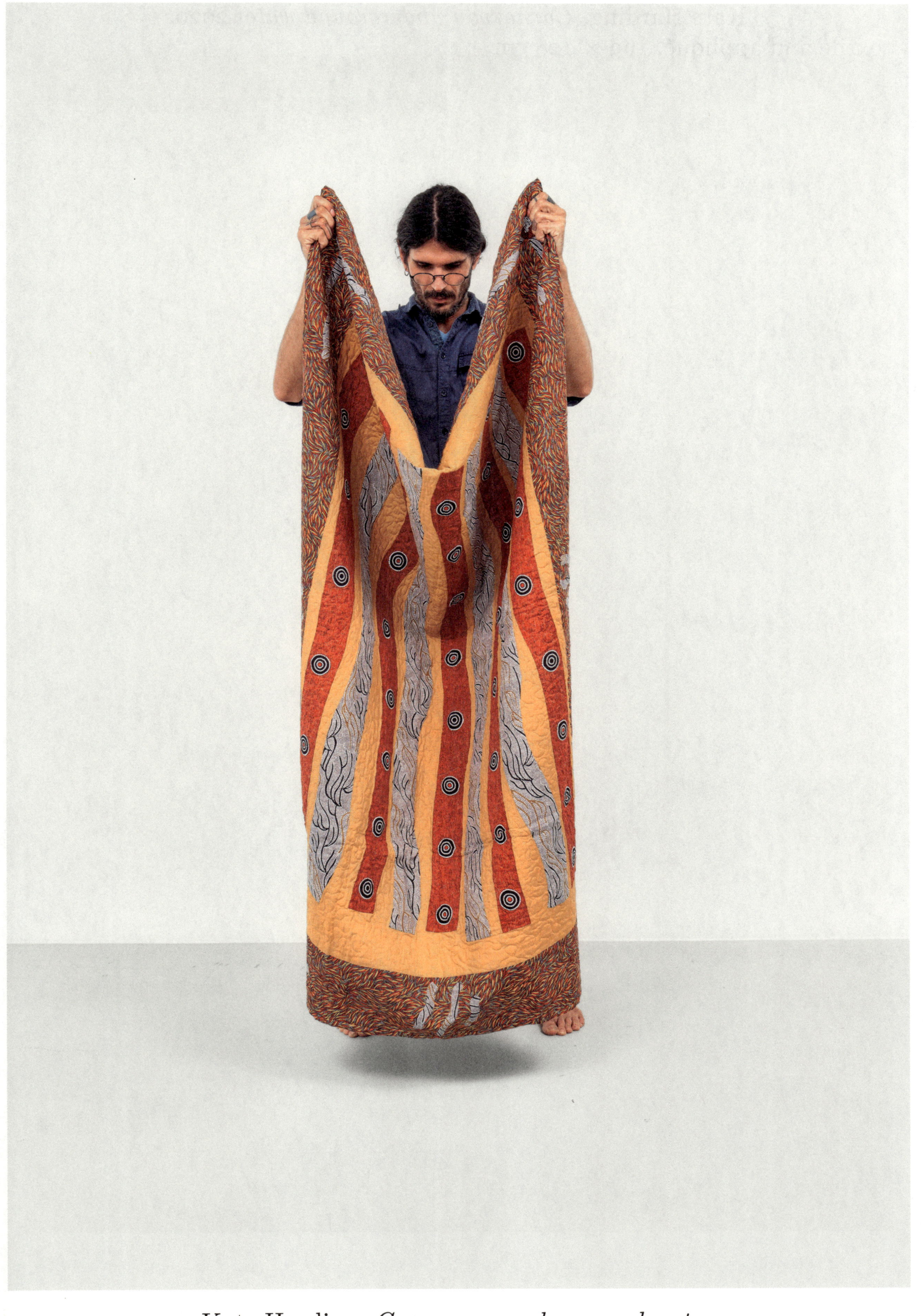

Kate Harding, *Carnarvon underground water*

Kate Harding, *Carnarvon underground water* 2020,
textile and appliqué, 169 × 128 cm

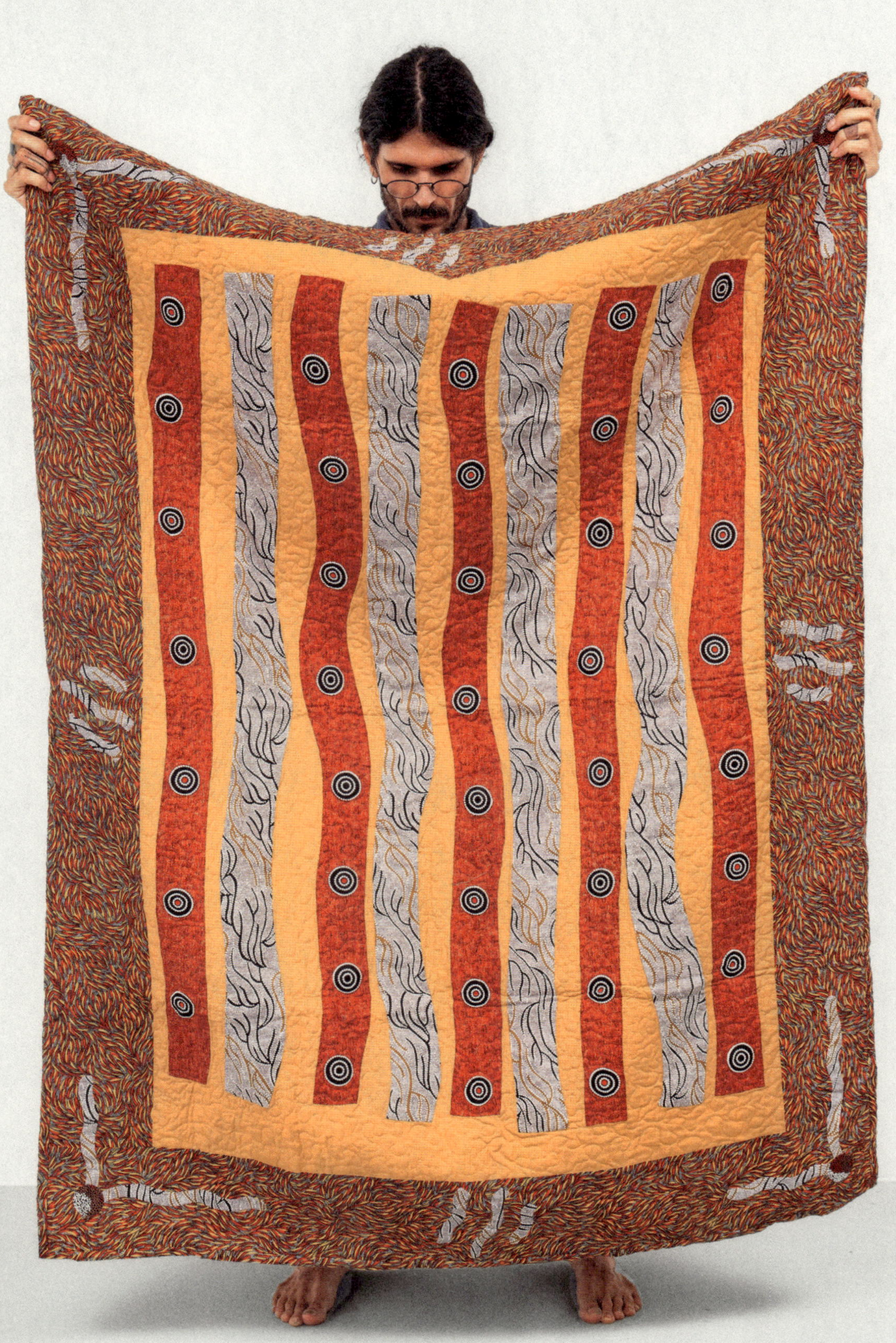

Kate Harding, *Tribute to women—
past, present and future* 2019,
textile and appliqué, 171 × 160 cm

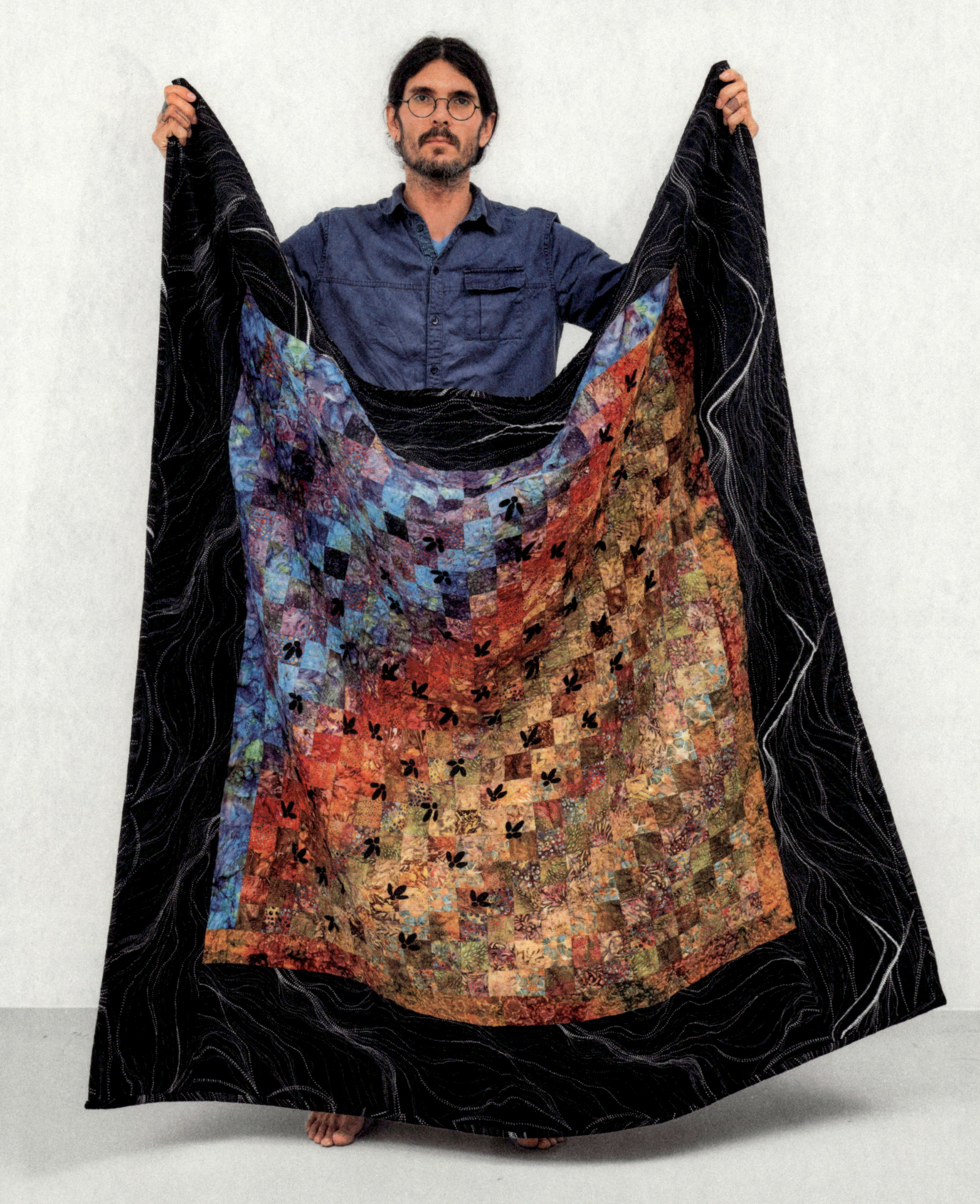

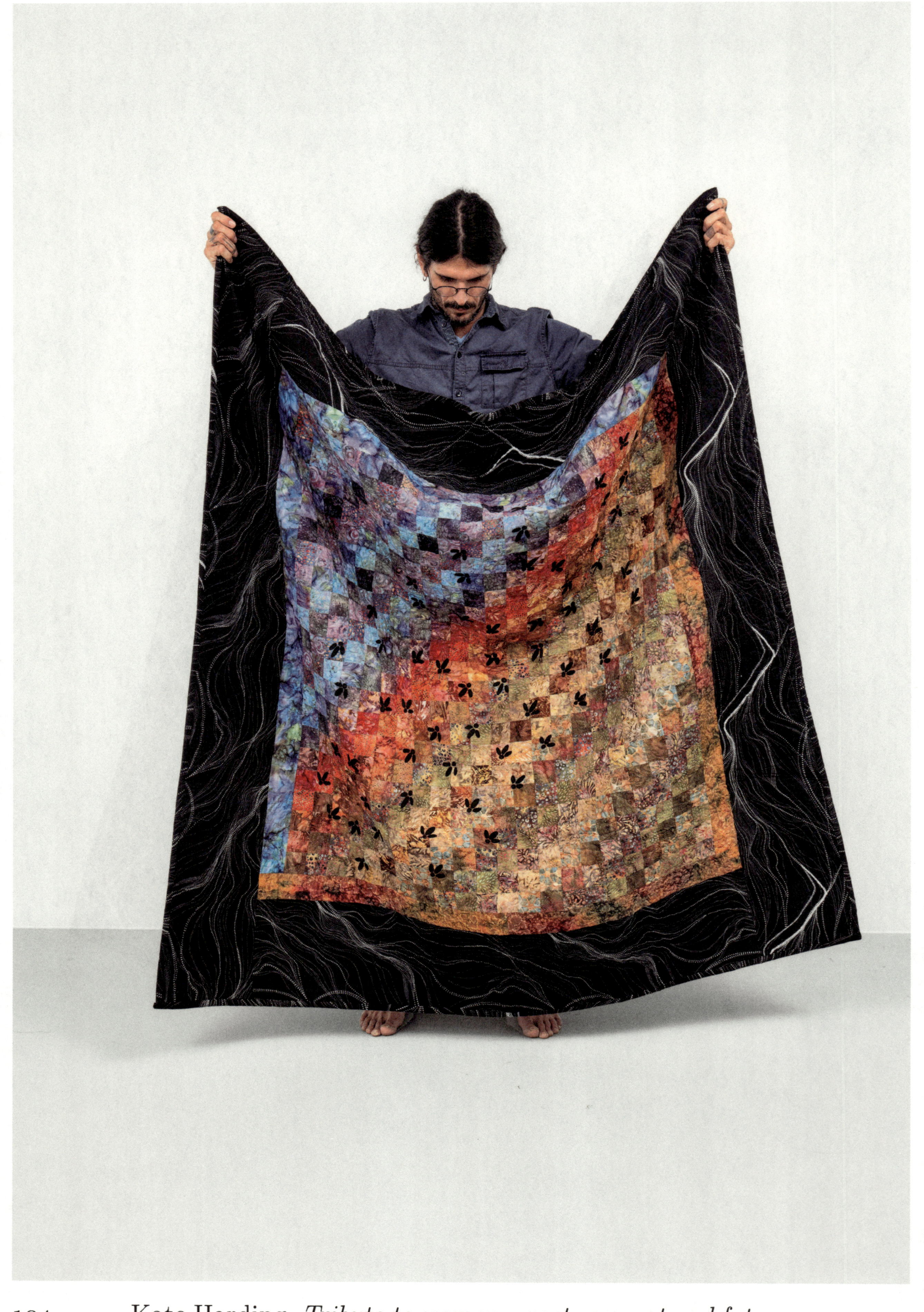

 Kate Harding, *Tribute to women—past, present and future*

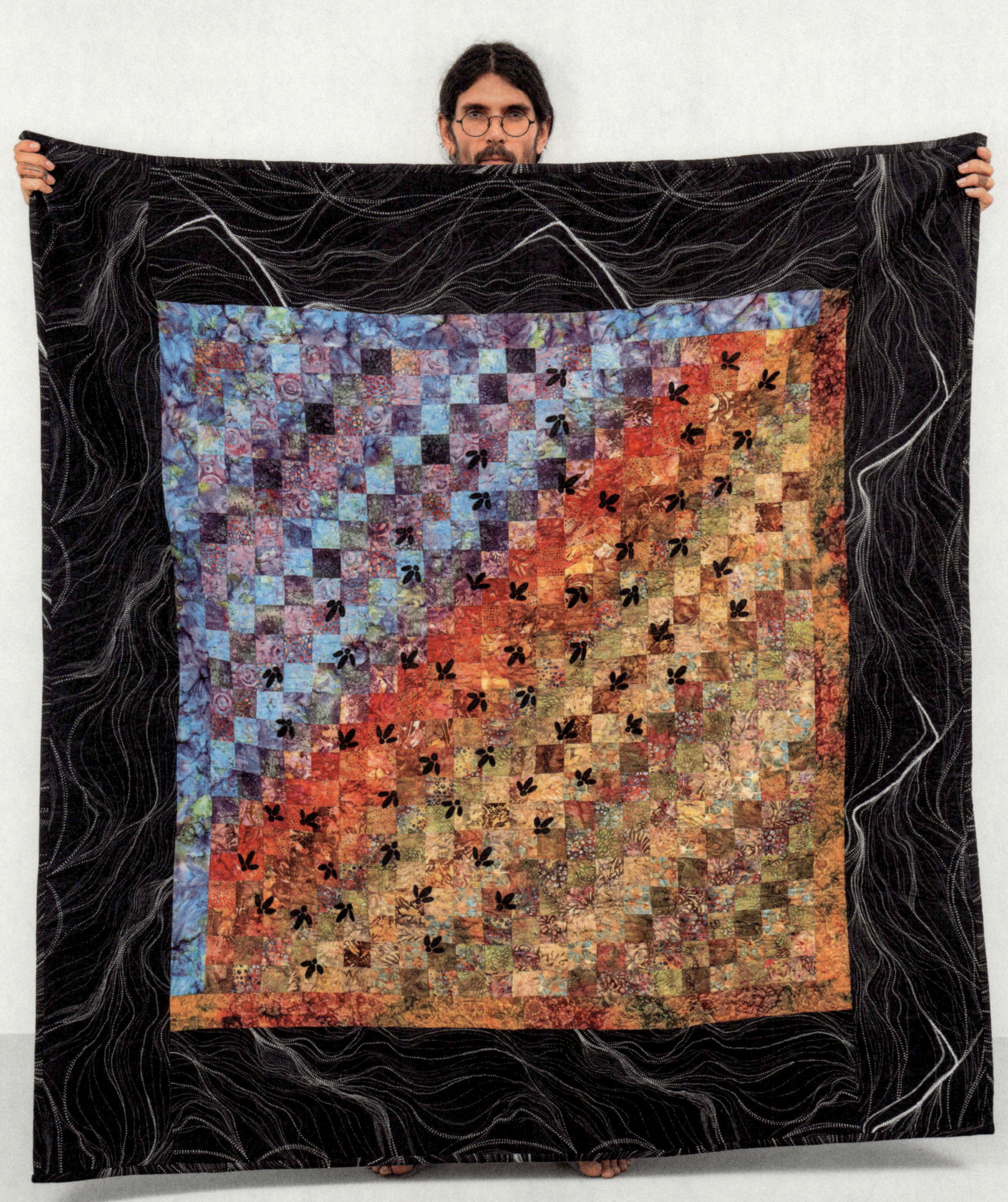

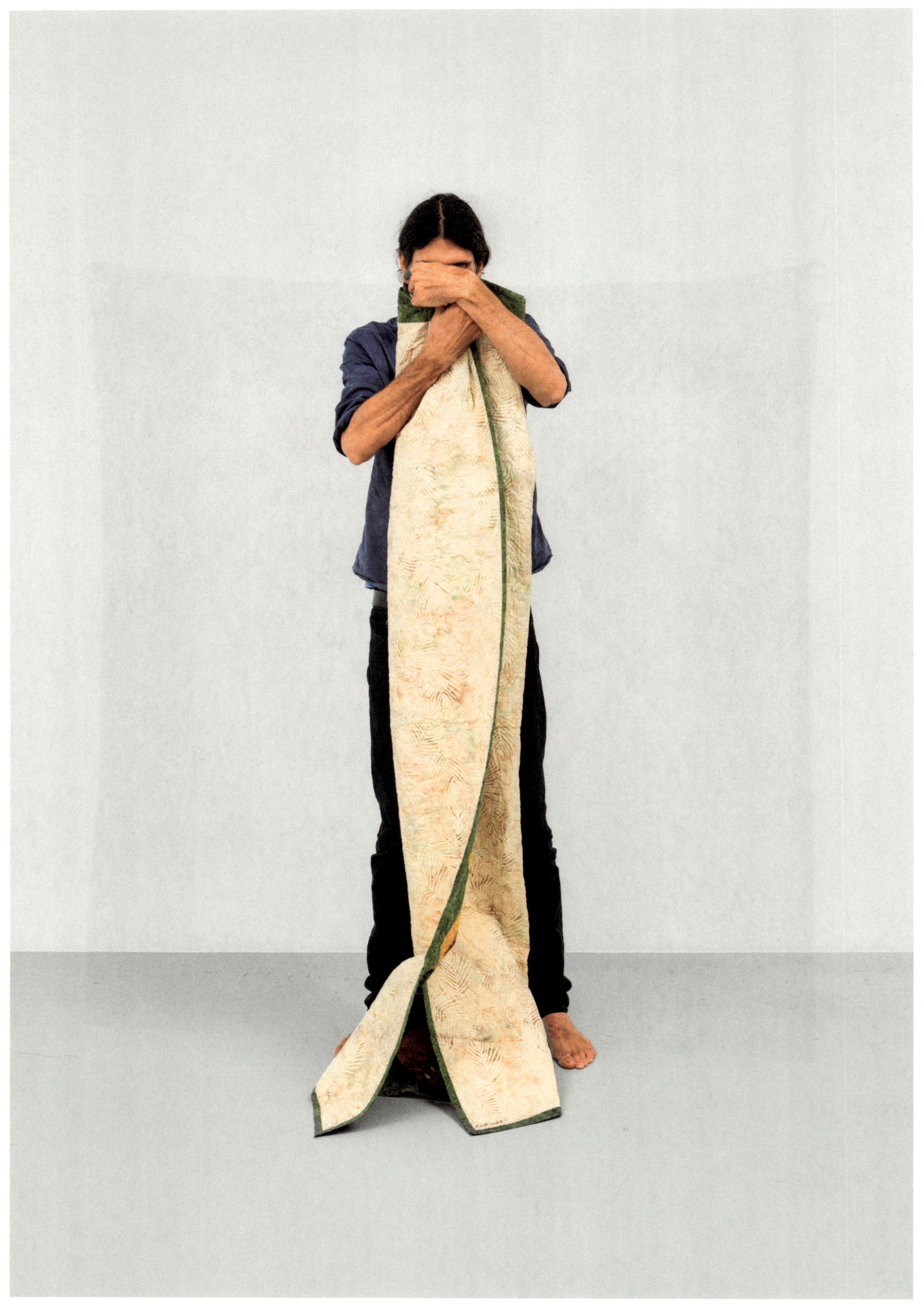

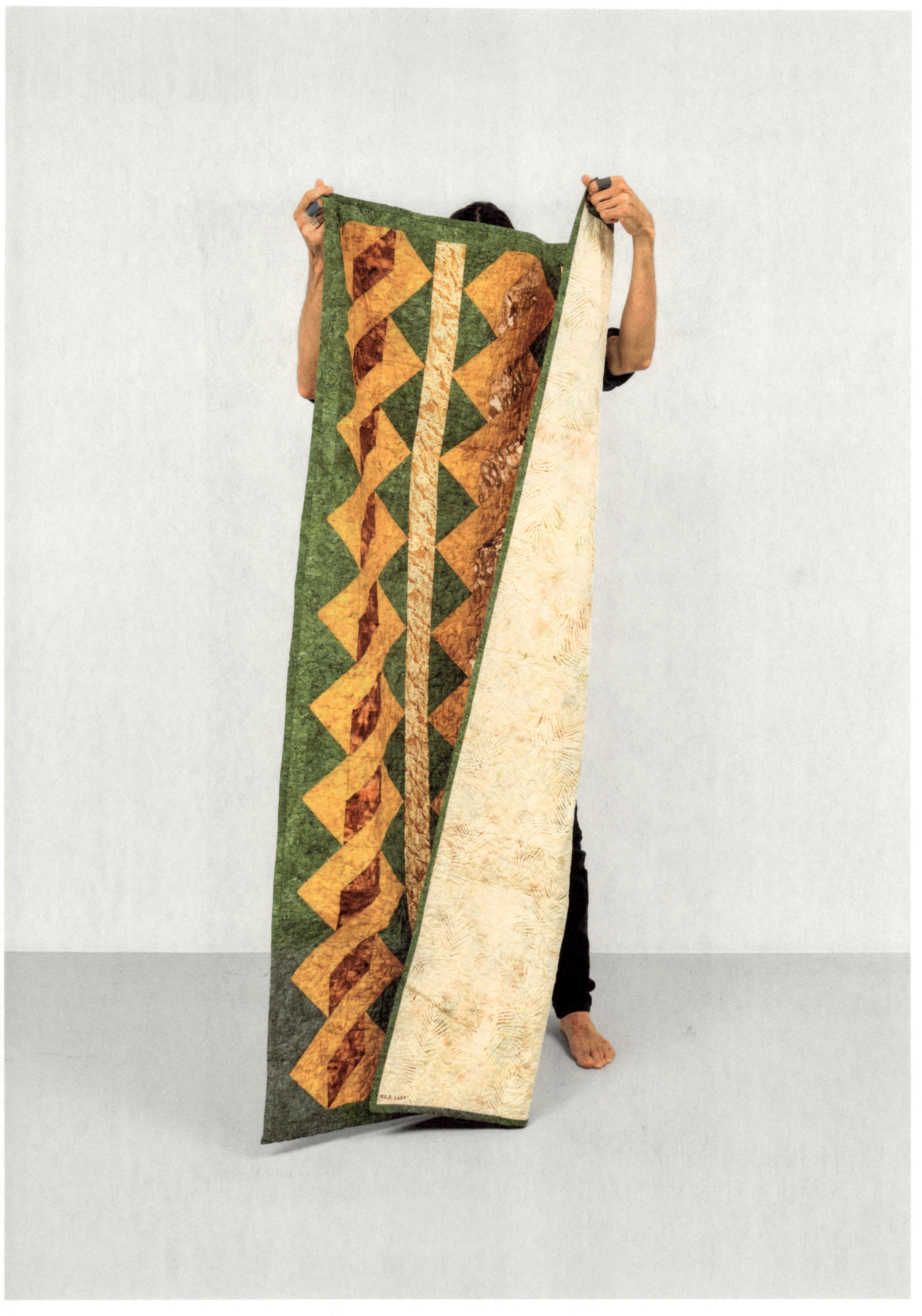

Kate Harding, *Cylinders*

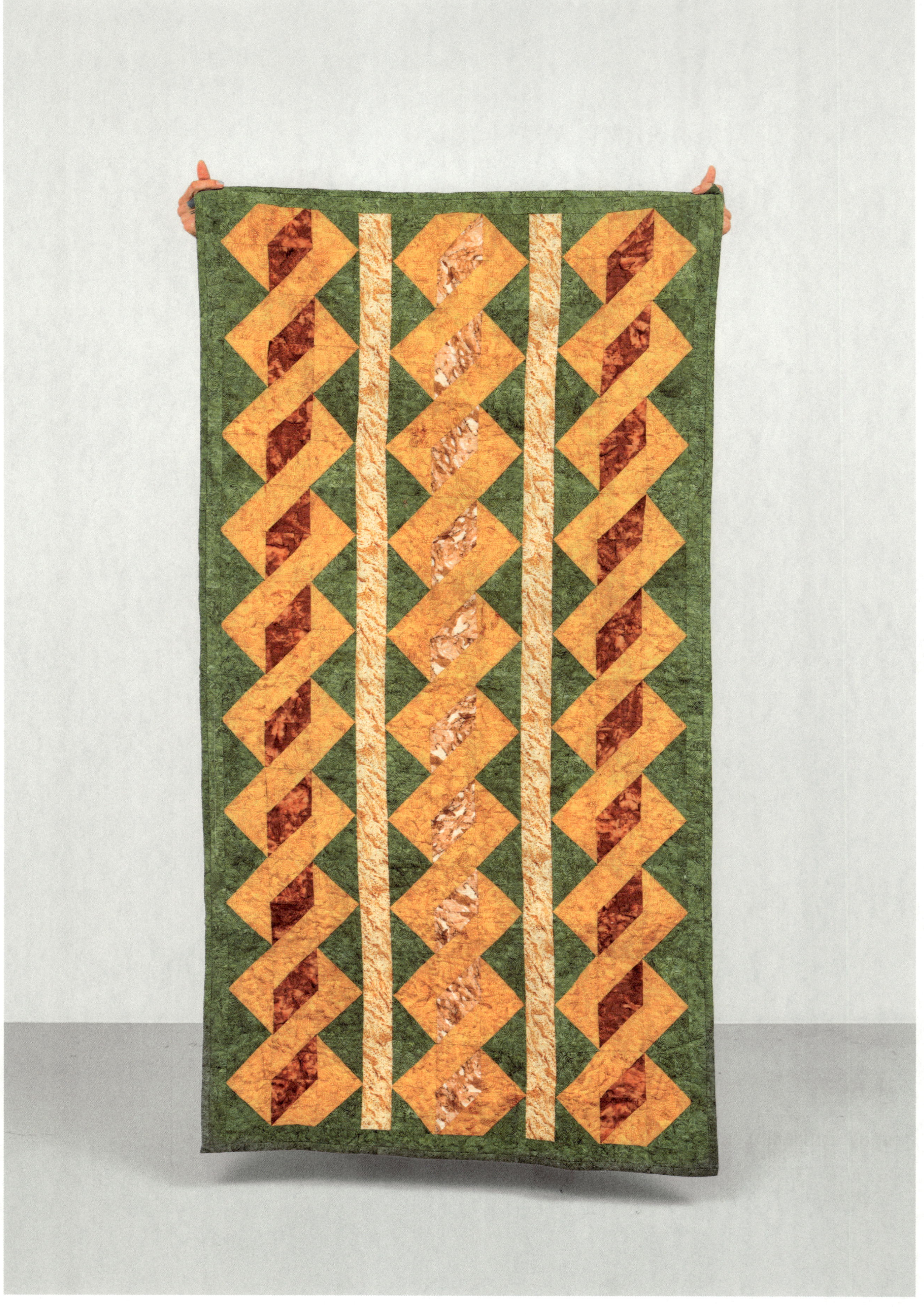

Kate Harding, *Cylinders* 2020,
textile, 187 × 100 cm

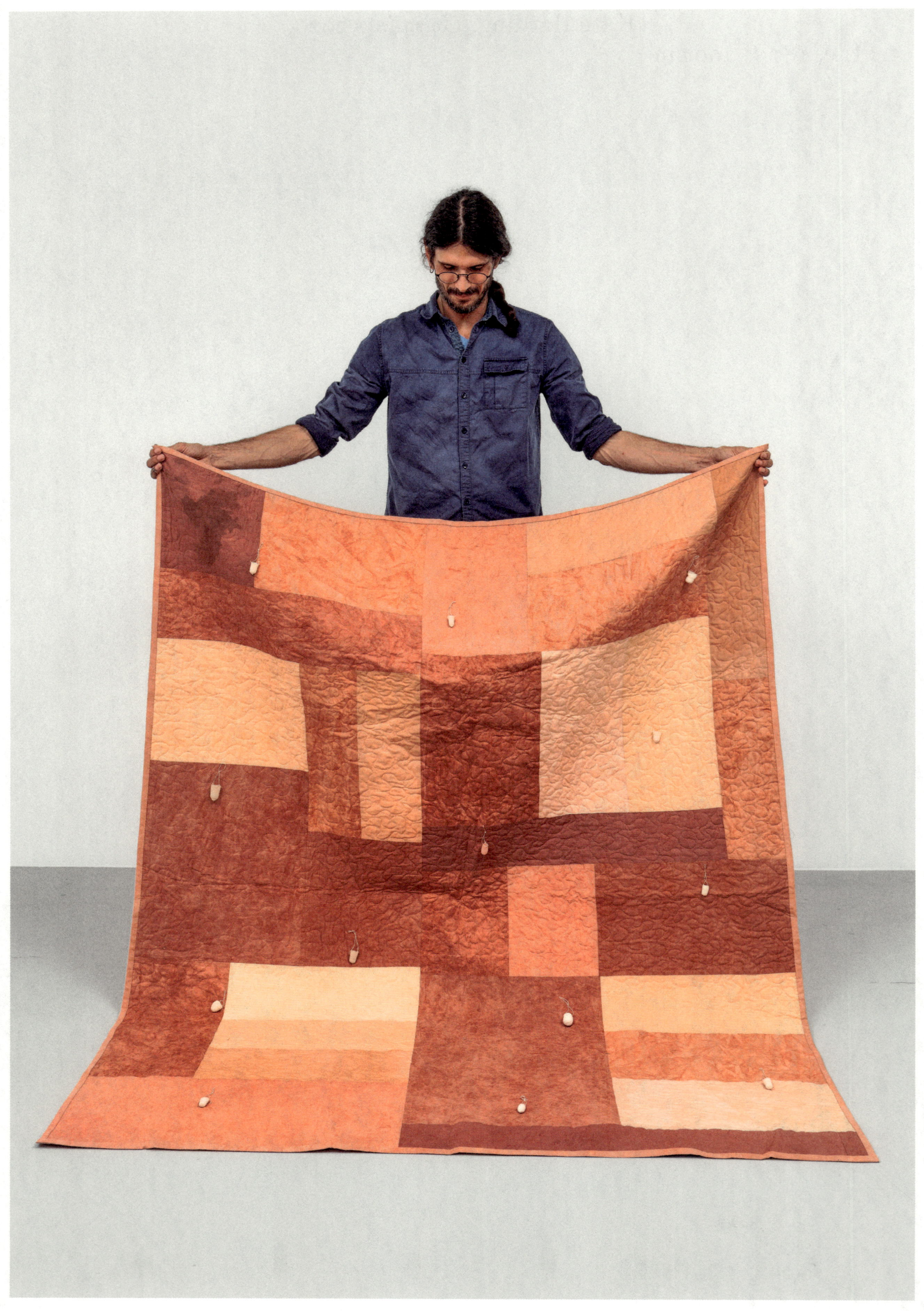

Kate Harding, *Carnarvon*

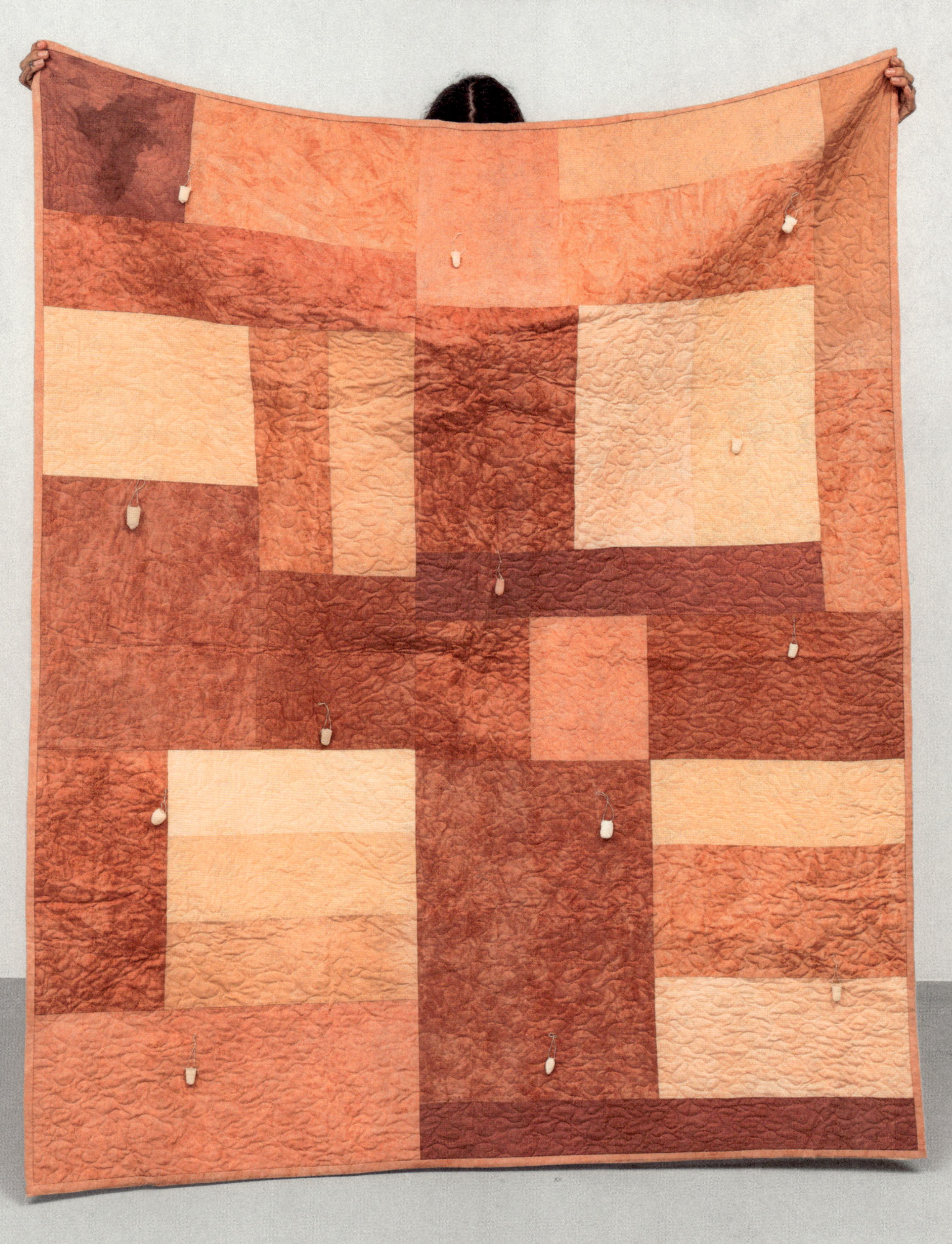

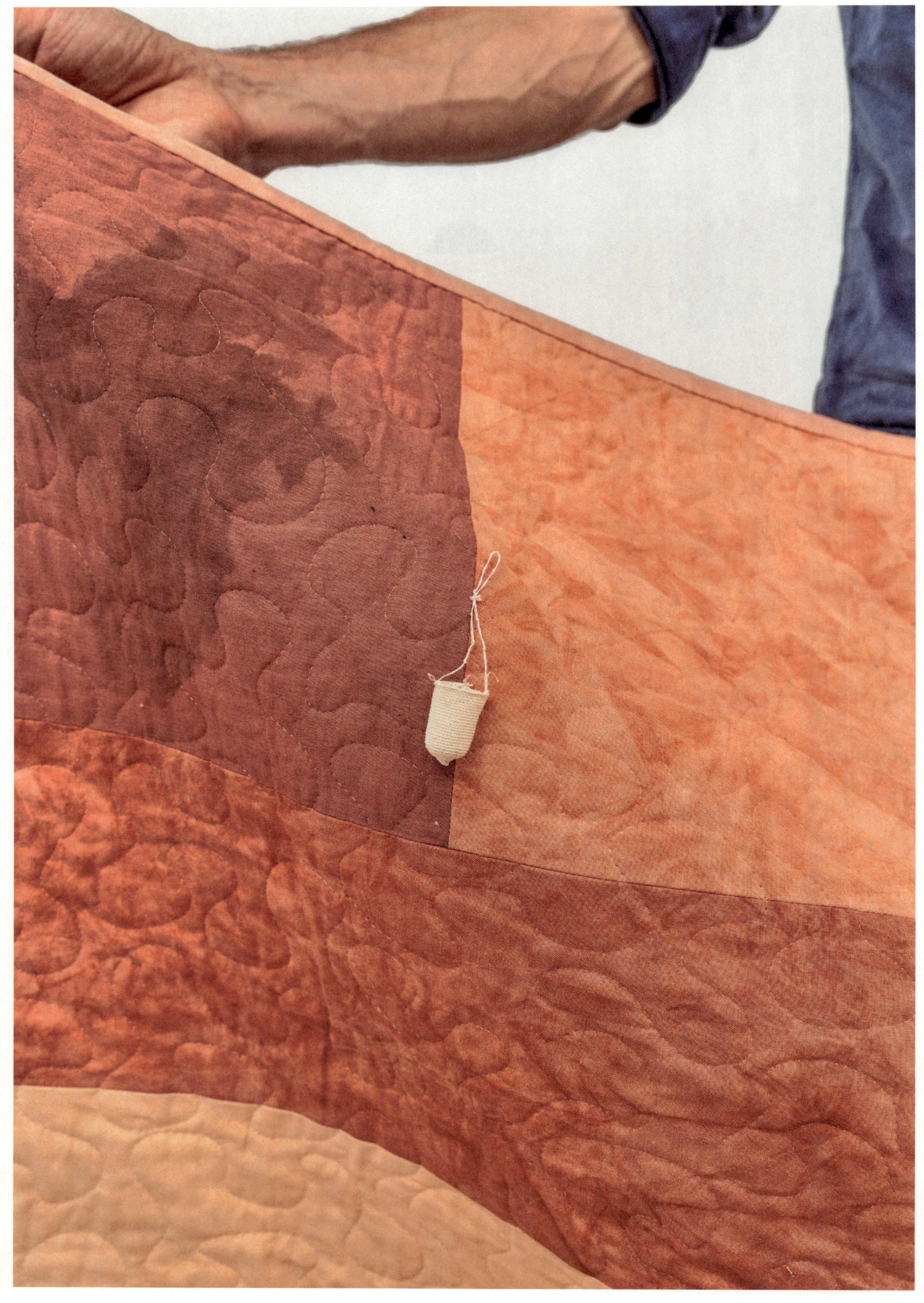

(detail)

Kate Harding, *Carnarvon* 2020,
textile and appliqué, attached thread bags, 188 × 157 cm

Kate Harding, *White Hill—looking for food at Clermont* 2020, textile, ochre dyes, hessian and thread, 125 × 93 cm

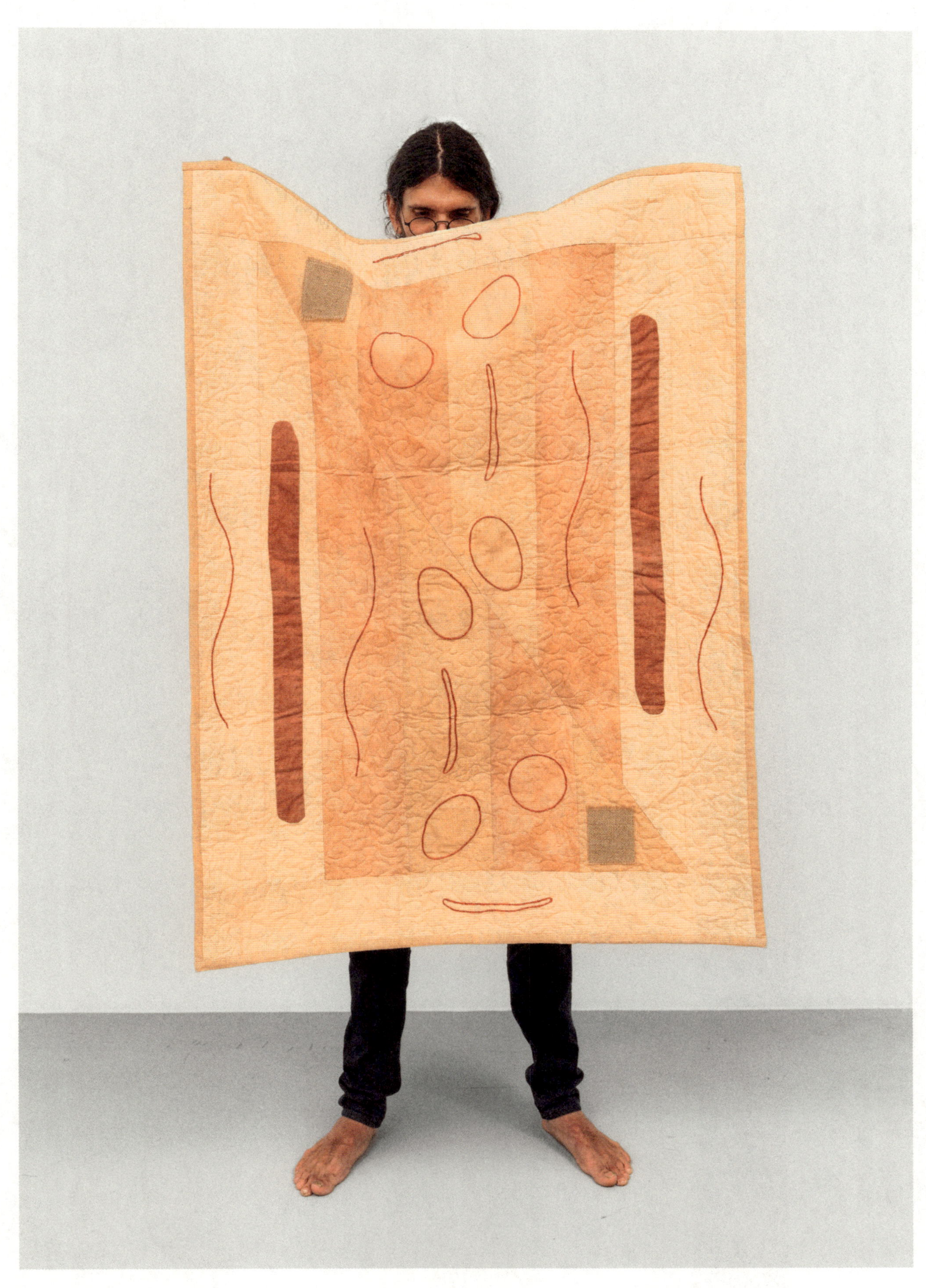

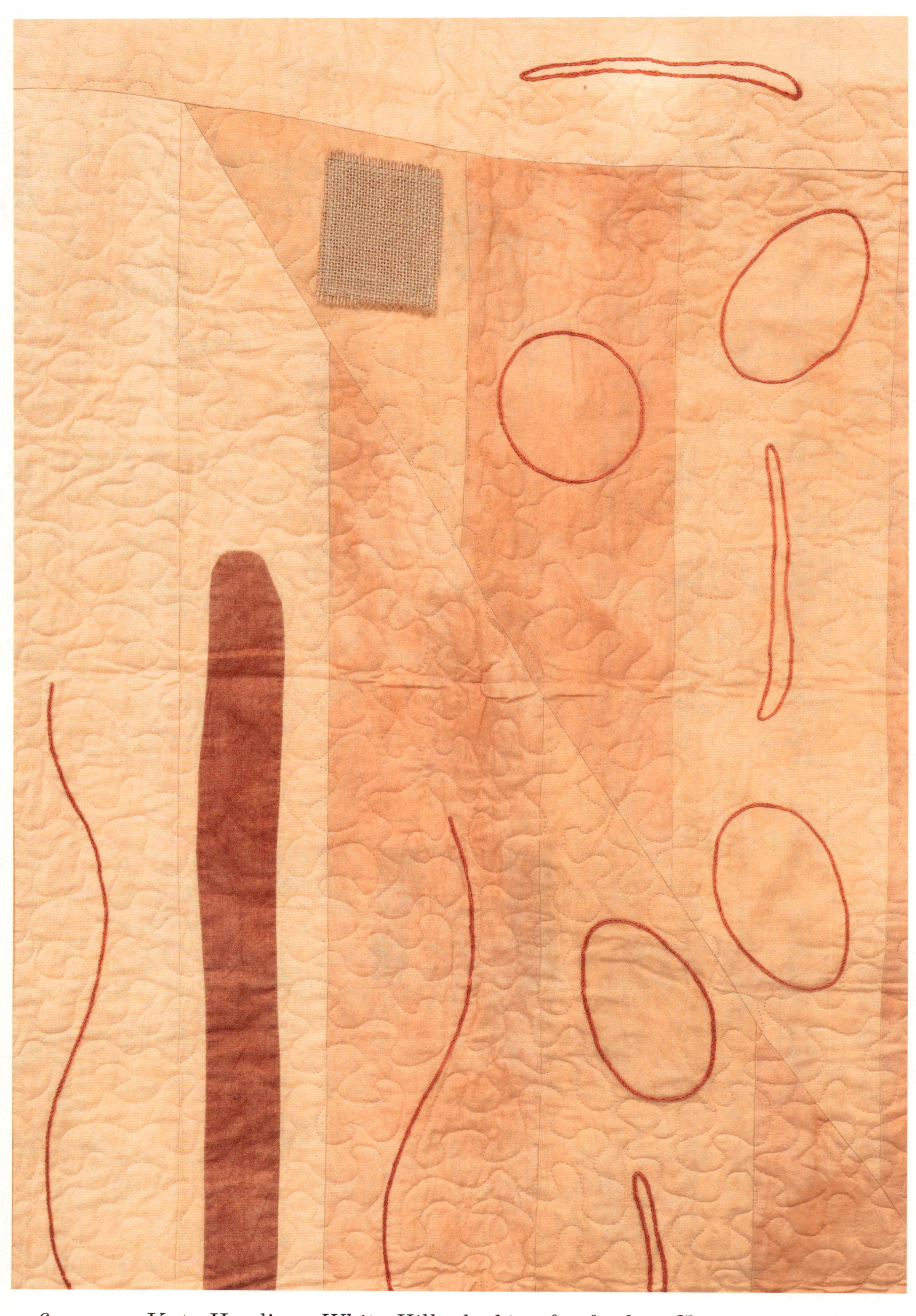

   Kate Harding, *White Hill—looking for food at Clermont*

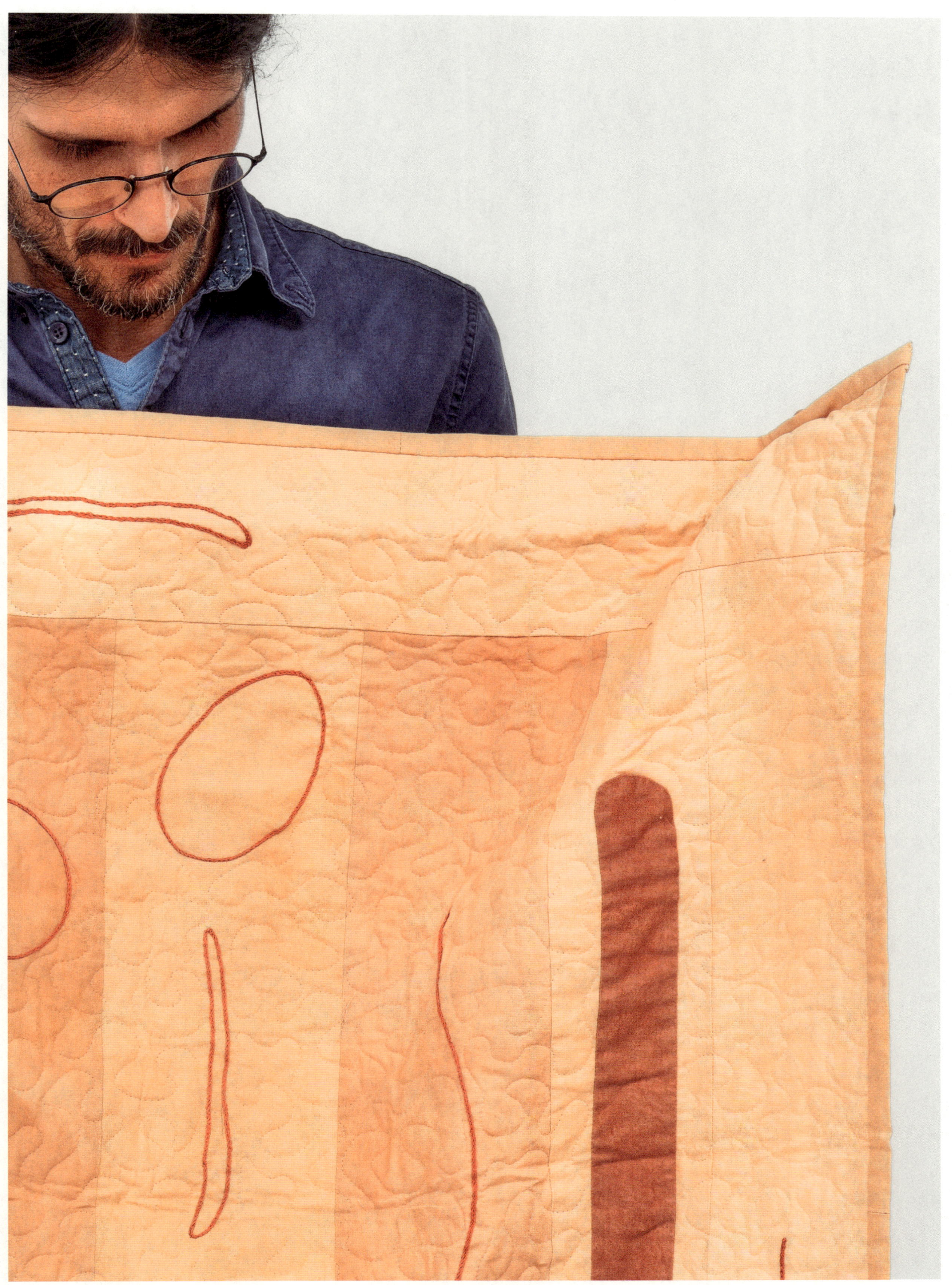

(details)

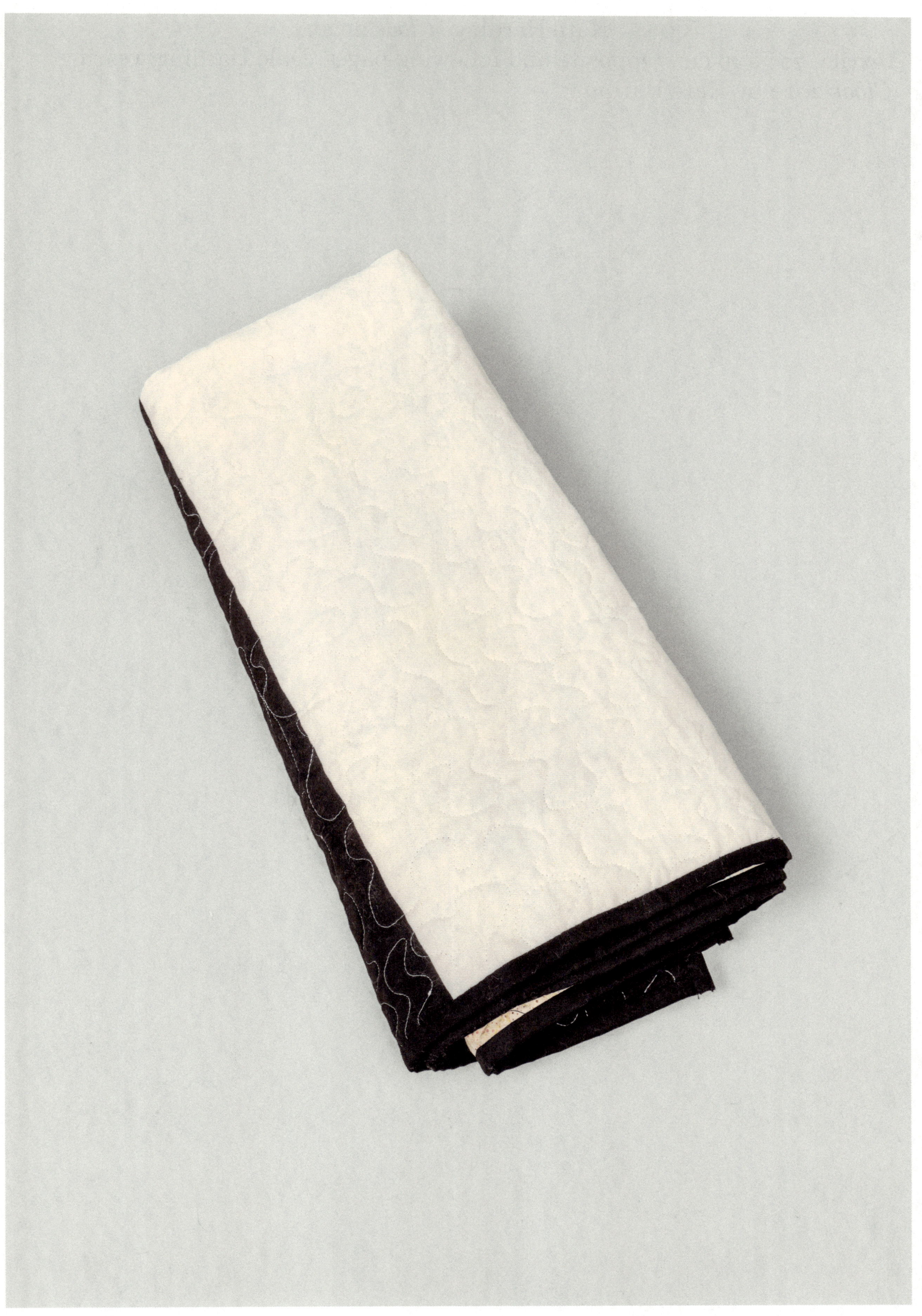

Kate Harding, *Cloak*

Kate Harding, *Cloak* 2020,
textile, 70 × 40 cm. Opposite and following pages: Dale Harding wearing
Cloak 2020 by Kate Harding

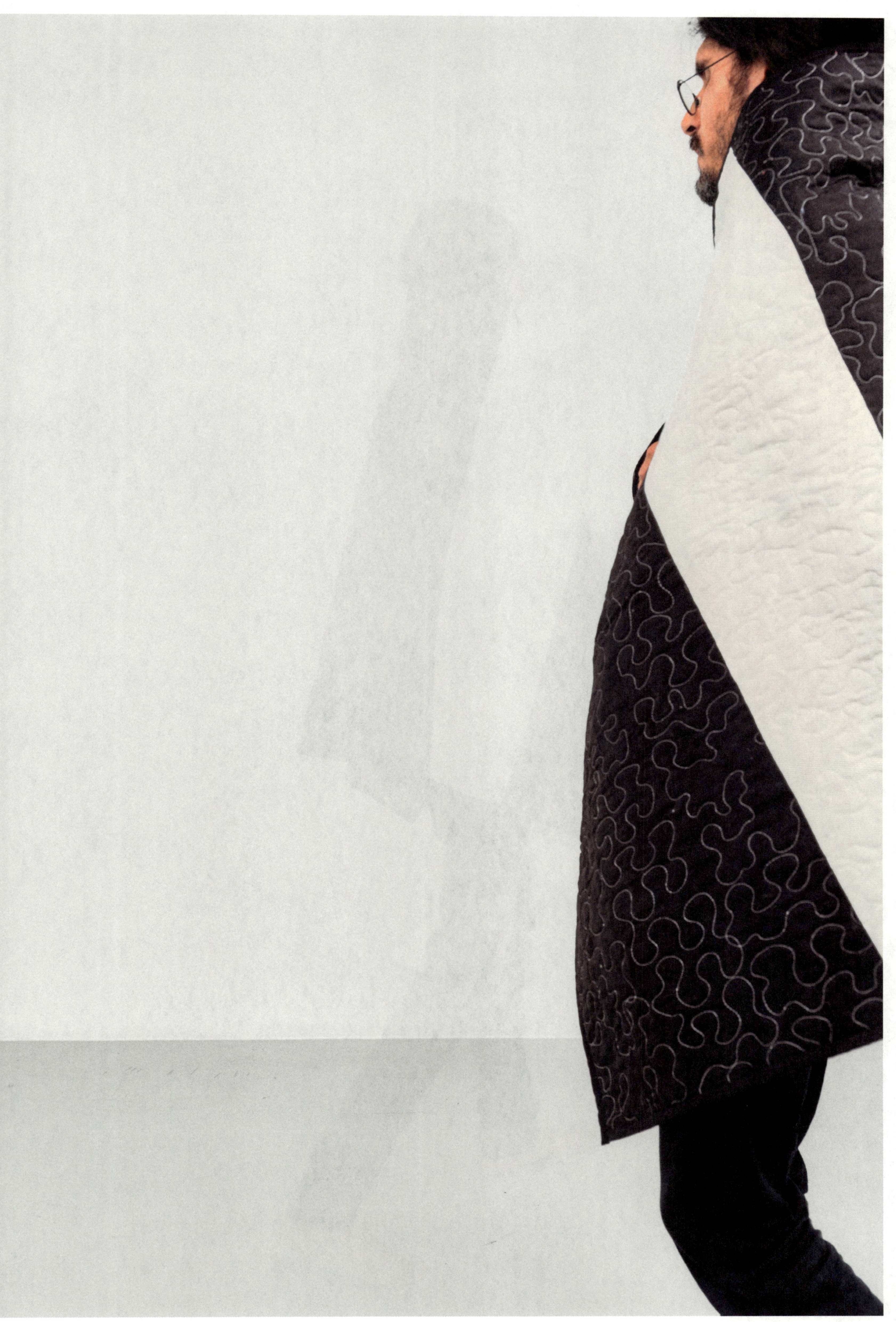

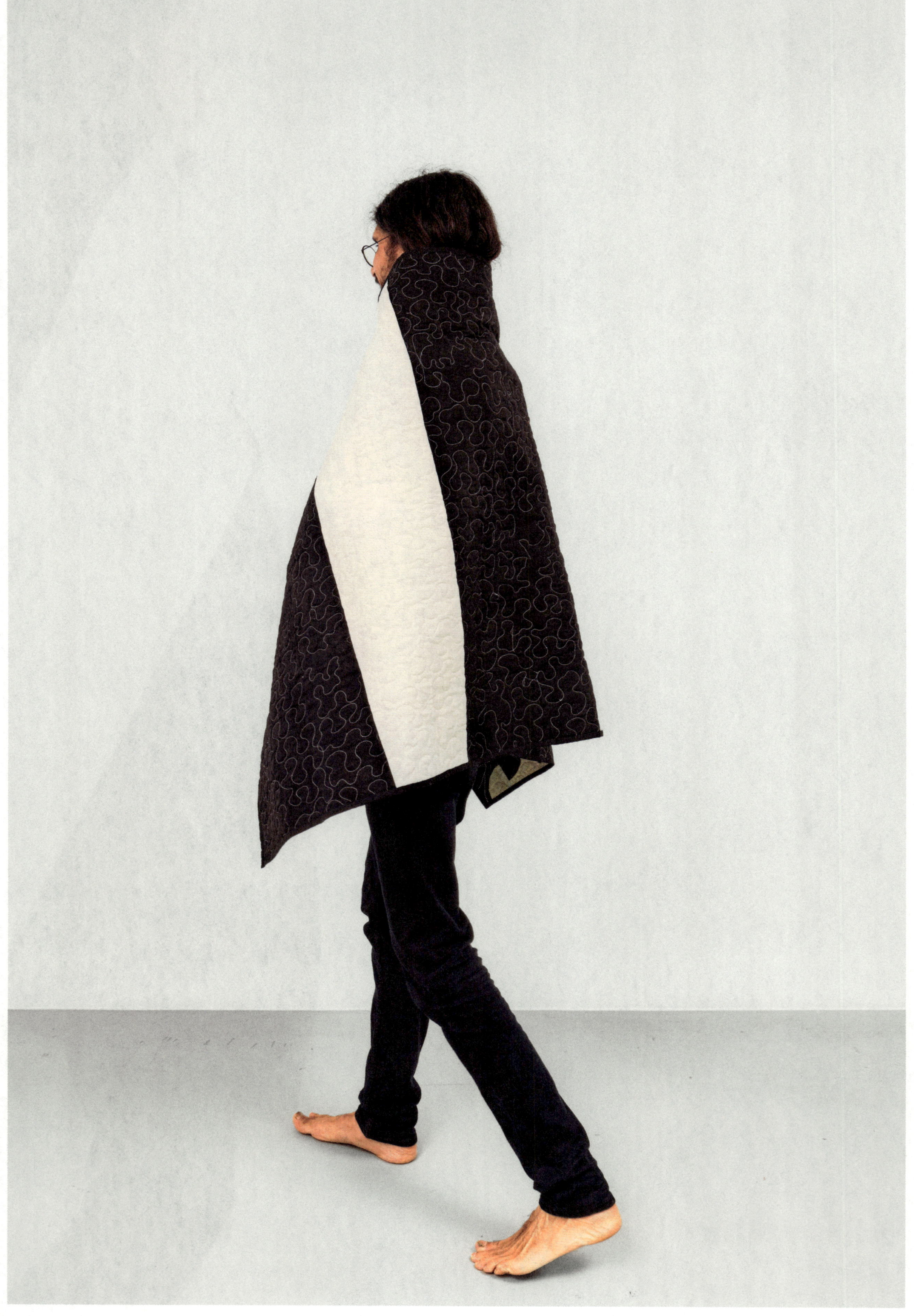

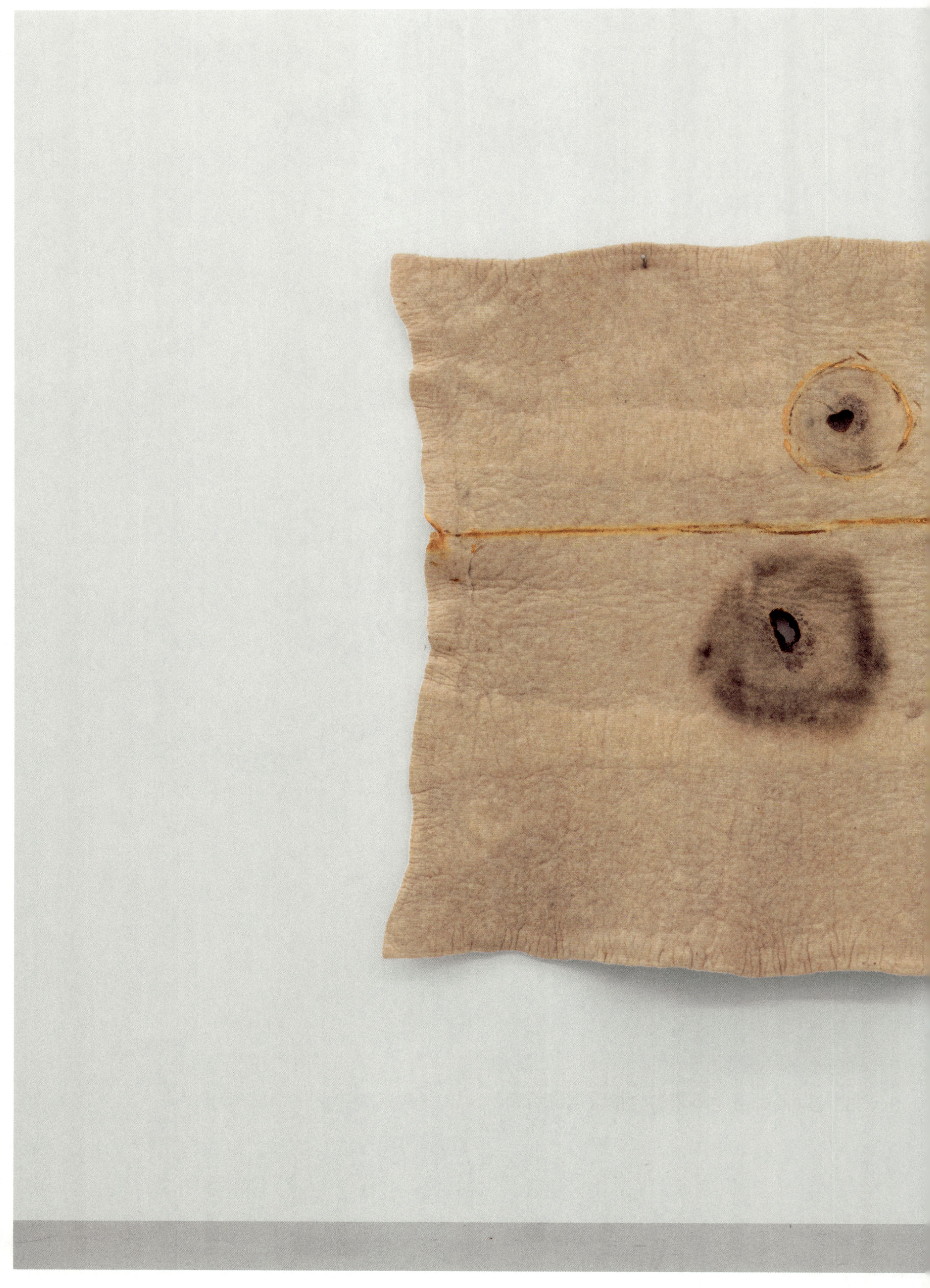

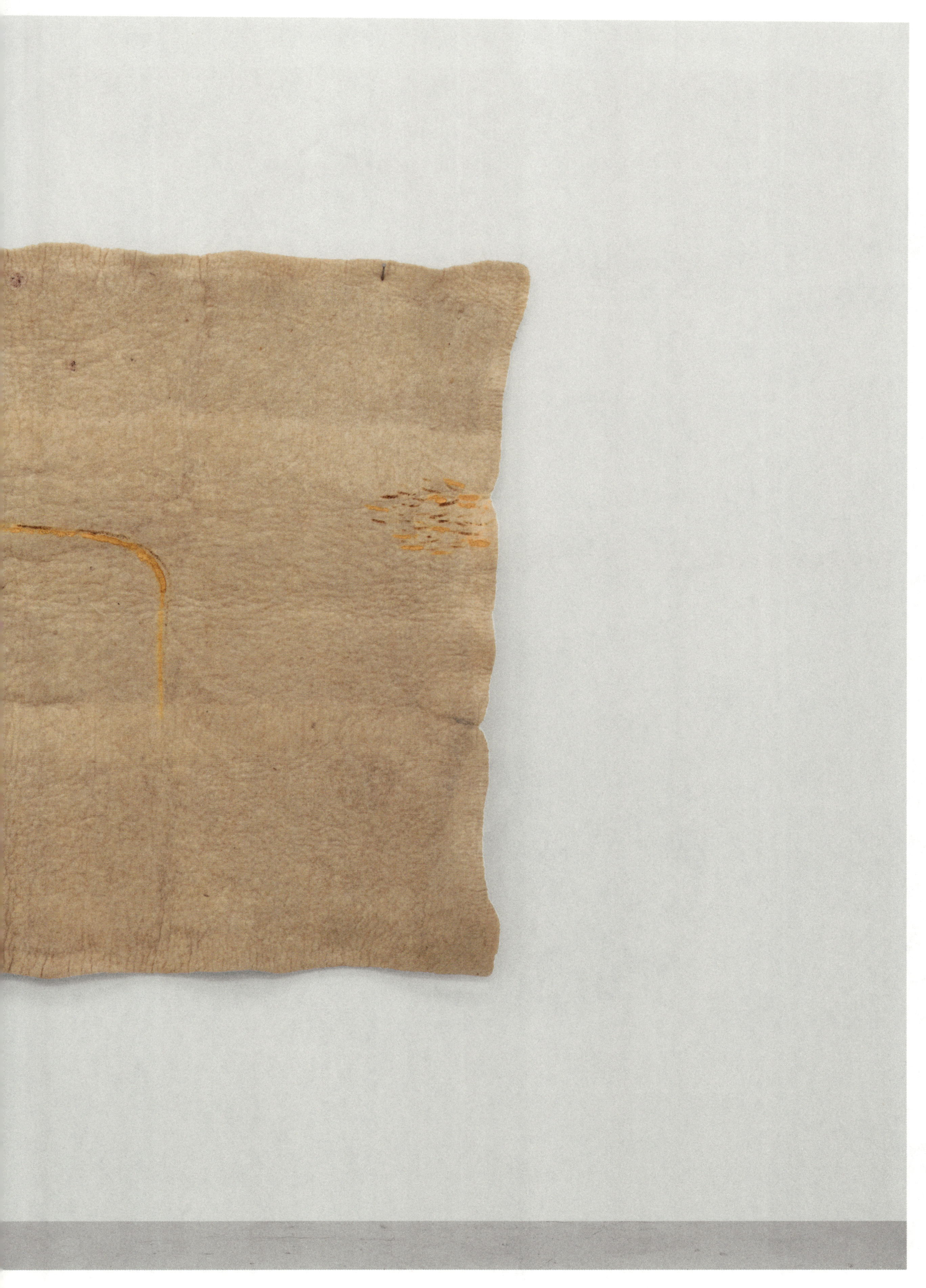

Dale Harding, *F1 (Saddler's contract)*

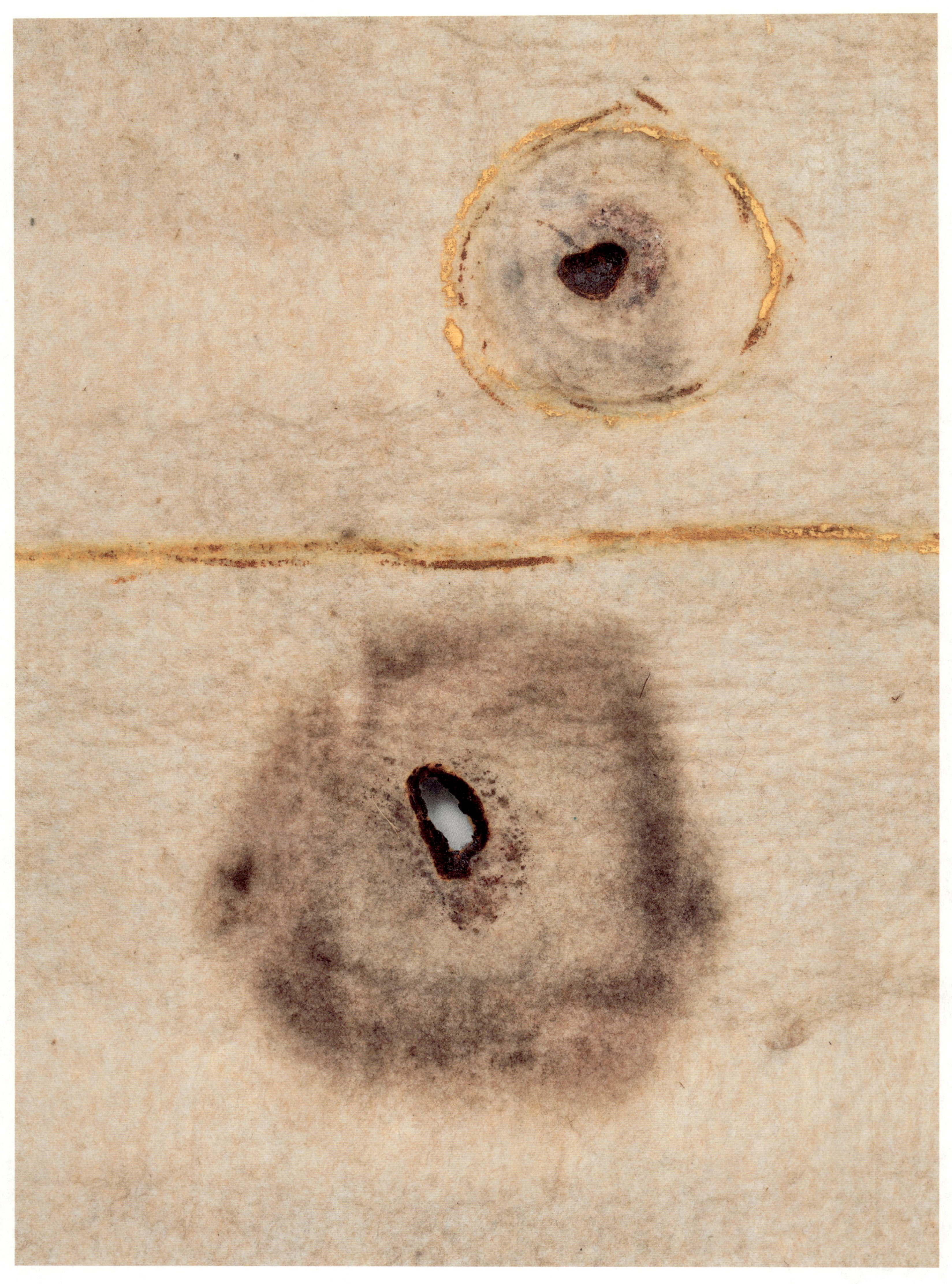

(detail)

Dale Harding, *F1 (Saddler's contract)* 2020,
wool felt made by Jan Oliver, gum arabic, yellow ochre and scorching,
104 × 162 cm

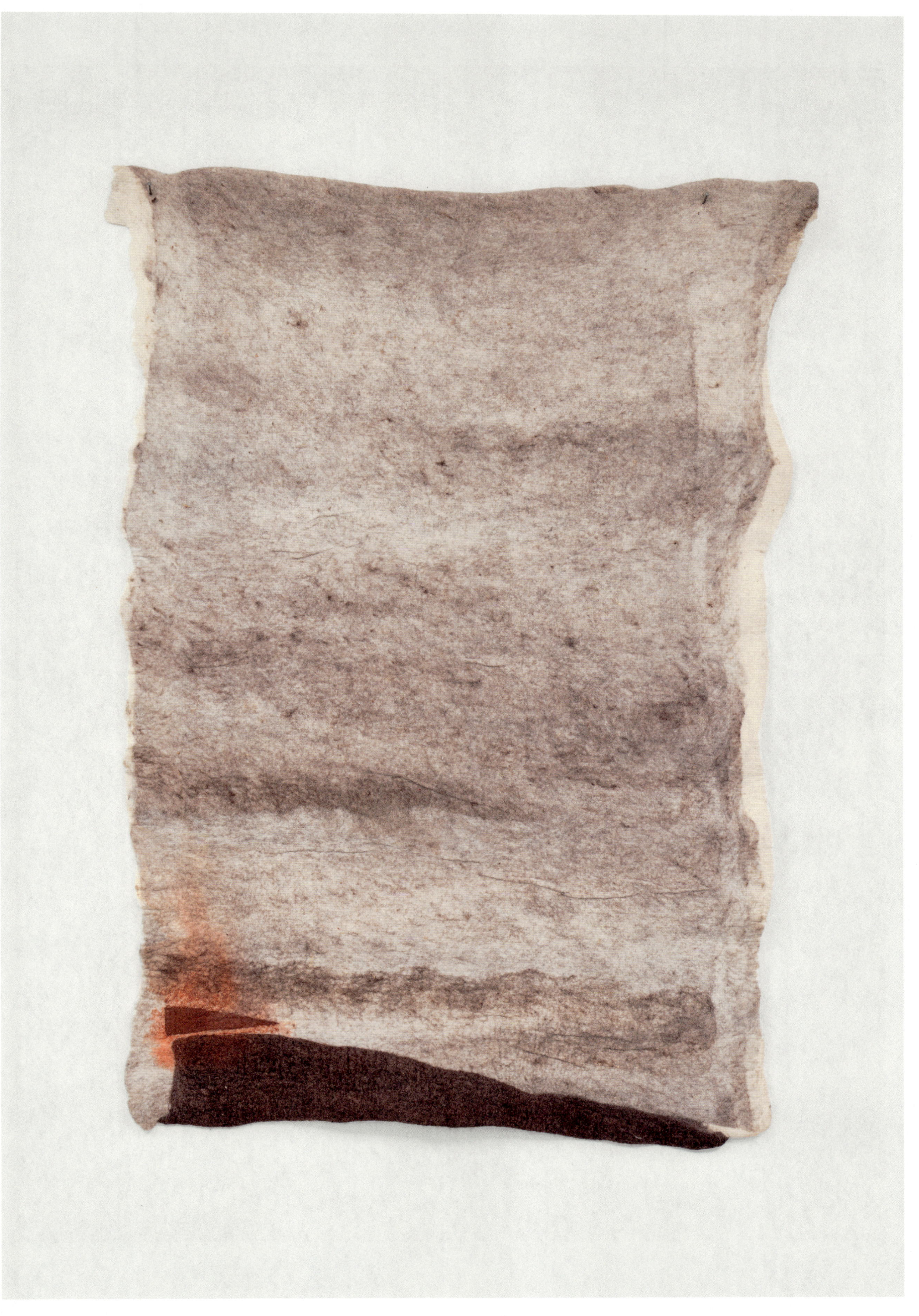

Dale Harding, *F2 (Mt Hetty fire viewed from Bandanna)*   131

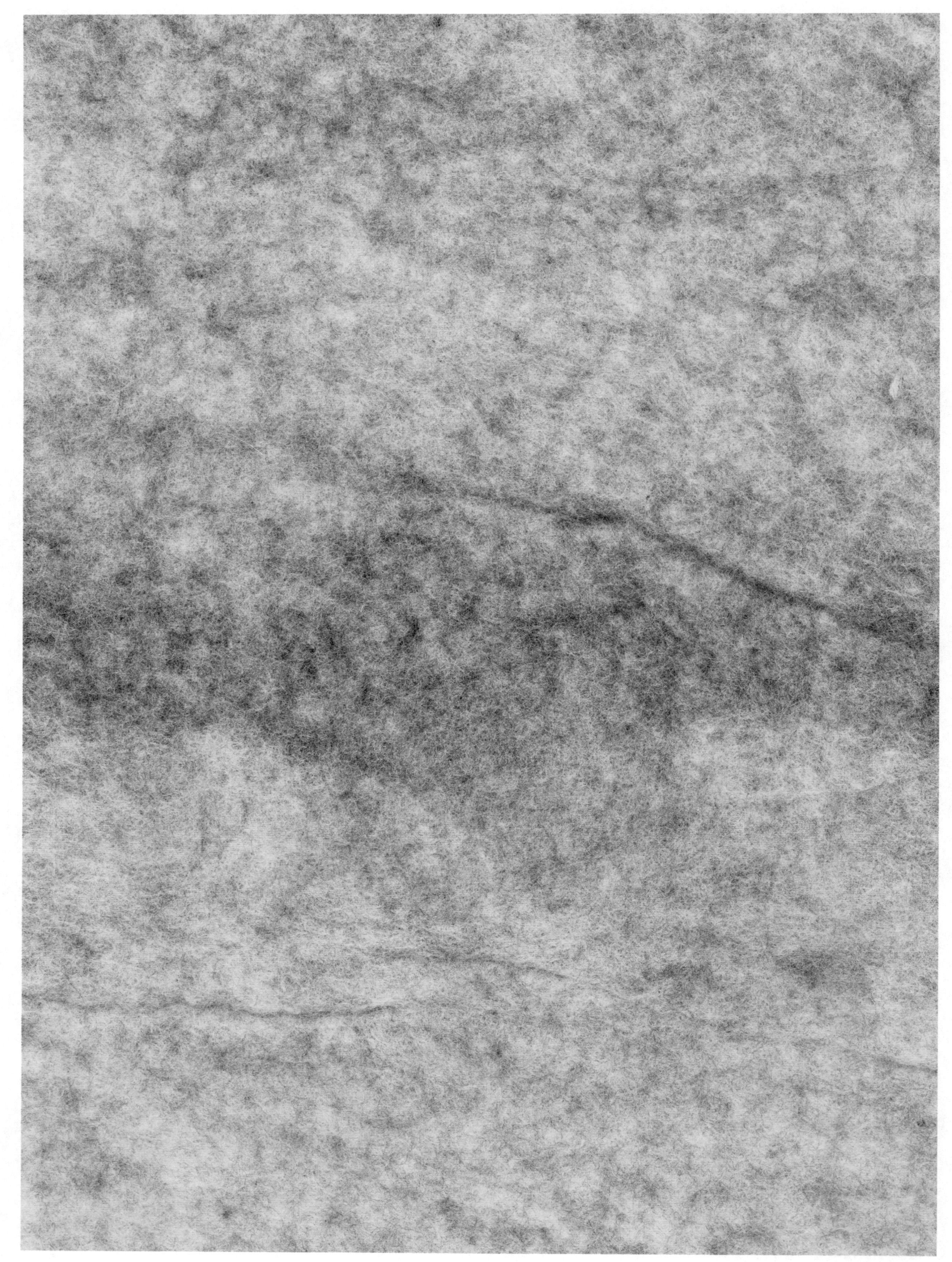

(detail)

Dale Harding, *F2 (Mt Hetty fire viewed from Bandanna)* 2020, wool felt made with Jan Oliver, gum arabic and hematite, 160 × 115 cm

Dale Harding, *Extractive painting 2* 2021,
gum arabic and dry pigment on linen, 150 × 120 cm

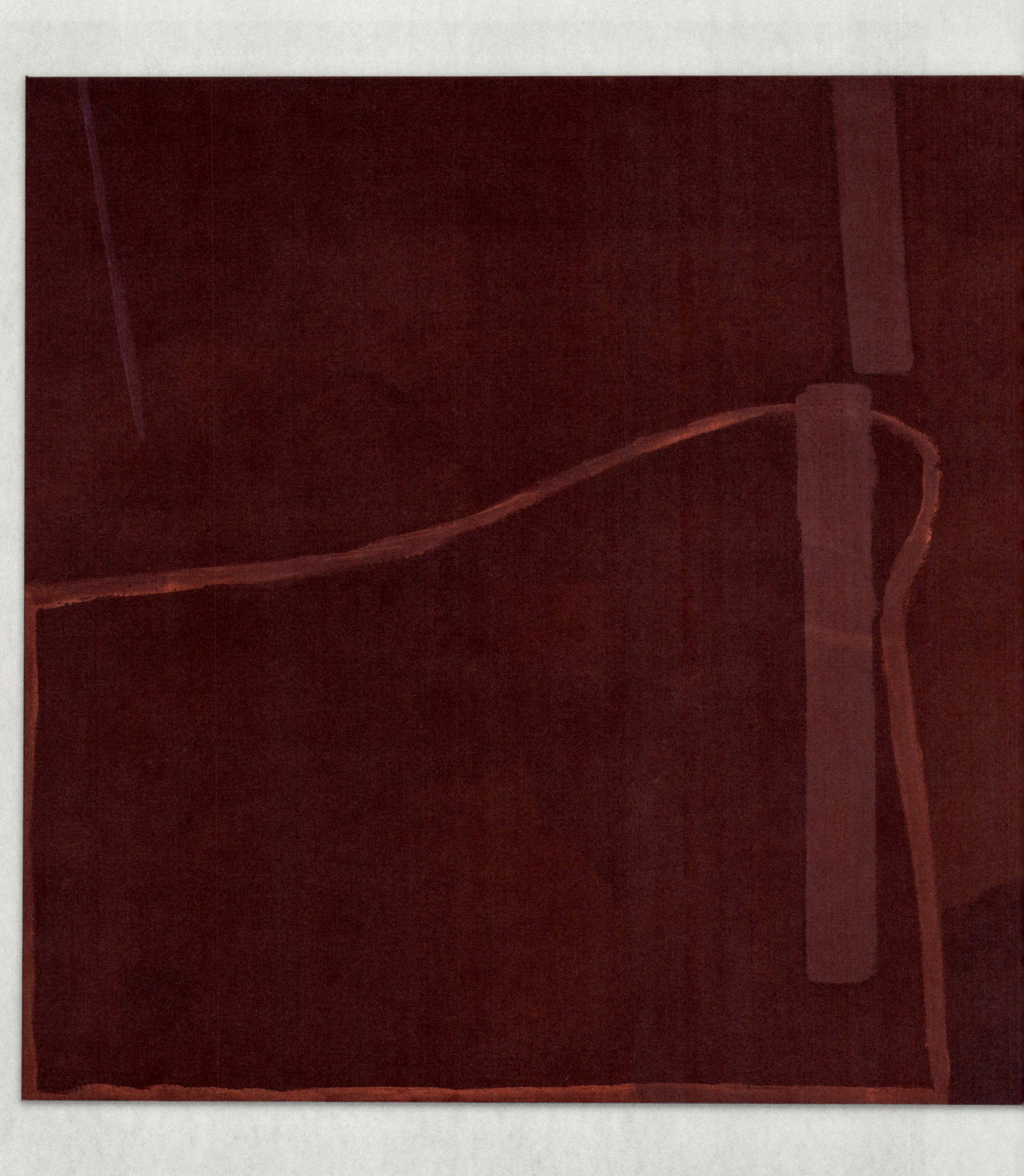

Dale Harding, *Emetic painting (International Rock Art Red and white)* 137

Dale Harding, *Emetic painting (International Rock Art Red and white)* 2020, acrylic binder, dry pigment and gum arabic on linen, 2 parts: 150 × 180 cm; 150 × 120 cm

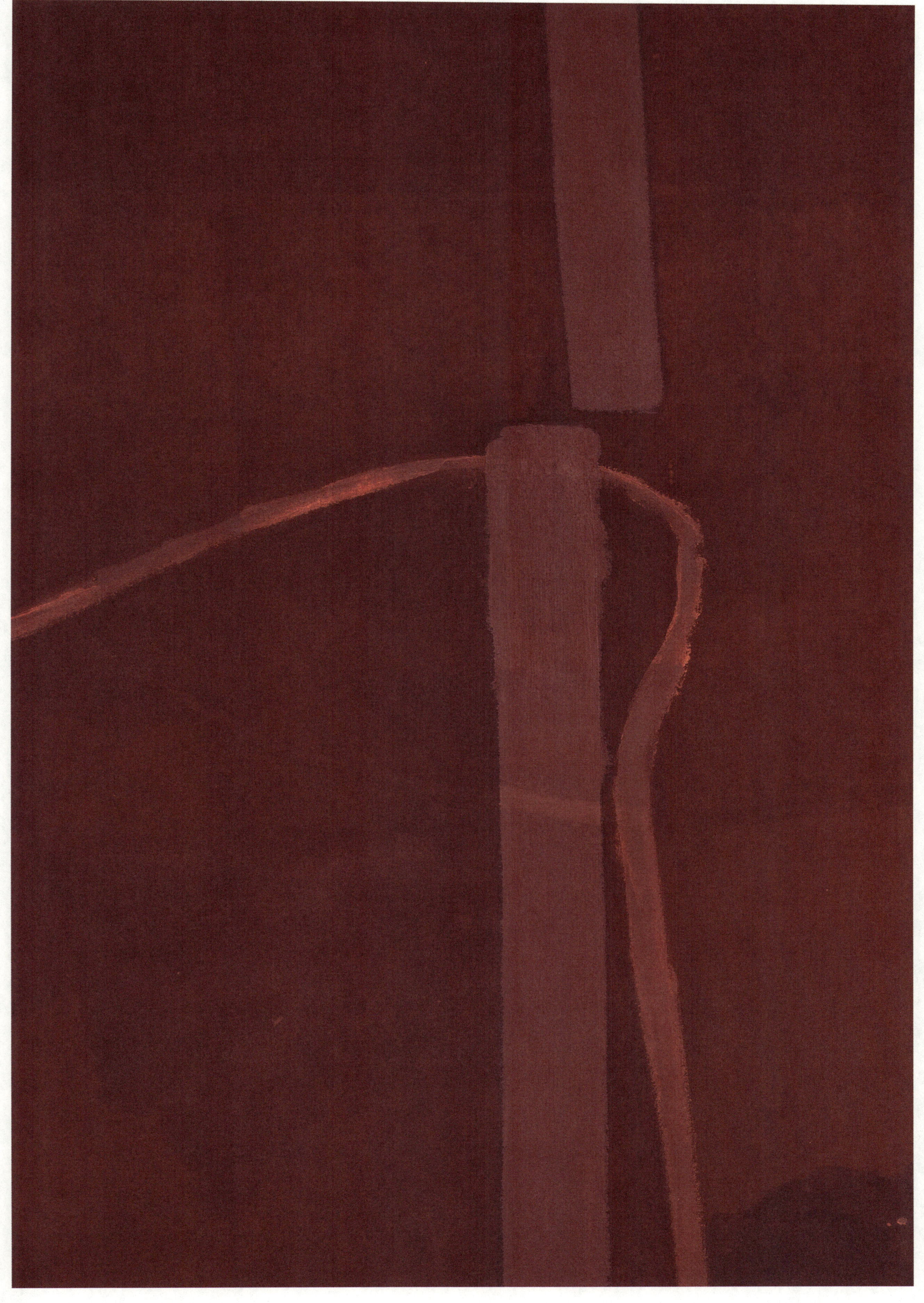

DALE HARDING

All works are courtesy of the artist and Milani Gallery, Brisbane, unless otherwise stated. All photos by Carl Warner, unless otherwise stated.

Blue ground/dissociative 2017
Reckitt's Blue and white ochre on linen
180 × 240 cm
Private collection, Brisbane
Cloaks (mortua and mortuus) 2018
cotton blanketing, gum arabic and powdered pigment
205 × 310 cm overall, displayed folded
Moonda and The Shame Fella 2018
glass, xanthorrhoea resin and lead
3 parts: glass 12 × 210 x 2 cm;
lead 5 × 215 × 15 cm;
plinth 200 × 120 × 20 cm
Repression cloak (ceremony for a gay wedding)
2018
synthetic powdered pigment, ochre,
gum arabic, abrasion and pressure on
cotton blanketing
205 × 310 cm overall, displayed folded
What is theirs is ours now (I do not claim to own) 2018
Reckitt's Blue, ochre, dry pigment and binder on linen
2 parts, each 180 × 240 cm;
180 × 480 cm overall
Queensland Art Gallery |
Gallery of Modern Art, Brisbane
Purchased 2019, Queensland Art Gallery |
Gallery of Modern Art Foundation
Emetic painting 2019–20
ochre, xanthorrhoea resin, grevillea robusta
gum and acrylic on linen
180 × 240 cm
Emetic painting (International Rock Art Red and white) 2020
acrylic binder, dry pigment and gum arabic on linen
2 parts: 150 × 180 cm; 150 × 120 cm
F1 (Saddler's contract) 2020
wool felt made by Jan Oliver, gum arabic,
yellow ochre and scorching
104 × 162 cm
F2 (Mt Hetty fire viewed from Bandanna) 2020
wool felt made with Jan Oliver, gum arabic
and hematite
160 × 115 cm
Extractive painting 2 2021
gum arabic and dry pigment on linen
150 × 120 cm
Xanthorrhoea resin on glass 2021
xanthorrhoea botanical resin and glass
on window
dimensions variable;
glass: 201 × 12 × 1.9 cm

KATE HARDING

All works are courtesy of the artist.
All photos by Carl Warner.

Tribute to women—past, present and future 2019
textile and appliqué
171 × 160 cm
Carnarvon 2020
textile and appliqué, attached thread bags
188 × 157 cm
Carnarvon underground water 2020
textile and appliqué
169 × 128 cm
Cloak 2020
textile
70 × 40 cm
Cylinders 2020
textile
187 × 100 cm
White Hill—looking for food at Clermont 2020
textile, ochre dyes, hessian and thread
125 × 93 cm

DALE HARDING WITH HAYLEY MATTHEW

Untitled (private painting H1) 2019
dry pigment, acrylic and gum arabic on
linen
6 parts, overall dimensions variable
Panel 1: 150 × 250 cm
Private collection, Brisbane
Panel 2: 150 × 150 cm
Private collection, Brisbane
Panel 3: 150 × 250 cm
The University of Queensland, Brisbane
Purchased 2019
Panel 4: 150 × 150 cm
Monash University Collection, Melbourne
Purchased 2019
Panel 5: 150 × 250 cm
Griffith University Art Collection, Brisbane
Purchased 2019
Panel 6: 150 × 150 cm
Private collection, Sydney

DALE HARDING

All works are courtesy of the artist and Milani Gallery, Brisbane, unless otherwise stated. All photos by Carl Warner, unless otherwise stated.

Spine 2 2018
Gosford sandstone, off-form concrete and
hematite oxide
wedge-shaped plinth 113 (to 200) × 1200
× 130 cm; front block 139 × 150 × 150 cm;
back block 150 × 150 × 150 cm
The University Art Collection, The
University of Sydney
Site Surveys / International Standard 2019
acrylics, dried pigments, gum arabic and
glass
dimensions variable
Untitled 2020
xanthorrhoea resin on glass
2 parts, each 18 × 14 cm

Baloon Cave visit and assessment, Carnarvon Gorge, Queensland
Fieldwork Report, 7 February 2019

Paul S.C. Taçon
PERAHU, Griffith Centre for Social and Cultural Research
Griffith University, Queensland

1   Background

On 2 January 2019 Dale Harding (Bidjara, Garingbal and Ghungalu peoples), who is a member of Griffith University's Place, Evolution and Rock Art Heritage Unit (PERAHU) Indigenous Advisory Group, contacted PERAHU Director Professor Paul S.C. Taçon by email to inform him about fire damage to Baloon Cave, Carnarvon Gorge National Park, that occurred in December 2018. After a phone conversation later that evening and a series of emails, as well as conversations between Dale Harding and community members concerned about Baloon Cave, Professor Taçon was invited to visit the site by Dale Harding, Milton Lawton and other community members.

After flying to Roma on 9 January, Taçon and Harding drove to Carnarvon Gorge where they were met by Fred Conway (senior Bidjara elder and Carnarvon Gorge National Park Ranger for over 30 years; see Figure 1), Milton Lawton (Bidjara), Darren McLeod (Garingbal) and Will Lawton (Bidjara; Milton's youngest son). All members of the group are passionate about their heritage, especially the rock art sites but Fred (now 75 years of age), in particular, has been active much of his life in looking after his people's rock art. As the Queensland Government states on its website for Carnarvon Gorge "Fred is an Indigenous Elder and tireless advocate for protecting Indigenous cultural sites, particularly the rock art sites in Carnarvon National Park in central west Queensland" (https://parks.des.qld.gov.au/parks/carnarvon-gorge/ranger.html). In 2014, he was given a 'Queensland Great Award' for his service.

After introductions and a welcome to Country the group proceeded to Baloon Cave. Public access to the site was closed but permission had been obtained from Queensland Parks and Wildlife (QPWS) staff, some of whom we later met with on site, including Brett Roberts. This report focuses on the results of the visit including recommendations discussed in the field.

2   ARC Laureate Project: Australian rock art history, conservation and Indigenous well-being

This fieldwork was also part of an Australia-wide research program focusing on rock art. The project 'Australian rock art history, conservation and Indigenous well-being' is part of Professor Paul Taçon's Laureate award from the Australian Research Council (FL160100123). The overall aim of the Laureate research project is to ensure that rock art landscapes are better conserved, appreciated and understood for the benefit of local communities and future generations. We are currently exploring questions such as:

1   How can we contribute to better conservation and management of rock art landscapes for the benefit of future generations?
2   In areas with vast landscapes of rock art - how can we help communities make decisions on where to focus their time, energy, and resources for rock art conservation and management?
3   Why are rock art complexes important for Indigenous people, and especially for Indigenous well-being today?

For further information on this larger program please visit: https://www.griffith.edu.au/humanities-languages/place-evolution-rock-art-heritage-unit/

3 Why rock art is powerful and relevant today

The Laureate project is aligned with <u>The Rock Art Network</u>, an international alliance of individuals and organisations, of which Professor Taçon is a member. In 2015, they published a seminal volume on how we can better protect the valuable and vulnerable heritage of rock art (Agnew et al. 2015) and in 2018 produced the following about why rock art is important:

> Rock art – ancient paintings and engravings on rock surfaces – is a visual record of global human history. It is a shared heritage that links us to powerful ancestral worlds and magnificent landscapes of the past. It tells the story of the birthplaces of art, the dawn of artistic endeavors. It creates connections to significant places and depicts encounters with the surrounding living world. Through its existence nature and culture are connected in the landscape. It resonates with our individual and collective identity while stimulating a vital sense of belonging to a greater past. Rock art illustrates the passage of time over tens of thousands of years of environmental and cultural change. It incarnates the essence of human ingenuity and facilitates contacts today between cultures and aspects of spirituality. Rock art is artistically compelling and full of meaning. This fragile and irreplaceable visual heritage has worldwide significance, contemporary relevance and for many indigenous peoples is still part of their living culture. If we neglect, destroy, or disrespect rock art we devalue our future.

The Network abides by eight important principles which set a foundation for rock art conservation (Agnew et al. 2015:4):

Principle 1 – Work actively to promote rock art as a valuable heritage for everyone, and allocate sufficient resources specifically to its future care

Principle 2 – Manage to protect all values

Principle 3 – Preserve and manage rock art as an inherent part of the landscape

Principle 4 – Safeguard cultural rights and practices

Principle 5 – Involve and empower Indigenous owners and local communities in decisions about rock art management and conservation

Principle 6 – Use recognised ethics, protocols and standards for documentation, conservation and interpretation as the basis for management practice

Principle 7 – Give priority to preventive and protective conservation

Principle 8 – Make effective communication and collaboration a central part of management

These foundation principles lead to the four 'pillars' which make for strong rock art policy and conservation when it is applied in practice (Agnew et al. 2015:4-5):

Pillar 1 – Public and political awareness

There is a need to raise awareness about rock art, the range and severity of threats to it and the need for effective responses to these threats. Public and political awareness of rock art is vital for successful planning and budgeting for conservation and management.

Pillar 2 – Effective management systems
Systems are required to manage rock art sites and groups of rock art sites in their landscapes. This includes identifying the significance of sites, their management needs and the development of strategies for their long-term conservation. A key to the development of such systems is the active involvement of all key stakeholders especially traditional owners, site custodians, and local communities and the allocation of the capable human resources required to look after rock art sites.

Pillar 3 – Physical and cultural conservation practice
Careful guidance is needed for the work of physically protecting and, if necessary, undertaking conservation work on rock art sites. The same applies to the cultural practices that secure the physical and spiritual integrity of rock art sites. Physical conservation and cultural conservation need to be considered, planned and undertaken in dialogue with each other. In each case, it is important that people with suitable expertise are available, that expert knowledge is respected and that informed decisions are made regarding the physical and cultural benefits and impacts of actions.

Pillar 4 – Community involvement and benefits
An important way of conserving and celebrating rock art is through appropriate and well-managed economic, social and cultural development initiatives by and for indigenous, local and regional communities.
Genuine community involvement can result in greater awareness of rock art, increased economic opportunities and higher quality display and interpretation for visitors.

* The Rock Art Network, established by the Getty Conservation Institute and the Bradshaw Foundation, comprises individuals and institutions committed to the promotion, protection, and conservation of rock art globally.

4   Baloon Cave viewing platform history

Initially access to Baloon Cave was via a stone and soil walking track, with low handrails separating visitors from the art panels. However, some vandalism occurred with lines and letters scratched over and into stencils. To facilitate better access and to better protect the rock art a large viewing platform and walkway was installed at Baloon Cave in 2014 (Figure 2 and see https://www.wagner.com.au/main/our-projects/baloon-cave-viewing-platform for photos immediately after installation). REPLAS Enduroplank recycled plastic products (see http://www.replas.com.au/tag/balloon-cave/) were used with composite fibre structural components. On the REPLAS website the Enduroplank is promoted as a low maintenance endurable material suitable for Baloon Cave (http://www.replas.com.au/carnarvon-national-park-upgraded-replas-enduroplank-viewing-platform/):

The perfect fit-for-purpose as a low maintenance, long lasting product lies Replas Enduroplank™, an upgrade for the pathway near this cave. This recycled plastic decking solution gives better access to the National Park's guests.

144

Not only is this recycled product low maintenance and long lasting, it is
durable enough to handle to walkers, hikers, and even 4WD vehicles to head
right into the heart of this country!

It also is promoted as fire retardant but fire testing undertaken in December
2017 appears to have limited mixed results (see Abraham 2018, available on the
REPLAS website).

Recycled plastic had been used for a rock art viewing platform at Nganalang, Keep River
National Park, Northern Territory. It too was said to be fire retardant but in 2008:

> once the plastic material ignited, the severe heat generated caused the painted
> rock surface to shatter and disintegrate, falling to the floor of the shelter. The
> follow up conservation action in consultation with Traditional Owners was
> confined essentially to a clean up, placing the shattered material near the
> entrance of the shelter and to initiate baseline monitoring to assess the need
> for any future intervention (Lambert and Welsh 2011:47).

In December 2018 the Baloon Cave viewing platform and walkway was burnt to the
ground. At both Nganalang, Keep River and Baloon Cave, Carnarvon it appears a hot fire
melted and then ignited part of the infrastructure, resulting in an extremely hot explosive
fire with heat so intense that massive exfoliation of nearby rock surfaces resulted,
destroying or severely damaging rock art in the process, as well as coating areas with
soot.

5   Results of inspection

During the visit we inspected the walkway infrastructure leading up to Baloon Cave,
including the remains of both recycled plastic and wooden walking tracks and bridges
(Figure 3). One of our first observations was that the recycled plastic infrastructure was
badly burnt and melted but much of the wooden infrastructure, although blackened, was
largely intact (Figure 4).

The fire was particularly devastating where the viewing platform and walkways leading
up to it once stood. This infrastructure was completely destroyed, severely damaging the
rock shelter in the process. The heat must have been very intense as much of the rock
shelter surface exfoliated and collapsed. Black soot covers remaining parts of the shelter
wall and ceiling (see Figures 5–8).

Rock art at the site was heavily impacted. Damage to the main panel consists of
exfoliation to the left, right and above right; cracking at the upper right; and a coating of
soot over most of the stencilled hands and all of the hafted axe stencils (see Figures
9–10). As one approaches the panel, at first it appears it is completely blackened but
closer inspection and photography with the light at the right angle reveals the stencils
underneath.

Damage to the rare hafted stone axe stencils is pronounced as not only have they been blackened but also where two of them are located the rock has both cracked and exfoliated. The cracked portion at the left looks as if it could easily collapse (see Figures 11–12). It may be possible to remove the soot and to consolidate the panel but this needs further investigation and assessment (see recommendation 5 below). Should it be decided to attempt this it should be undertaken cautiously, so as to not create new damage. More generally, physical intervention at rock art sites should always be a last resort, carefully considered and undertaken only by knowledgeable/experienced professionals.

6   Recommendations

A number of recommendations came out of discussions that took place immediately after visiting Baloon Cave. They include:

1   Fred Conway was very angry about what happened but wants healing now. He would like the site to be used as an example/case study of what can happen at sites with improper infrastructure. For this he would like the site left pretty much as is, after the remains of the platform are removed, so people can see the damage European mismanagement of sites/heritage that has occurred. He said Baloon Cave could be used for educating people about how important these places are and what can happen to them.

2   Milton Lawton said everyone has been spiritually wounded by the fire event. The past couple weeks he has had disturbing dreams and after he saw what the fire did to Baloon Cave he and his family became physically sick/ill for 6 days. He also said it is now time for healing and that everybody should work together for positive outcomes.

3   The clean-up of the site and removal of the remains of the walkway and viewing panel should only be undertaken with appropriate Aboriginal community members present.

4   Everyone agreed we should try to make 3D models and possibly some sort of small 3D replicas from existing high resolution photographs if enough from different angles taken before the fire can be collected from a range of individuals.

5   Paul Taçon should consult rock art conservation experts as to whether the soot coating over the main panel of stencils can be removed and the panel consolidated without doing further damage. If the community agrees the first action might be an off-art test of soot removal. Fred asked if chemicals would be used but hopefully all that would be needed is water, perhaps applied with cotton buds and/or a special cloth.

6   Uncle Milton would like to see a new relationship between the community and Parks, like the way it was some time ago. He said the viewing platform was installed without proper community consultation.

7   A full site history and conservation/remediation assessment should
     take place.

8   Input from a broader range of Bidjara and Garingbal community members
     needs to take place, especially from women.

9   Ideally, an agreed media strategy should be developed so everyone is
     talking from the same page. This could include a media statement and
     designated spokespeople. Among other things, a post could be placed on
     the Bradshaw Foundation web site (http://www.bradshawfoundation.
     com/), an organisation that disseminates information about world rock art,
     at the appropriate time to alert the world to the dangers of using recycled
     plastic products at rock art sites.

10   Everyone in the group would like collaborative academic publications
     about what occurred to tell the world and to help prevent such material
     (i.e. recycled plastic, etc.) being used at any other site in Australia. This
     report could be used as a resource for such publications.

11   An initial online search suggests recycled plastic products have been
     installed at many park and heritage locations but not at other rock art
     sites. An audit of Australian rock art sites with walkways and viewing
     platforms should be undertaken to see what materials they are made from
     and if recycled plastic for any aspect.

12   The nature of existing infrastructure at other Carnarvon Gorge rock art
     sites, and more generally throughout Queensland, should be reviewed.

13   All future conservation and management decisions about Baloon Cave
     and other Carnarvon Gorge rock art sites should have Aboriginal
     community involvement and approval. It should also follow the principles
     set out by Agnew et al. 2015 (see above).

14   National Parks organisations across Australia should be alerted so that
     recycled plastic is not used when old viewing platforms and walkways are
     upgraded and new infrastructure for public access is installed.

7   Conclusions

Of course, the main conclusion is that recycled plastic products should never be used
again at rock art sites, especially for walkways and viewing platforms. However, wooden
infrastructure is also problematic and there have been many instances in Australia and
overseas where wooden platforms and/or walkways caught fire and then caused
damage to rock art panels. As Lambert and Welsh (2011:48) conclude:

> Clearly, new boardwalks should no longer be constructed using combustible
> material, and old wooden boardwalks need to eventually be replaced with a
> non-combustible material or design.

Metal walkways and viewing platforms, although more expensive, might be the way forward for some sites. One of the best examples was installed at the Jibbon rock art site on the edge of Royal National Park, New South Wales (Williams et al. in press [2019]).

At Baloon Cave, the main central panel, once immediately above the viewing platform, suffered the most damage, especially to two of the three hafted stone axe stencils, with a covering of soot, exfoliation and cracking. There is a risk that the rock above the major new crack could sheer off and fall to the ground, taking portions of the stencils with it. It also poses a health and safety risk to visitors, staff and contractors rehabilitating the site, as well as conservators addressing both this issue and the soot over the panel in the future.

Rock art conservators should be employed by QPWS to undertake a detailed conservation assessment and to decide what remedial action could be implemented. Previous interpretative material installed at the site was excellent but if the site is reopened to the public, and considering what happened, then very different new interpretive material will need to be developed in consultation with representatives of the Aboriginal community.

For any of the above to happen smoothly a stronger positive relationship between QPWS and the larger Bidjara-Garingbal Aboriginal community needs to be fostered.

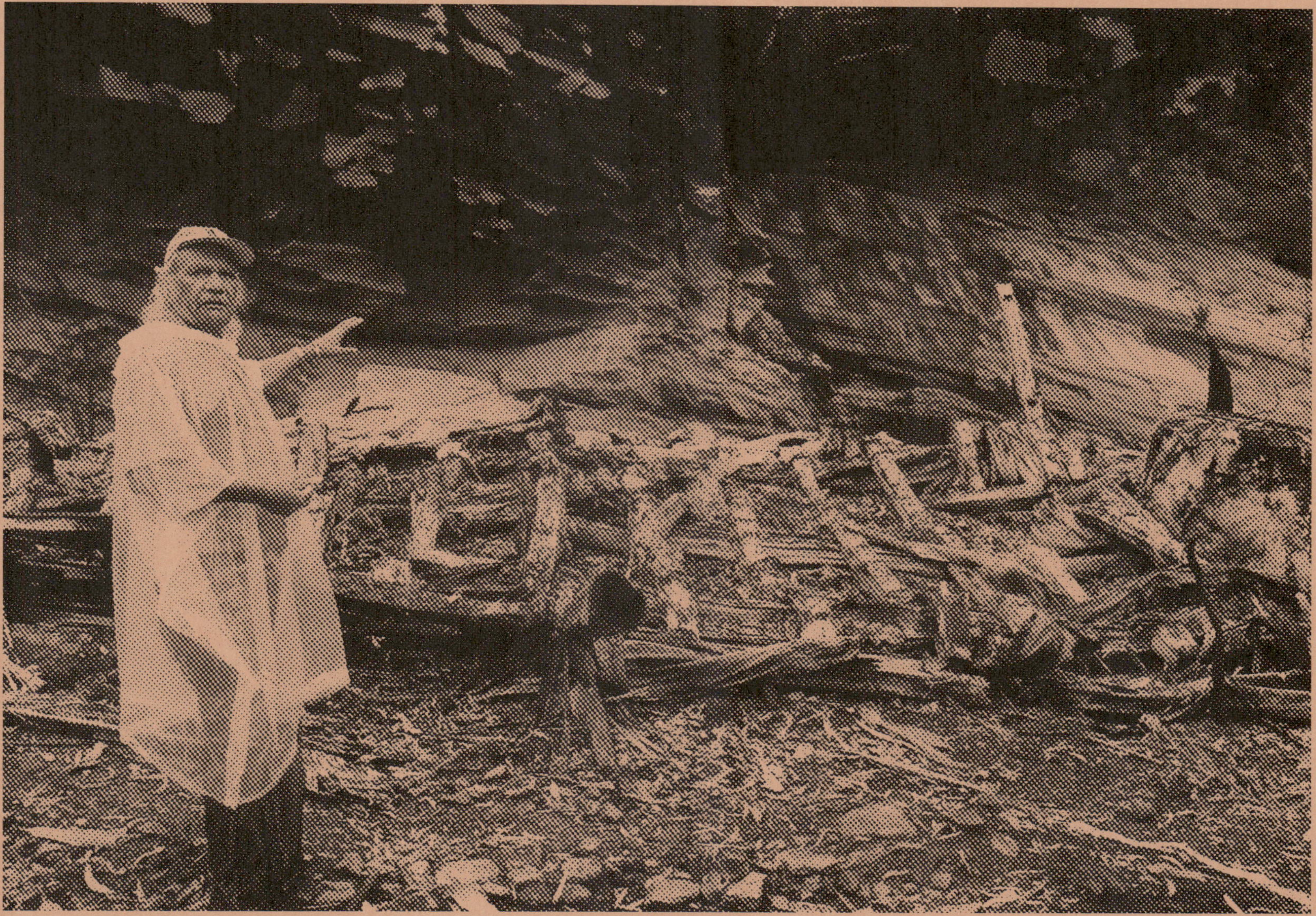

Figure 1: Fred Conway at Baloon Cave with remains of viewing platform behind.

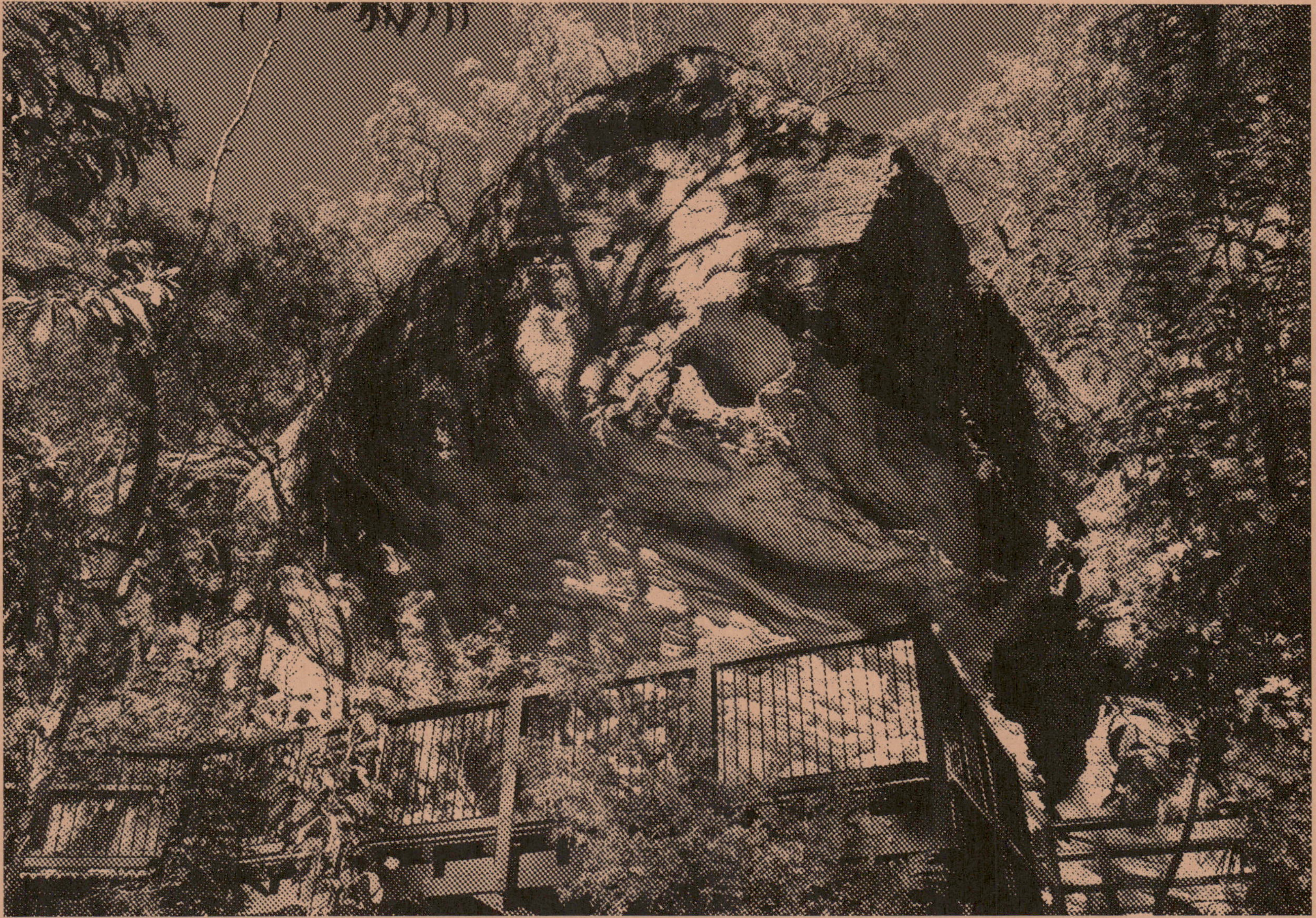

Figure 2: Baloon Cave with viewing platform in July 2018 before the fire (photo: Selina Goodreid and lifeoutsidework.com.au).

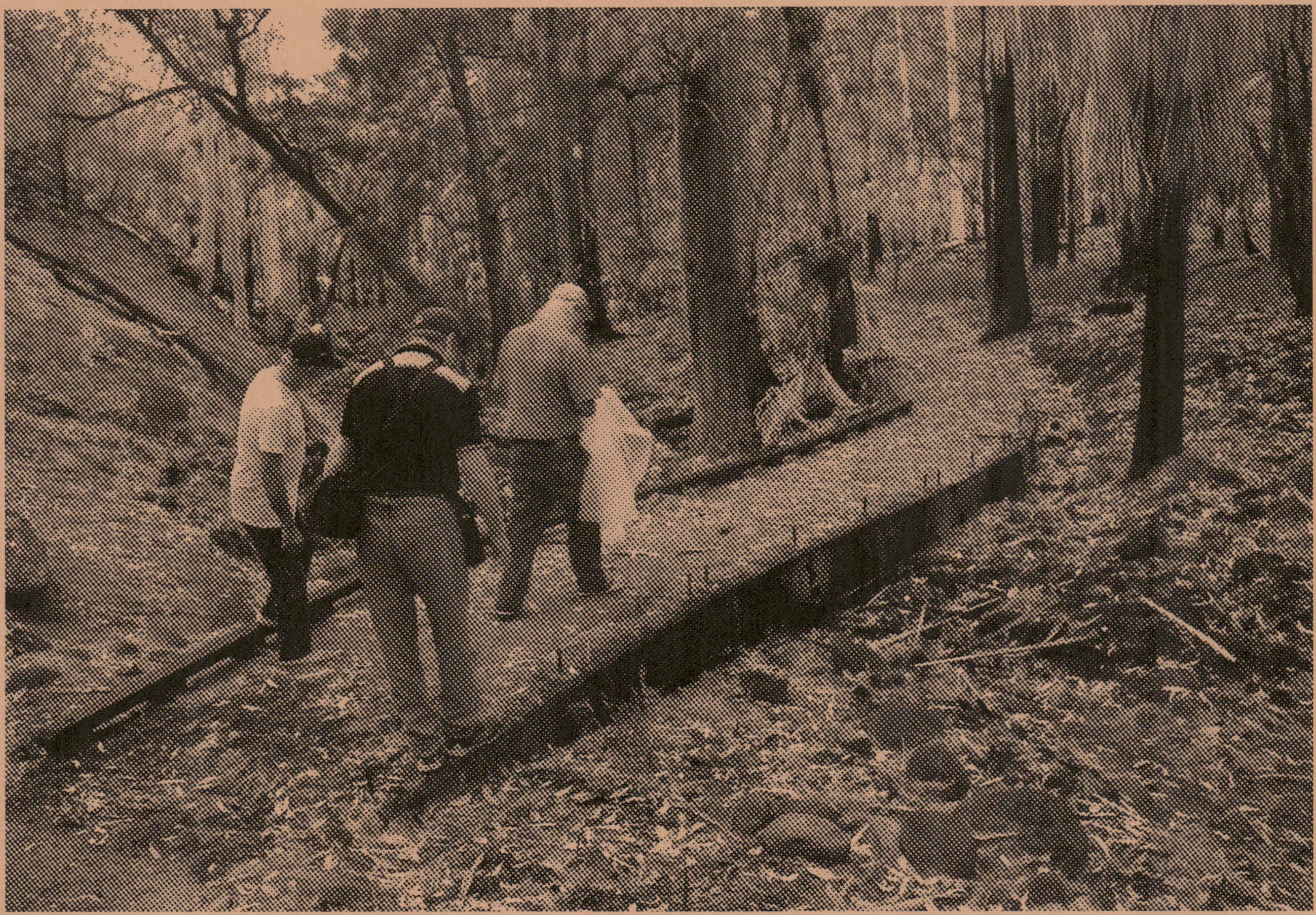

Figure 3: The plastic guardrail on the right that once was in the fire's path burnt and melted.

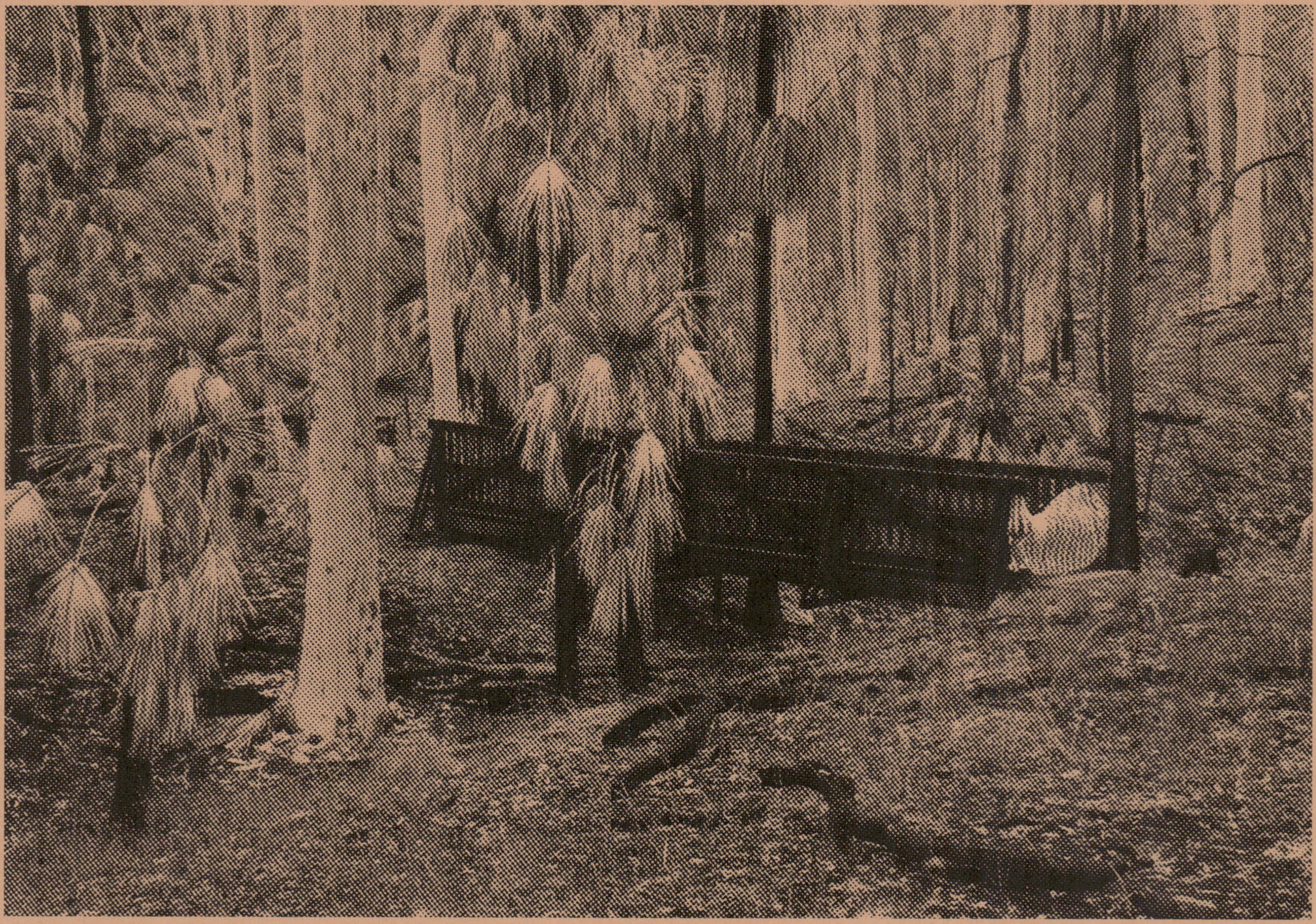

Figure 4: Wooden bridges, although scorched, survived largely intact, unlike plastic infrastructure.

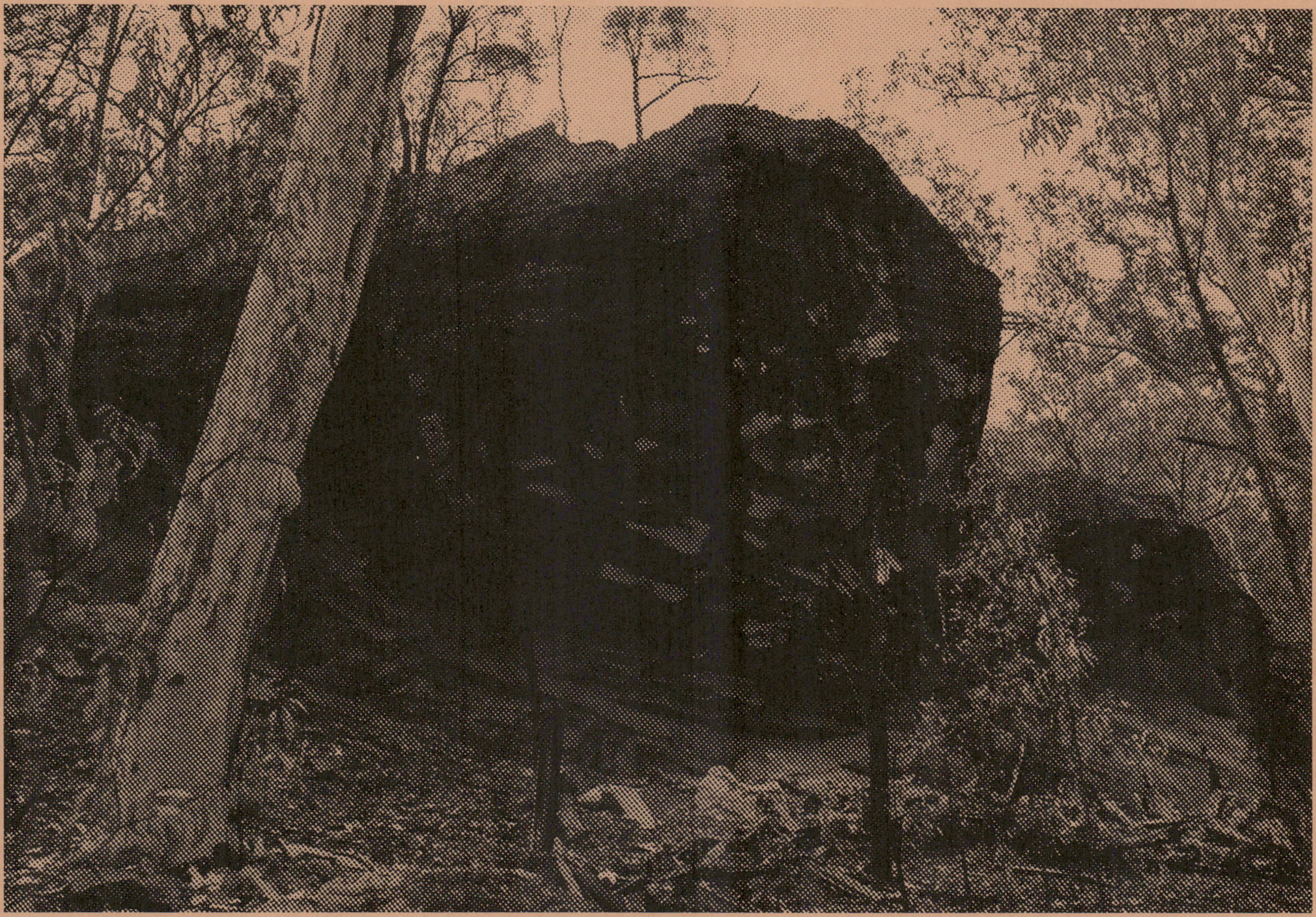

Figure 5: View of Baloon Cave after the fire facing into the shelter.

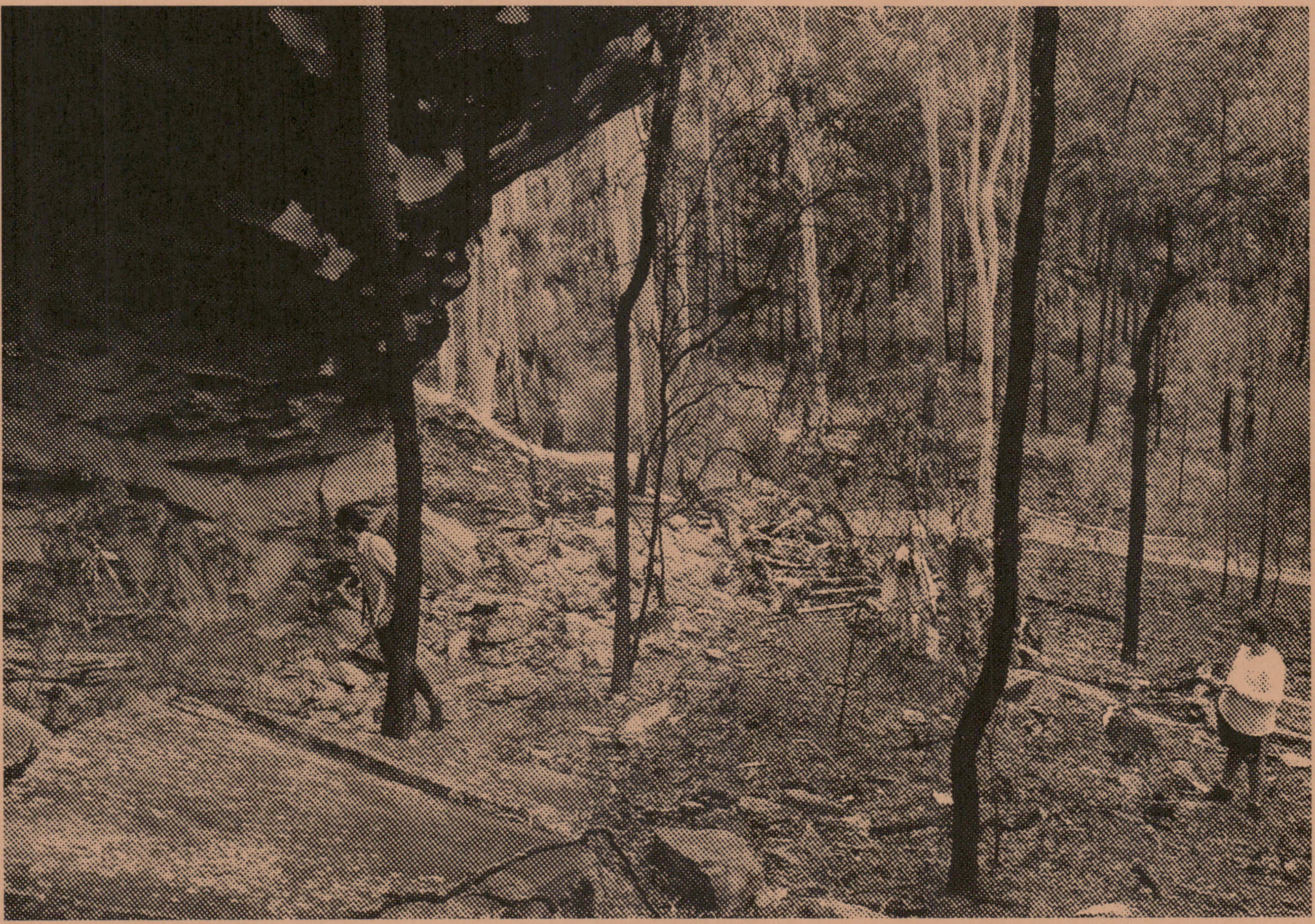

Figure 6: Dale Harding (left) and Will Lawson (right) inspecting Baloon Cave.

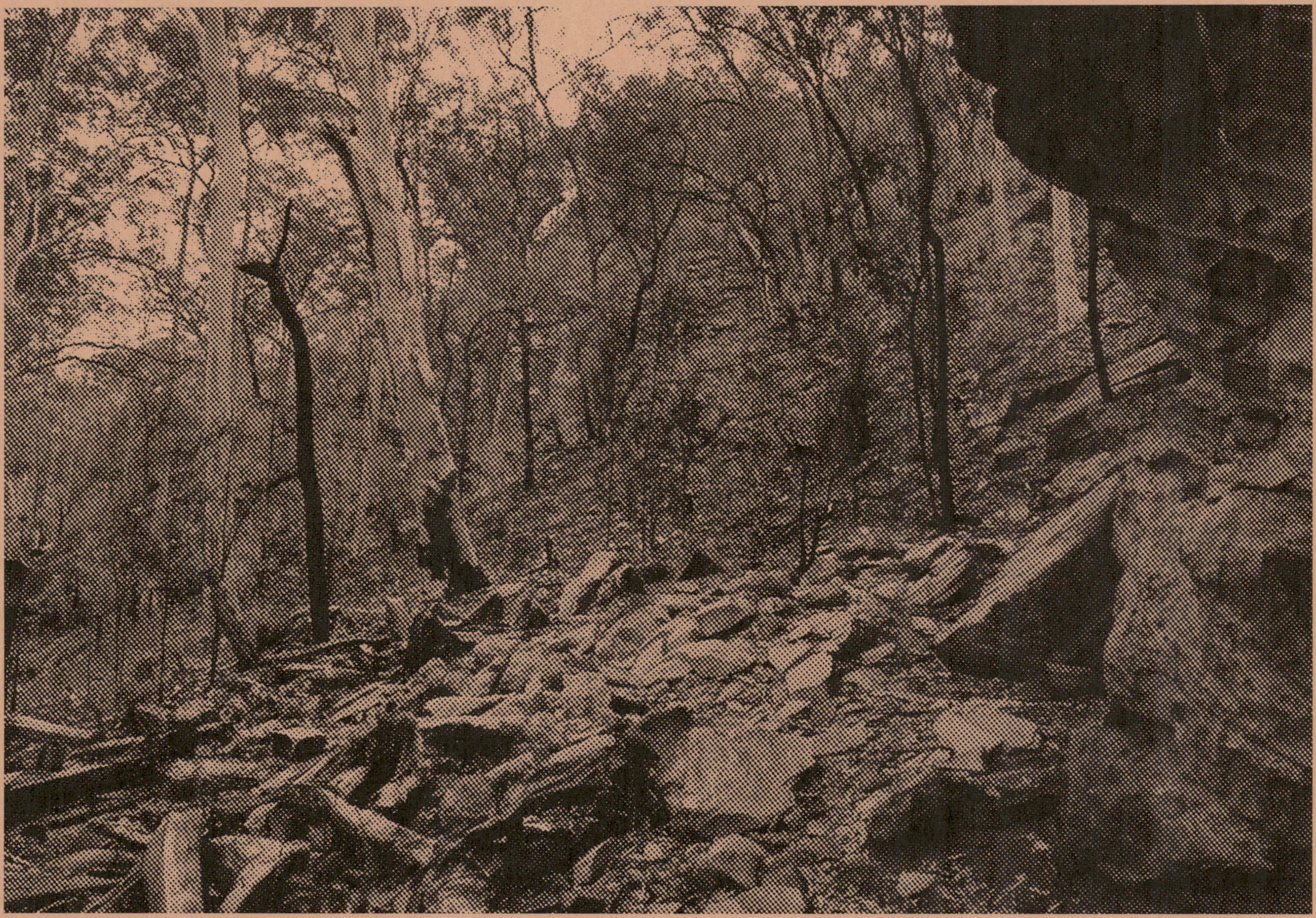

Figure 7: Baloon Cave where the viewing platform once stood with collapsed wall on floor.

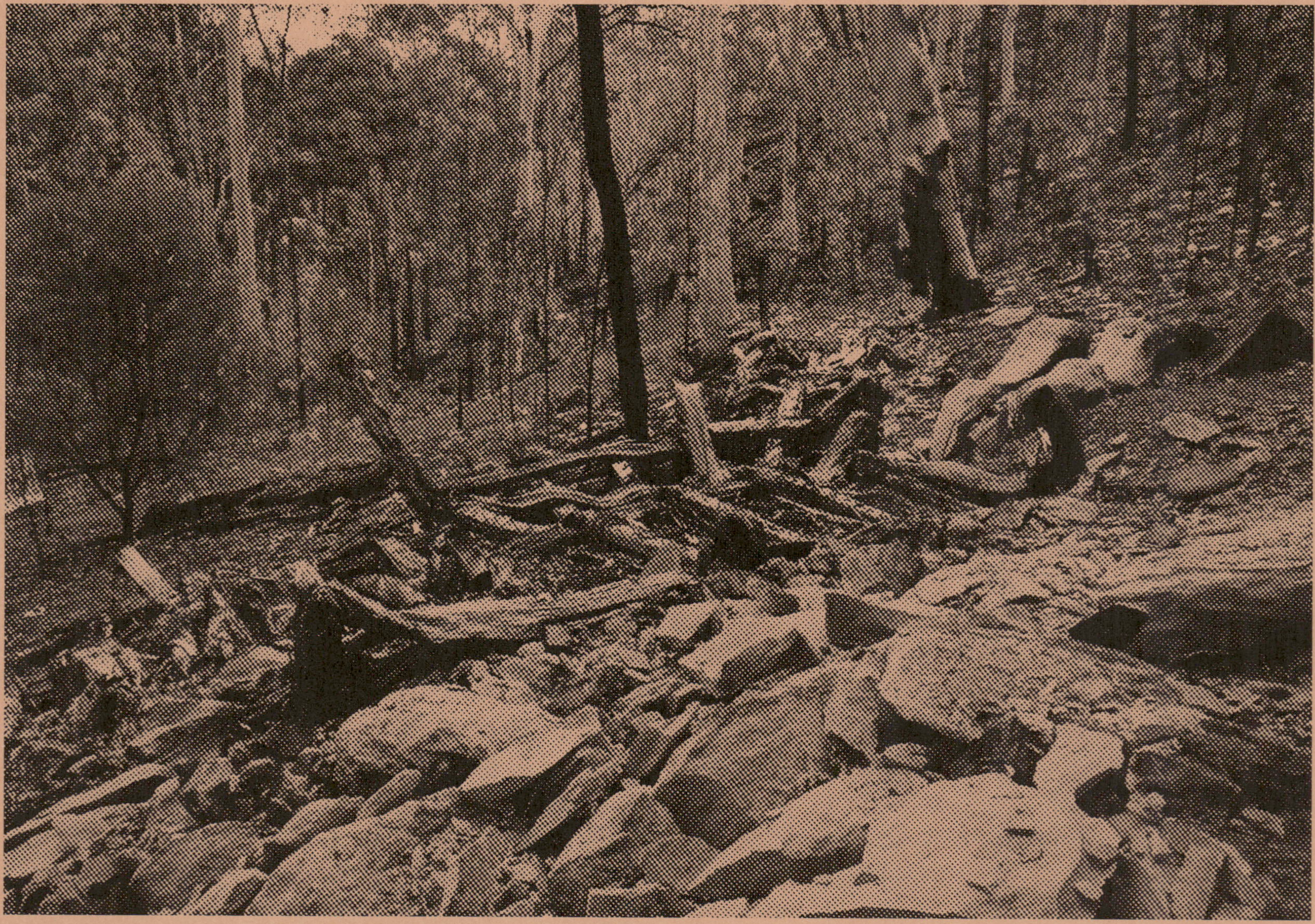

Figure 8: View looking out from the back of the shelter.

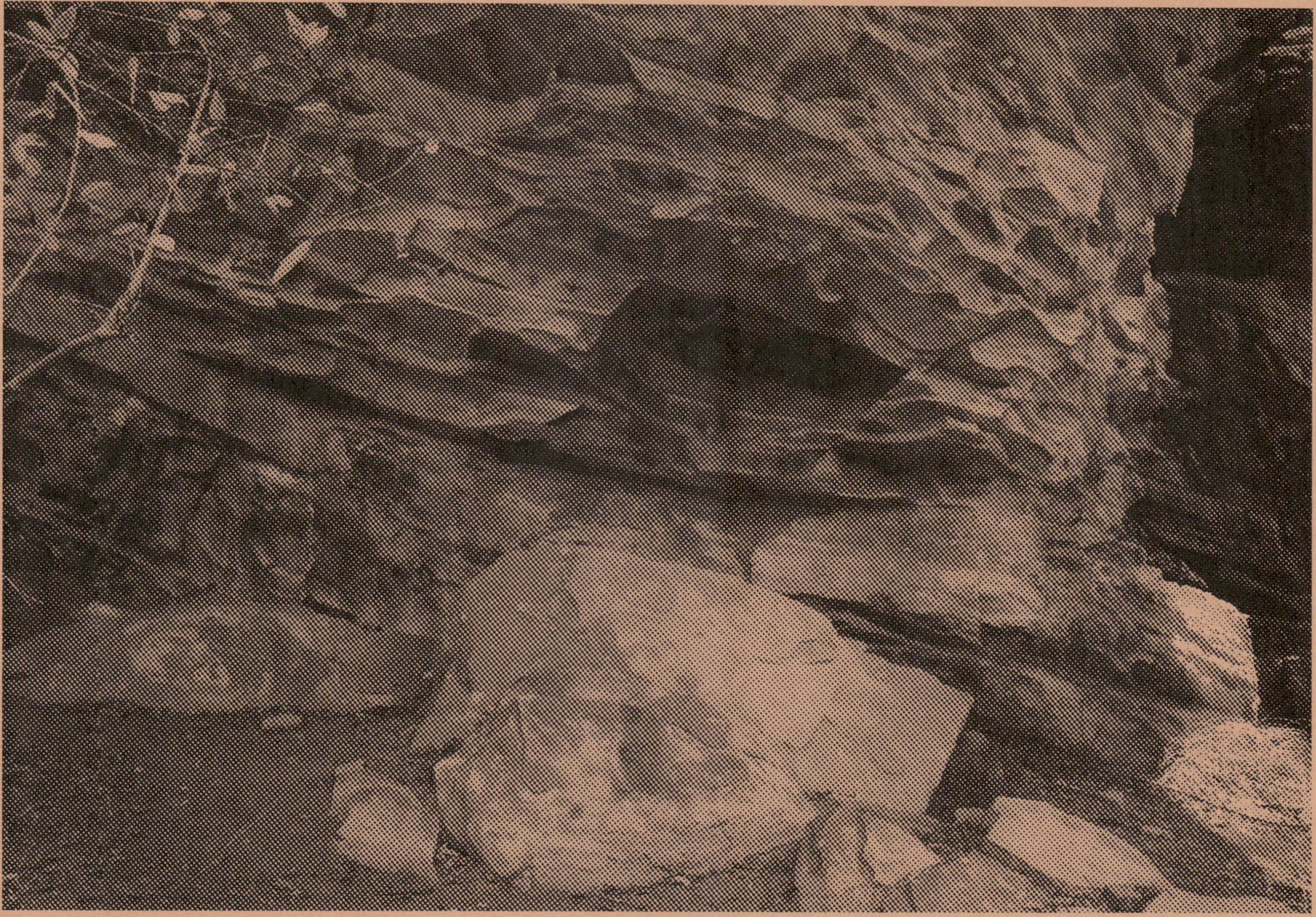

Figure 9: The main panel (centre) before the fire (photo: Marisa Giorgi).

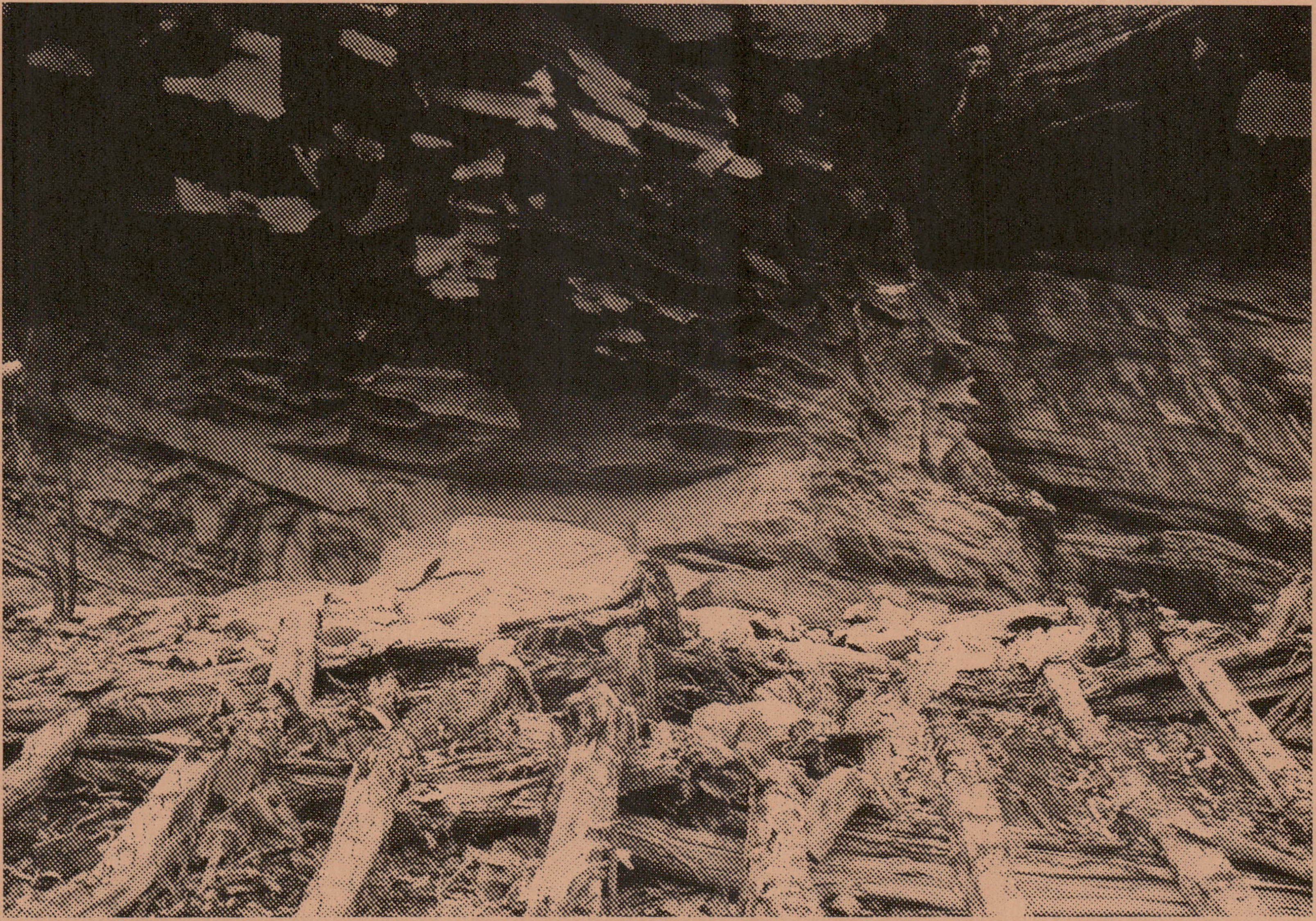

Figure 10: After the fire. At first the main panel (centre) appears totally blackened.

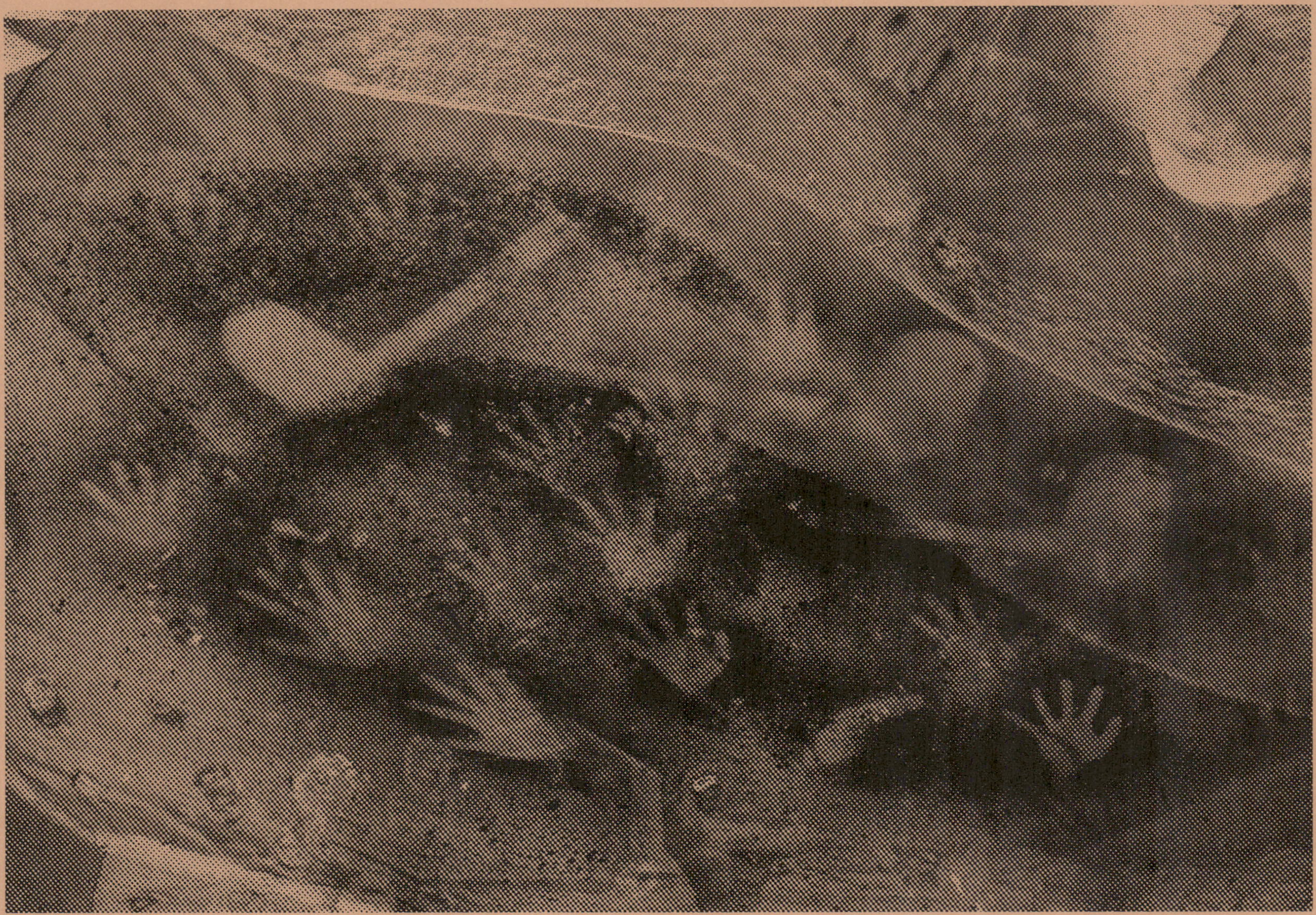

Figure 11: Baloon Cave main stencil panel before the December 2018 fire (photo: Dale Harding).

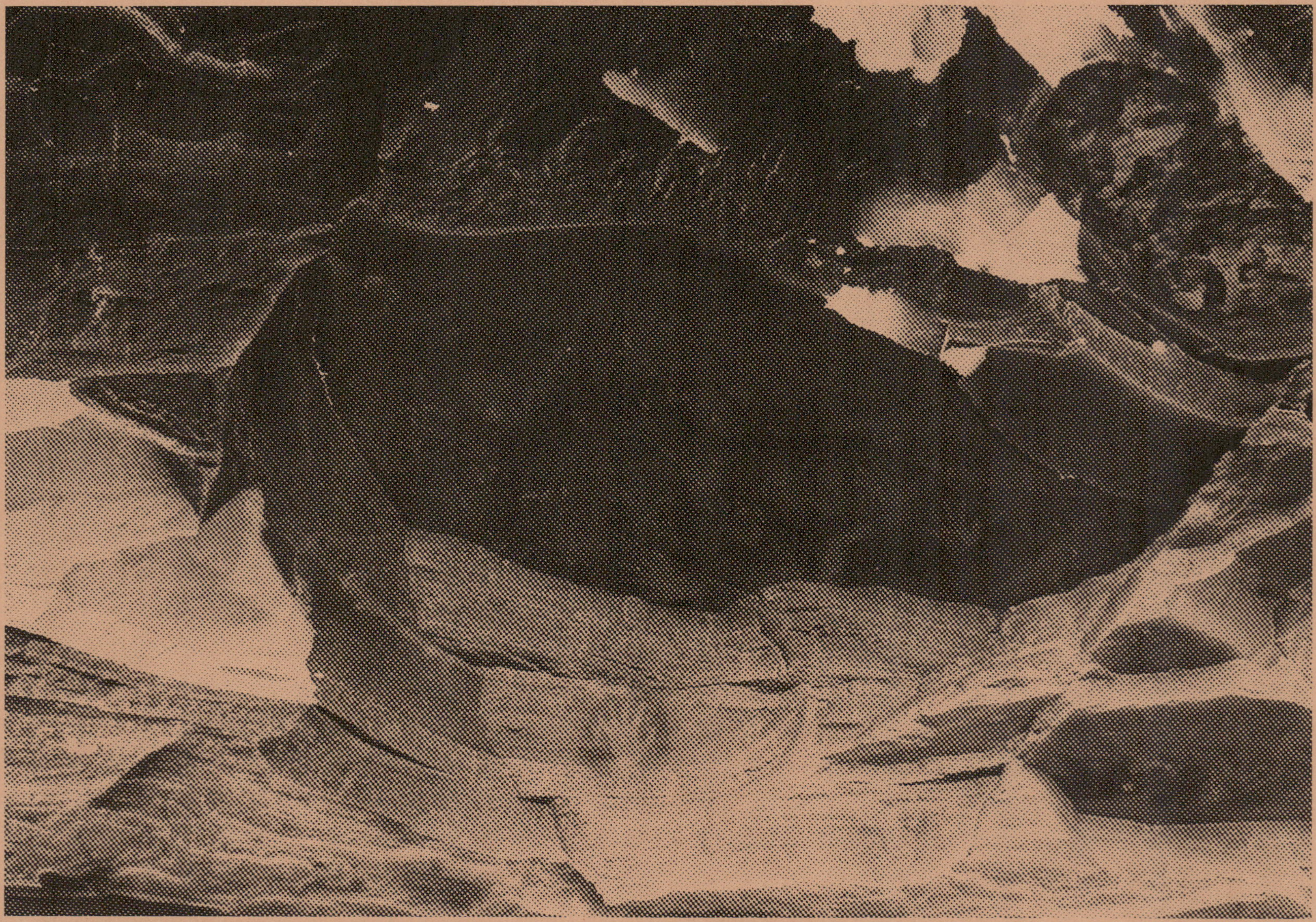

Figure 12: Baloon Cave main stencil panel after the December 2018 fire.

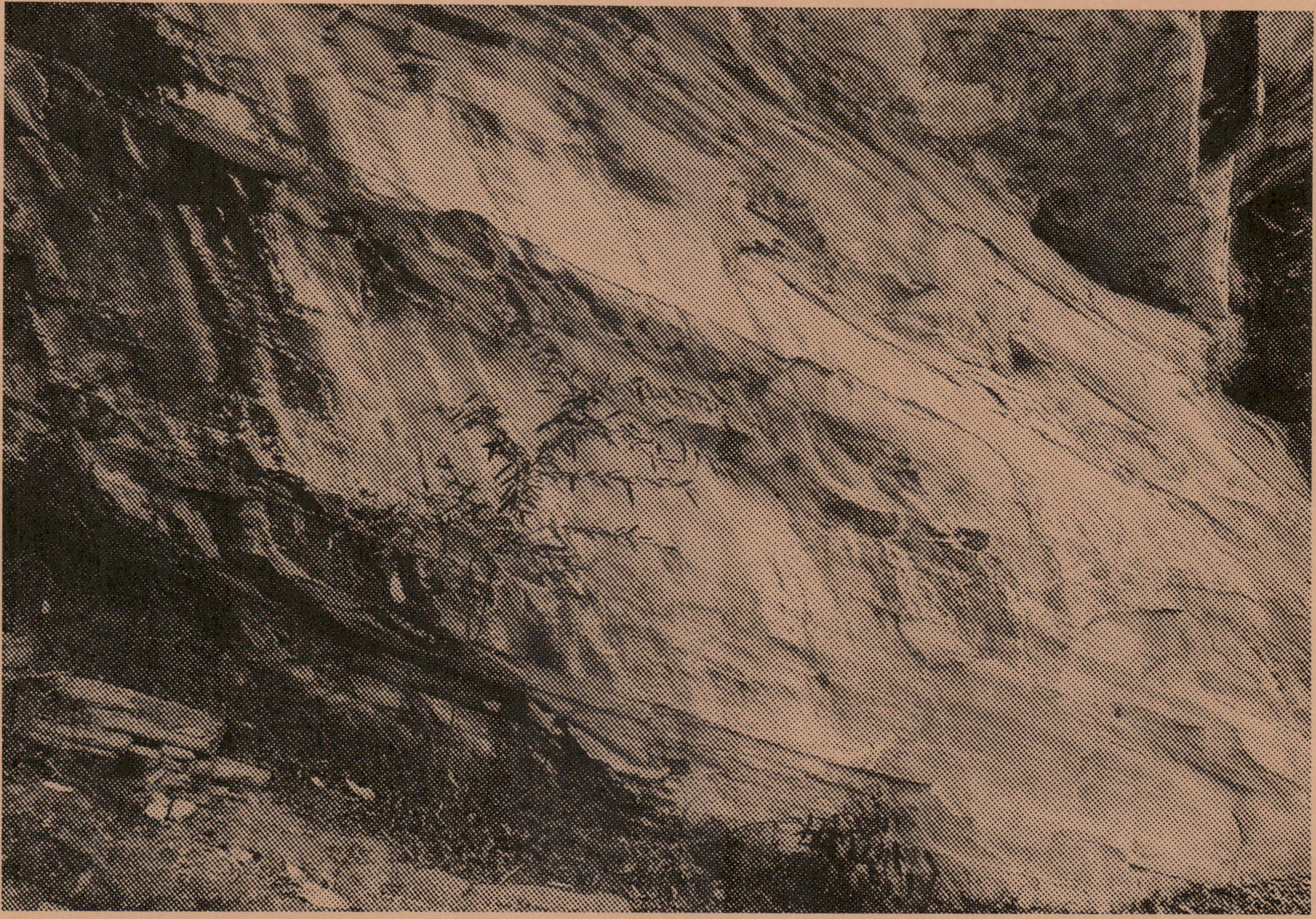

Figure 13: The lower right panel before the fire (photo: Marisa Giorgi).

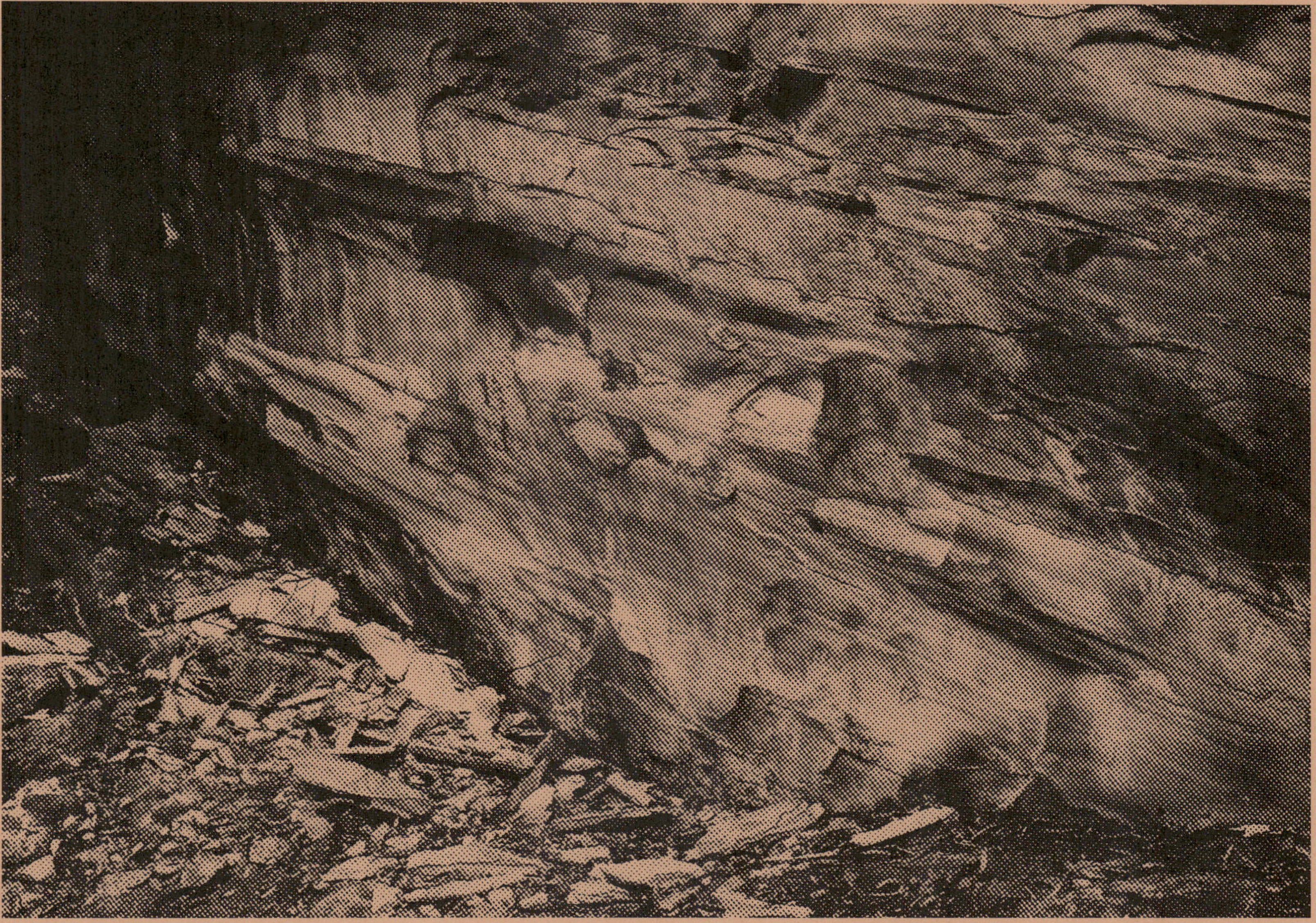

Figure 14: The lower right panel after the fire.

References cited

Abraham, J. 2018. Cone calorimeter tests for REPLAS at 25kW/m2 in accordance with AS3837:1998. Fire testing report. Revision B. 20 February 2018. Clayton South: Infrastructure Technologies, CSIRO.

Agnew, N., Deacon, J., Hall, N., Little, T., Sullivan, S. and Taçon, P.S.C. 2015. Rock art: a cultural treasure at risk. How we can protect the valuable and vulnerable heritage of rock art. The Getty Conservation Institute, Los Angeles (available free at: http://www.getty.edu/conservation/publications_resources/pdf_publications/pdf/rock_art_cultural_treasure.pdf).

Lambert, D. and B. Welsh. 2011. Fire and rock art. Rock Art Research 28(1):45-48.

Williams, S., Koeneman, T. and P.S.C. Taçon. In press (Nov 2019). The importance of conserving rock art: a conversation at the Jibbon petroglyph site, Royal National Park. Rock Art Research 36(2).

Further information

Prof. Paul S.C. Taçon
ARC Laureate Professor, PERAHU, Griffith Centre for Social and Cultural Research, Griffith University, Gold Coast campus, QLD 4222
P +61 07 555 29074; 0432981552
E p.tacon@griffith.edu.au

Editorial note: This report has been minimally modified for the present publication. The original report includes additional photographs documenting the 2019 Baloon Cave site visit and examples of metal infrastructure at a New South Wales site.

Monash University Museum of Art | MUMA and Dale Harding acknowledge the Wurundjeri and the Boon Wurrung peoples of the Kulin Nation and the Jagera and Turrbal peoples of the Brisbane regions as the first and continuing custodians of the lands and waters on which this exhibition and book were produced. We pay respect to their Elders, past and present.

The project *Dale Harding: Through a lens of visitation* provides us with the opportunity to experience the artist's practice at a crucial moment of connection. Through it, Harding draws out a number of artistic, personal and cultural links: to the artmaking and strong matriline of his own mother, Kate Harding; to Australian art history—specifically to two of its key protagonists, the artists Margaret Preston and Sidney Nolan; and to Carnarvon Gorge, a site that the Hardings—along with Bidjara, Ghungalu and Garingbal/Karingbal ancestors over millennia and their descendants today—hold as sacred, a spiritual home and an important place of learning.

It is testament to Dale Harding's emphasis on relationality—to his family, community and Country—that his solo survey at MUMA takes such a form of expanded engagement, and connects to a number of works he has made in recent years. This is complex terrain to navigate but this territory is vital to him and to us at MUMA, too. It is one of our responsibilities to better interweave our histories with contemporary conditions, and to make space for important revisions and revelations with new storylines.

The new works by Dale and Kate Harding have been co-commissioned by MUMA and the Chau Chak Wing Museum at the University of Sydney, and will be presented in their newly opened galleries in late 2021. We are thrilled to partner with the team at Chau Chak on this occasion and acknowledge their relationship with Dale over a number of years, manifesting in the multifaceted public artwork, *Spine*, on the University of Sydney campus in 2018.

We appreciate Dale Harding's trust in us to prepare this exhibition and publication with him. It has been a real pleasure to be guided through his practice. We also extend our acknowledgement to Kate Harding for the exhibition of her textile works as part of this project, and acknowledge Dale's other collaborators, Hayley Matthew and Jan Oliver, who are represented in the selection of works.

A project of this scope only comes together through the investment and commitment of many people. Our sincere thanks to the dedicated staff of Milani Gallery who have been so integral to this project. In particular, we thank Josh Milani and Jenna Baldock, who worked closely with Dale to secure major support from the Queensland Government through Arts Queensland. We are also grateful to Dale's studio assistant Grace Jeremy for her insight and support. All have provided valuable assistance to both the exhibition and the publication.

It was important to us to be able to bring a number of Dale's earlier works together to create a conversation with this new project, and we sincerely thank the many lenders who made this possible. We acknowledge the private collectors who have allowed their works to be included in the exhibition and the public collections who provided loans: Griffith University Art Collection, Brisbane; Queensland Art Gallery | Gallery of Modern Art, Brisbane; and The University of Queensland, Brisbane.

This book, which accompanies the exhibition of the same name, includes existing and newly commissioned writing by a selection of senior experts in their fields. We are grateful to Aunty Jackie Huggins AM FAHA for allowing us to reprint her article from 1995 and for writing a new introduction. Thanks also to Professor Paul S.C. Taçon FAHA FSA for allowing his report to be republished. For entering into dialogue with Dale's practice and illuminating its art-historical context, we thank the writers Deborah Edwards, Dr Ann Stephen FAHA and Dr Nancy Underhill.

We are grateful to Carl Warner for his lively photographs of Dale's and Kate's works and we acknowledge the many other organisations whose images have contributed to the visual richness of this publication: Art Gallery of New South Wales, Sydney; Art Gallery of South Australia, Adelaide; Art Gallery of Western Australia, Perth; Axel Poignant Archive, London; Canberra Museum and Gallery; Lyon Contemporary Art Biennale; Museum of Old and New Art (Mona), Hobart; National Gallery of Australia, Canberra; National Library of Australia, Canberra; Queensland Art Gallery | Gallery of Modern Art, Brisbane; Sharjah Art Foundation; The Sidney Nolan Trust, Presteigne, United Kingdom; State Library of Victoria, Melbourne; Tate, London; The University Art Collection, The University of Sydney; and The University of Western Australia Art Collection, Perth. We are grateful also to the Copyright Agency for their assistance, and to Ruark Lewis, Dr Chris Wright and Professor Lynette Russell for helping us to secure images from the Axel Poignant Estate.

Thanks to publication designers Stuart Geddes and Žiga Testen for their careful design of this book and their respect for the valuable knowledges it holds, and to Kay Campbell for her astute copyediting work. We also thank our co-publisher, the Power Institute, who will inaugurate their exciting new imprint—Powered by Power—with this book.

Special thanks go to all MUMA staff for their support of this project, particularly Curator Exhibitions, Francis E. Parker for his management of exhibition logistics, and to our talented install team.

Dale Harding and MUMA acknowledge the financial support of the Queensland Government through Arts Queensland. Dale would also like to acknowledge: the Harding, Lawton, and Kemp families, the Bidjara, Ghungalu, and Garingbal/Karingbal communities, Hayley Matthew, Paul Hey, Aileen Burns and Johan Lundh, Bruce McLean, Professor Sue Best, Angela Goddard, the Yeronga Artists and the Vincent Family.

Charlotte Day, Director, MUMA
Hannah Mathews, Senior Curator, MUMA, and curator of *Dale Harding: Through a lens of visitation*

Dale Harding is a descendant of the Bidjara, Ghungalu and Garingbal peoples. His early works give priority to documenting the oral accounts and lived realities of discrimination enacted against Aboriginal communities, in particular those inherited from matrilineal figures. Recent work is focused on enacting cultural continuum through practices that originate in Central Queensland. His practice encompasses textile, sculpture, film and painting, both in the form of discrete canvases that draw on Colour Field and Minimalism and in site-specific installations that reveal a sensibility for materials and social context. In July 2020 Harding was awarded a Post-Doctoral Fellowship from Queensland College of Art (QCA), Griffith University, Brisbane.

Harding's significant solo exhibitions include: *Dale Harding: Current iterations*, Institute of Modern Art, Brisbane, 2018; *The golden mile*, Gertrude Contemporary, Melbourne, 2018; and *White collared*, Institute of Modern Art, Brisbane, 2015. He has also shown regularly at Milani Gallery, Brisbane, since 2016.

Harding has participated in a number of significant national and international group exhibitions including: *Things entangling*, Museum of Contemporary Art Tokyo, Japan, 2020 (with KADIST); *15th Lyon Biennale: Where water comes together with other water*, France, 2019; *Surface tension*, Sharjah Art Foundation, United Arab Emirates, 2019; *Liverpool Biennial 2018: Beautiful world, where are you?*, United Kingdom; *TarraWarra Biennial 2018: From will to form*, TarraWarra Museum of Art, Healesville, Vic.; *documenta 14*, Athens and Kassel, 2017; *The national: New Australian art*, Art Gallery of New South Wales, Sydney, 2017; *Defying Empire: 3rd National Indigenous Art Triennial*, National Gallery of Australia, Canberra, 2017; *11th Gwangju Biennale: The eight climate (what does art do?)*, Korea, 2016; *String theory: Focus on contemporary Australian art*, Museum of Contemporary Art Australia, Sydney, 2013; *My country, I still call Australia home: Contemporary art from black Australia*, Queensland Art Gallery | Gallery of Modern Art, Brisbane, 2013; and *unDisclosed: 2nd National Indigenous Art Triennial*, National Gallery of Australia, Canberra, 2012.

CONTRIBUTOR BIOGRAPHIES

Kate Harding's parents were Bidjara and Ghungalu Elders and she maintains her Garingbal matrilineality. Harding works in a wide variety of textile media, specialising in embroidery techniques including silk ribbon embroidery and stumpwork. Recently, she has been invigorating the ancestral practices of basketry and bag forms, in particular the pityuri bag. Harding's work was exhibited in *Tradelines* at Bundaberg Regional Art Gallery in 2019 and a suite of her contemporary bag forms foregrounded Dale Harding's 2018 exhibition *The drive home* at Milani Gallery, Brisbane. Harding has been central to her son Dale Harding's material working processes for exhibitions including the 11th Gwangju Biennial in Korea in 2016, and the National Indigenous Triennial at the National Gallery of Australia, Canberra in 2017.

Dr Nancy Underhill established the Department of Art History and The University Art Museum at the University of Queensland. She has been a Visiting Fellow at the Humanities Research Centre, Australian National University, Canberra and Research Associate at the Menzies Centre, Kings College, London. Her books include *Sidney Nolan a life* (2015), *Nolan on Nolan: Sidney Nolan in his own words* (2007), *Letters of John Reed*, co-edited with Barrett Reid (2001) and *Making Australian art 1916–49* (1991).

Dr Deborah Edwards was Senior Curator of Australian Art, Art Gallery of New South Wales from 2002 to 2016. She has also been a curator at Queensland Art Gallery | Gallery of Modern Art and a tutor at the University of Sydney. She has written major monographs on a number of Australian painters and sculptors, including Margaret Preston, and is now a consultant curator with research interests in modernism, twentieth-century sculpture and Indigenous art.

Dr Ann Stephen FAHA is Senior Curator, Art at Chau Chak Wing Museum, University of Sydney, with responsibility for the university's public art commissions. She has curated many exhibitions, including those accompanying the publications *Bauhaus diaspora and beyond: Transforming education through art, design and architecture* (with Goad, McNamara, Edquist, Wunsche), Melbourne University Press (MUP) and Power Publications, 2019; *Jacky Redgate: Mirrors* (with Robert Leonard), Power Publications, 2016; *Modern times: The untold story of modernism in Australia* (with Goad and McNamara), MUP, 2008; and *On looking at looking: The art and politics of Ian Burn*, MUP, Melbourne, 2006.

Dr Jackie Huggins AM FAHA is a Bidjara and Birri Gubba Juru woman from Central and North Queensland. She is a historian, author and advocate who has spent four decades working in Aboriginal Affairs, particularly reconciliation, women's issues, history and literacy. She was Deputy Director of the Aboriginal and Torres Strait Islander Unit at the University of Queensland (1997–2010) and has been a member of several important councils and enquiries including chair of Reconciliation Australia, co-chair of the National Congress of Australia's First Peoples and co-chair of Queensland's Treaty Working Group. She has published numerous essays and studies on Indigenous history and identity and her books include *Sistergirl* (1998) and the acclaimed biography written with her mother, *Auntie Rita* (1994).

Professor Paul S.C. Taçon FAHA FSA is an ARC Australian Laureate Fellow (2016–21), Chair in Rock Art Research and Professor of Anthropology and Archaeology at Griffith University, Brisbane. He also directs Griffith University's Place, Evolution and Rock Art Heritage Unit (PERAHU) and leads research themes in the Griffith Centre for Social and Cultural Research and Griffith's Research Centre of Human Evolution. He co-edited *The archaeology of rock-art* with Dr Christopher Chippindale and has published over 280 academic and popular papers on rock art, material culture, colour, cultural evolution and identity. In 2016, he was awarded the Rhys Jones Medal for Outstanding Contribution to Australian Archaeology and the Griffith University Vice-Chancellor's Research Excellence Award for Research Leadership.

MUMA STAFF

Charlotte Day, Director
Hannah Mathews, Senior Curator
Alicia Renew, Gallery Manager (parental leave)
Meredith Turnbull, Gallery Manager
Emma Neale, Collection Manager
Francis E. Parker, Curator Exhibitions
Melissa Ratliff, Curator Research
Warisa Somsuphangsri, Communications Coordinator
Kate Barber, Public Programs
Melissa Bedford, Education
David Thomas, Museum Officer
Trent Crawford, Museum Officer
Alkira Kinchela, Administrative Assistant (Indigenous Trainee), Office of the Pro Vice–Chancellor (Indigenous)
Museum Assistants: Isabella Darcy, Cathryn Ross, Rachel Schenberg
Installation: Benjamin Crowley, Beau Emmett, Gian Manik, Hayden Stuart, Simone Tops
Volunteers: Marcie Bakker, Mia Bell, Nishita Desai, Nishadi Fernando, Pallas Hocking, Angela Liang, Elsie Preston, Noni Salazar, Anna Smith, Megan Tan, Anna Venosta

MUMA COMMITTEE

Professor Shane Murray (Chair), Dean, Faculty of Art, Design and Architecture, Monash University
Charlotte Day, Director, Monash University Museum of Art
Professor Louise Adler AM, Vice-Chancellor's Professional Fellow, Monash University
Professor Wendy Brown, Chair, Department of Surgery, Monash University and Central Clinical School, Alfred Health
Professor Jacinta Elston, Pro Vice-Chancellor (Indigenous), Monash University
Damien Farrell, Vice-President (Advancement), Monash University
Maudie Palmer AO, Founding Director, TarraWarra Museum of Art and Heide Museum of Modern Art
Renaye Peters, Vice-President (Campus Infrastructure and Services), Office of Chief Operating Officer, Monash University
Professor Kathy Temin, Head of Fine Art, Faculty of Art, Design and Architecture, Monash University

COLOPHON

Through a lens of visitation
Published on the occasion of the exhibition *Dale Harding: Through a lens of visitation* at Monash University Museum of Art, Melbourne, from 26 April to 26 June 2021 and Chau Chak Wing Museum, University of Sydney, in late 2021.

Through a lens of visitation is supported by the Queensland Government through Arts Queensland and the Chau Chak Wing Museum and Power Institute at the University of Sydney.

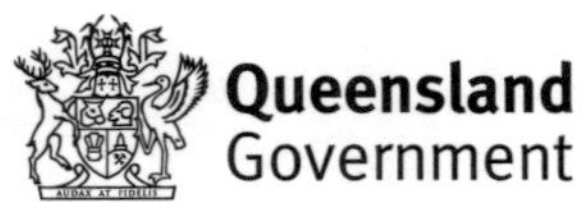

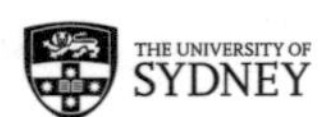

Curated by Hannah Mathews
Editors: Hannah Mathews and Dale Harding
Design: Stuart Geddes and Žiga Testen
Lithography: Sebastiaan Hanekroot, Colour & Books
Print production: Jos Morree Fine Books
Printing: Wilco Art Books
Copyediting: Kay Campbell, The Comma Institute
First edition of 500
ISBN 978-0-6481529-8-9

Published by
Monash University Museum of Art | MUMA
900 Dandenong Road, Caulfield Campus
Caulfield East VIC 3145
Australia
monash.edu/muma

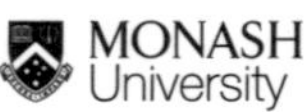

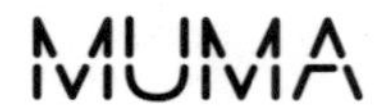

Powered by Power
An imprint of Power Publications
Power Institute Foundation for Art and Visual Culture
University of Sydney
NSW 2006 Australia
powerpublications.com.au